P9-DND-242

I'm Chocolate, You're Vanilla

I'm Chocolate, You're Vanilla

Raising Healthy Black and Biracial Children in a Race-Conscious World

Marguerite A. Wright

JOSSEY-BASS
A Wiley Imprint
www.josseybass.com

FIRST PAPERBACK EDITION PUBLISHED IN 2000.

Published by Jossey-Bass
A Wiley Imprint
989 Market Street, San Francisco, CA 94103-1741 www.josseybass.com

Jossey-Bass books and products are available through most bookstores. To contact Jossey-Bass directly call our Customer Care Department within the U.S. at 800-956-7739, outside the U.S. at 317-572-3986, or fax 317-572-4002.

Jossey-Bass also publishes its books in a variety of electronic formats. Some content that appears in print may not be available in electronic books.

Library of Congress Cataloging-in-Publication Data

Wright, Marguerite A.
I'm chocolate, you're vanilla: raising healthy Black and biracial children in a race-conscious world / Marguerite A. Wright.
— 1st ed.
p. cm.
Includes bibliographical references and index.

ISBN 978-0-7879-5234-1 (pbk.)
1. Race awareness in children—United States. 2. Afro-American children—Psychology. 3. Afro-American children—Attitudes. 4. Afro-American children—Ethnic identity. 5. Racially mixed children—Psychology. 6. Racially mixed children—Attitudes. 7. Racially mixed children—Ethnic identity. I. Title.
BF723.R3 W75 1998
155.8'2—ddc21
98–19700

15 14 13 12

Contents

Acknowledgments

Many people over several years supported me in making this book possible. I am particularly grateful for the unwavering support, generosity, and belief in my work of the late Dr. Jean V. Carew, who became my mentor while she was a visiting professor at Harvard University.

Professor Sara Lawrence Lightfoot of Harvard University provided valuable guidance and encouragement during the early phase of my work. I appreciate Professor Robert Selman's indispensable advice on the developmental aspects of my work on how children construct their concept of race. Along with Dr. Carew, Drs. Lightfoot and Selman guided my doctoral thesis, which formed the beginnings of the book.

Laurie Harper, my agent, helped me reach my goal of publishing this book through her enthusiasm and enduring faith in this project. Her confidence in this work did much to boost my spirit along the way.

Dr. Stephen M. Schoen introduced my book to Jossey-Bass, and senior editor Alan Rinzler got behind it from the start.

Katie Levine, my editor, grasped ideas I was trying to convey even when they were not yet fully formed. Her insightful criticism and thoughtful suggestions have been tremendously helpful.

Robert Aquinas McNally gave critical advice on some early chapters that helped me translate psychological jargon into understandable language for a nonprofessional audience.

Several other people helped me with various aspects of the early research, including Professor Joan Bissel, Mary Lynn Vaillume, Terry Tivan, Jan Stiberg, Judy Czarkosky, Gail Bates, and the late Cynthia Longfellow Lincoln and Marie Peters. Professor Edward Zigler of Yale University encouraged me to continue my research on race.

Several people provided ideas and support in the later phase of this work, including Ellen Pinderhughes, Susan Payne, Karen Cox, Wanda Davis, Emmy Petterson, Cherese Macedone, and my colleagues at Children's Hospital Oakland. Joanne Clapp Fullagar provided great production advice. Thanks also to Dr. Kimberly Edelin of the United Negro College Fund, who provided me with research assistance. I also appreciate the teachers and school administrators who shared their views with me.

My family's love and support made it possible to write this book. My dear children, Nicole, Elena, Davi, and Matthew, whose stories, laughter, cheerful notes, and yummy snacks, brought to me during my work at the computer, brightened my days. Nicole also provided cheerful research assistance. Very special thanks go to my soulmate, my husband Brian, whose brilliant advice, optimism, and infinite kindnesses made it much easier to write this book.

Finally, my deepest appreciation to the many families in the San Francisco Bay Area, New Haven, Connecticut, and Cambridge, Massachusetts, who welcomed me into their homes and shared with me some of their most intimate thoughts on race and parenting. I will be forever grateful to the parents who allowed me to talk with their children. It is the children's compelling voices that form the essence of this book.

Oakland, California
July 1998

MARGUERITE A. WRIGHT

I'm Chocolate, You're Vanilla

To my mom,
Evelyn Eugenie,
for inspiring me to reach for my dreams

Introduction

I could sense the anger rising in Mrs. Lee* as she spoke. A dark-skinned foster mother, she had been caring for Malcolm, a light-skinned preschooler, for nearly six months.

"Do you know, that child has the nerve to keep telling me that he's white?" Mrs. Lee said. "Who does he think he is? I keep saying, 'No, Malcolm, you're black.' He looks at himself and shakes his head and says, 'Uh-uh, I'm white.'

"He thinks he's better than the rest of us black folks," she continued. "I don't know what to do with him."

Because I am a psychologist who counsels children and families, I've heard this kind of story about black children many times from adults of all races. It has become the common wisdom that even the youngest black children loathe their race and would prefer to be white. The media regularly report that black children suffer from low self-esteem springing from negative feelings about their skin color.[1] Many black adults believe that by the time their children are learning to talk and read, they are already ashamed of their race and therefore themselves.

---

*The names of all adults and children have been changed to protect their privacy.

But is this really the case? My own research and life experience tell me that it's not. In fact, I'm certain that low self-esteem is less a reality than a firmly held but mistaken assumption with which many adults approach black children. Children like themselves the way they are; it's adults who can't see the facts of the matter.

"I know it seems to you that Malcolm thinks he's white and better than you," I said to Mrs. Lee, "but children sometimes don't look at things the same way we adults do."

"What do you mean?" she replied, eyeing me suspiciously.

"Children perceive skin color very differently from the way we adults do. When Malcolm says he or someone else is 'white,' it doesn't mean the same thing as when you and I and other adults say it. This isn't about him thinking he is better or worse than you. It's about the fact that as a little boy, he just sees skin color differently than the way we do."

I had held several counseling sessions with Mrs. Lee by this time and given her some other parenting advice that she seemed to find helpful. I was gradually gaining her trust, and so I hoped that she would believe me now. Over the next few counseling sessions, I talked more with her about the developmental stages through which children pass and how they gradually learn about skin color and race. What I told her made all the difference. Indeed, one of my most gratifying therapeutic experiences was watching the relationship between Mrs. Lee and Malcolm gradually improve as she came to understand that because of the developmental stage he was in, his perceptions of skin color did not carry the adult biases she attributed to him.

~

Part of my motivation for writing *I'm Chocolate, You're Vanilla* is to show that most young black children are not ashamed of their race. Indeed, like young children of other races, they are incapable of feeling shame about their color or race unless they have been unduly sensitized about the issue or somehow traumatized. As a black clinical psychologist and mother of four school-age children, I am bothered that black children are routinely portrayed as disliking themselves and facing bleak futures simply because of their race. In my research and practice, I've observed just the contrary. Young black children are no different from youngsters of any other race.

For almost two decades, I've been a practicing psychologist, specializing in children and family issues. I've counseled hundreds of children of various races in mental health centers, clinics, and schools on both coasts. What has struck me time and time again is how emotionally, cognitively, and socially similar children of different races are in their early years. In spite of the bigotry and racism that black children will experience as they mature, as youngsters they have that spark, that vibrancy, that "I can conquer the world" attitude that most children seem to be endowed with. Being black in and of itself is not the problem. What matters is how they are raised to deal with their identity and what opportunities are provided to them along the way. If children are provided the nurturance and guidance that are every child's birthright, I know from my own and many others' experiences that being black can be an asset rather than a liability.

In the pre–civil rights era, Kenneth and Mamie Clark found that young "Negro" children did not feel good about their race.[2] Of course, given all the obstacles that blacks faced back then because of institutionalized segregation, young blacks had obvious reasons to have negative feelings about their race. The Clarks' research contributed significantly to the landmark 1954 Supreme Court decision that struck down racial segregation in this country. Despite dramatic advances in the status of U.S. blacks over the past fifty years, research continued for several decades to show that black children had low self-esteem.[3] But at the same time, a body of research to which I contributed raised doubts about those findings and indicated that black children generally have positive self-concepts.[4] These positive findings have been supported by most studies conducted in the past two decades but are not given as much media play as those that show that black children have negative self-concepts. Thus the myth of the self-loathing black child (and adult) endures.

The notion that young African Americans dislike being black would not be so widely accepted were it not so plausible. It is patently obvious that to be born black in the United States is to be burdened with special disadvantages. Although the civil rights movement of the 1960s has resulted in major advances for black Americans, they still face considerable, although more subtle, discrimination in education, employment, housing, and other areas of life. The conservative backlash of the 1990s has resulted in the rollback of affirmative action programs, which some analysts say signals a change for the worse in our society's attitudes toward blacks. Nowhere is the situation of more concern than for black children, who on practically every measure of deprivation, whether in terms of family structure, family income, access to health care, or educational opportunities, fare worse than whites.

The daily experience of racial prejudice, in the form of major hassles or minor slights, places an enormous psychological toll on many blacks. The late tennis champion Arthur Ashe, a man not given to self-pity or hyperbole, said that being black was a much more difficult challenge than dealing with the dreaded AIDS infection that ultimately killed him.

Since race is such an important topic, especially for those subjected to or constantly threatened by prejudice, you would think that there would be loads of information about how children see race and lots of advice about how best to raise them and teach them to deal with racism. But until recently, race has been a taboo subject in the child-rearing literature. Even today, of the hundreds of books about parenting now available, few advise parents on how to teach their children about race. This oversight is lamentable because, along with gender and social class, race shapes a child's life more than anything else.

In my experience, young black children who have a poor sense of self-worth are no different from children of other races who have the same problem: they are harmed by insensitivity, abuse, and neglect within their own circle of family and friends. Most black children I've met who are well cared for have healthy self-images. Yet it is convenient, even politically correct, to blame most of the problems some black children experience on low self-esteem induced early in childhood by a "racist society."

Make no mistake: this book would not be necessary were racism irrelevant. Since racism remains very much a fact of U.S. society, responsible parents and caregivers need to reduce its impact on the development of the children they love and care for.

Tragically, when they misjudge children's responses to "racial" issues by relying on their own adult views, they run the risk of magnifying the significance of race problems in their children's lives and of reducing their children's initially high capacity to handle these issues in positive ways as they mature.

Few adults realize how frequently mismatches between their own perceptions of racial "reality" and the child's view of the world arise. Consider two more real-life situations. A young black single mother, bothered by the low self-esteem of her young son, Jonathan, considers enrolling him in a Black Muslim preschool that advocates racially separatist views in order to enhance his self-esteem. Crystal, a sweet, engaging six-year-old, begins to make negative comments about her "nappy" hair and dark skin. Her parents blame Crystal's feelings about her hair and skin on media propaganda promoting a white image of beauty.

For both these children, race was not the immediate cause of their low self-esteem. In Jonathan's case, it was his relationship with his own mother that was the problem. I learned from Jonathan's grandmother that his mother was not only overwhelmed with the responsibilities of parenthood but also ill-prepared to deal with them. As a result of her frustration, she often called him hurtful names—"brat," "butthead," and worse. She repeatedly told him that she should never have had him. Jonathan was too young to grasp the idea of race, let alone associate it with inferiority. But he was not too young to understand that his mother wished he had not been born.

What racist could match the power of that message to lower the self-esteem of a child of any race? Racial bias may well have contributed to the stress experienced by Jonathan's young single mother, but she needed to learn how much her own attitudes and behavior shaped her son's feelings about himself.

Something of the same sort was happening with Crystal. She confided to me that her own mother told her that her hair was "nappy" and a "trial" to comb. From conversations she overheard, she learned that her father favored her sister because of her lighter complexion. Crystal was copying her parents' expressed preferences; she herself had little conception of their racial connotations. Her parents needed to recognize that the preferences they found deplorable were not their daughter's but their own.

A child's concept of race is developmentally different from an adult's. Children, unless rigorously taught to do otherwise, start out making no distinction among people because of their skin color or race. It takes a good while before they are developmentally capable of seeing people primarily in terms of their race, in the way that too many adults do. This should come as no surprise to parents who, having heard their child talk about a buddy or a best friend, are later surprised to learn that the friend belongs to a different race. And how many times, when you have been to a playground or some other public place, have you observed adults of different races, with their children in tow, wary of coming too close to each other, while their young children are playing happily together, heedless of their parents' warnings not to play with "those kinds of kids"?

Over the years, I have also encountered children who seem unusually vulnerable to perceived and actual racism. Some of them obviously have to deal with an unusually heavy share of discrimination, but more often these children come from families who habitually blame their children's problems on race and who bring their children up to believe that they are victims because they are black.

Consider Marcus, a black father of five, who thought the best way to teach his children to deal with racism was to "toughen" them against racial realities. He repeatedly told his ten-year-old son that he'd have to work twice as hard as his white classmates to earn good grades and that teachers don't believe black children are as smart as Asian and white children. Unfortunately, some of what Marcus told his son is true: some teachers are prejudiced, expect blacks to do poorly in school, and thereby make it harder for black students to excel. Despite this reality, Marcus would have done a better job of parenting by encouraging his son to succeed instead of suggesting that the deck was stacked against him. Marcus's pessimistic message had the effect of emotionally debilitating his son. The boy believed that he and others who looked like him wouldn't do well in their schoolwork because all their teachers were prejudiced. Given the strength of this belief, he had no incentive to try to succeed.

When Marcus brought his son to me to get to the root cause of his poor grades, I found that his son's assumption of failure and resulting lack of effort, not the racial prejudice of his teachers, were the primary causes of his underachievement. Discouraged by the odds said to be against him, this child didn't feel it was worth trying to do well in school. For him, getting good grades was "a white thing."

One of my primary goals in this book is to help parents and other people who work with black and biracial children to understand that, developmentally, young children are not equipped to cope with the knowledge of pervasive racial discrimination. Children who are prematurely sensitized to the existence of racial bigotry have difficulty processing such information, much less coping with it. I believe that instead of telling their children how tough life will be for them, truly caring parents and other adults should shield them from this information for as long as possible. Don't we try to protect our children from other information we think they are too immature to handle?

I'm not saying that we should ignore racial discrimination and how it affects our children's lives. Far from it. We as adults should do whatever we can to reduce our children's chances of experiencing racial discrimination. For example, in Marcus's case, instead of lamenting the status quo, he would have done better to lobby his son's school to hire teachers who believe that black children, like any other children, have the ability to do well if they receive a quality education.

Dealing with the issues our children face regarding race requires an understanding of the developmental stages they pass through as they learn racial matters. Children are not simply miniature adults. Just as they learn to walk, talk, and think in definite and predictable stages, they likewise come to understand race in a series of stages.

Curiously, though, many people refuse to admit that racial awareness is a developmental issue even when they understand how development affects other aspects of growing up, such as sexuality. For example, not long ago, newspapers and TV gave considerable coverage to the plight of a five-year-old boy accused of sexual harassment and suspended from school for kissing a little girl in his kindergarten class. Most adults realized how ridiculous this all was; young children are simply incapable of manifesting adultlike sexism. Yet when it comes to race, many of us make the exact opposite assumption: we assume that everything a child says and does has the same meaning that it would have if said or done by an adult. With race, as with sexuality, children do not think or act like adults. They think and act like children. For us adults who parent and teach children, it is imperative to understand children as they are, not as we believe—or wish—them to be.

As black children develop from preschoolers to adolescents, they will confront tough issues relating to race. Navigating these racial waters can be treacherous unless parents and educators know how to guide their children safely through.

Some parents question whether it is even possible to raise psychologically healthy black and biracial children in this society. Like popular black novelist John Edgar Wideman, they give "a resounding no" to the question of whether one can stay "healthy and alive in this culture and be other than a white person."[5]

I solidly reject this negative view. Instead, in this book, I argue that *children who are loved, cared for, and shielded as much as possible from early experiences with racism grow up with a high sense of self-worth regardless of their race.* Black and biracial children who are emotionally nourished throughout their development preserve the resilience and optimism that most children seem to be born with. It is that sense that gave Alice Walker the belief that she could be an author when there weren't many black writers; that inspired Tiger Woods to believe he would one day be a great golfer when few people of color were even allowed to play the game; and that allowed Colin Powell, former chairman of the Joint Chiefs of Staff, to dream he could grow up to be anything he wanted to be at a time when the possibility of an African American becoming a five-star general, let alone a possible presidential candidate, seemed unimaginable.

Henry Louis Gates, author and chair of the Department of Afro-American Studies at Harvard University, distinguishes between the "structural" and the "behavioral" aspects of racism.[6] The structural aspects are those deeply rooted, societywide forms of institutional racism, in broad areas such as housing, employment, and education, that are slow to change. The behavioral aspects of racism include those practices (such as child rearing) that allow racism to prosper because blacks act in ways that perpetuate their own victimization. By improving the ways we perceive, parent, and educate our children, we could drastically lessen the impact of behavioral racism on them.

Much work remains to be done to make this country a more hospitable place for people of color. But there is much that can be done *right now* to enable our children to grow up with a proud and healthy sense of their color, race, and potential.

~

In this book, I cite many examples of both famous and ordinary black and biracial individuals who recall happy childhoods, some even spent in the hostile segregated South of the pre–civil rights era. They grew up with their self-esteem intact and went on to lead satisfying and accomplished lives. I quote from interviews with children, tell anecdotes, and draw on cases from my clinical work to demonstrate that children's awareness of skin color and race is dramatically different from that of adults. I follow children's development of race awareness though a series of predictable stages as they go from the preschool years through early adolescence. I hope that by sharing my insights about their attitudes to race, I can help readers enhance their children's healthy development and pass on attitudes that will help their children handle the racism they are sure to encounter.

I'm Chocolate, You're Vanilla offers a guide to parents, educators, and others who work with black and biracial children. It shows how an understanding of the child's perspective can help nurture and support the healthy self-images children bring to the world despite centuries of oppression and the enduring effects of racism in society today.

Myrlie Evers, widow of slain black civil rights leader Medgar Evers, said that when she suspected her husband had been killed by whites, she "really started to hate white people." These feelings festered until one day her children "sat me down and said, 'Dad died so people won't feel like that.' At that moment I learned to forgive."[7]

As Mrs. Evers discovered, by understanding our children's perspective, we can also become better able to deal with the racial animosity that is still our number one social problem.

In this book, I generally favor the term *black* over *African American* because it is a more inclusive term (referring not only to North American blacks but also to those of the Caribbean, Central and South America, and elsewhere). The names blacks have called themselves, and are called by others, have changed over the past century from *colored* to *Negro* to *black* to *African American*. There remains no clear consensus. For example, in both the black and the white media, the terms *black* and *African American* are used interchangeably. To my mind, not only is the term *African American* wordy, but it seems to put a qualifier on blacks' status as Americans. Unless they are recent immigrants, whites, regardless of national origin, are routinely regarded as Americans, not as Geman Americans, English Americans, Italian Americans, Scandinavian Americans, and so on. Shouldn't blacks be similarly regarded, especially since they have a longer history of living in America than many other groups of people? At the start of the twentieth century, over 98 percent of blacks in the United States were native-born—a much higher percentage than for whites. Blacks are as American as you can get.

PART ONE

That Magical Place

Race Awareness in the Preschool Years

CHAPTER ONE

Chocolate and Vanilla

How Preschoolers See Color and Race

It is only with the heart that one can see rightly;
what is essential is invisible to the eye.
—ANTOINE DE SAINT-EXUPÉRY, *The Little Prince*

Children don't start out as miniature adults. They don't see "reality" the way we grown-ups do. The preschoolers' world is an enchanted, magical place where imagination rules.

Race is an adult notion that means nothing to preschoolers. Even when they use adult words that refer to skin colors, young children understand these words quite differently. Wonderfully egocentric individuals that they are, they construct their own unique perspectives rather than conform to the ways adults expect them to see things. Only as they pass through a predictable series of developmental stages (see the Appendix) do children gradually come to share the views of racial matters held by their parents and other significant adults in their lives. The emotional baggage about race that so many of us carry around does not burden preschoolers.

WHEN DO CHILDREN BECOME AWARE OF THEIR RACE?

Babies are not born with knowledge of skin color or of race. According to conventional wisdom, most children have become aware of their own race by age three. However, my own work, as well as some other published studies, casts doubt on this conventional wisdom.[1]

Children this young cannot truly grasp the complexity of the idea of race. Just because a preschooler can tell us the color of her skin, it doesn't necessarily follow that she is also aware of her racial identity. Indeed, if you take the time to listen carefully to what your preschoolers themselves are saying about skin color, you'll quickly realize that race is the farthest thing from their minds.

Most of the preschoolers I interview about race do not have the slightest inkling of their race. For example, in a typical group of ten preschoolers I interviewed, only one, a four-year-old I'll call Josie, apparently regarded skin color as an important element in her self-image. Not one of the others seemed to have even a clue that skin color had a meaning beyond mere color. Seeing either themselves or others in terms of skin color simply is not natural for most preschoolers. Josie was a special case: her self-awareness regarding her skin color was the result of her mother's obsession with race.

Three-Year-Olds Don't Have a Clue About Their Race

To find out whether preschoolers are aware of their own skin color and race, I ask them to do several tasks. First, I show them a set of color cards (ranging in hue from pink to dark brown) and ask them to choose the card that most closely matches their own skin color. Next, I present photos of children of various races and ask them to choose the picture that looks most like them. Finally, I ask them to tell me their color and name their race.

The answers of three-year-olds will leave you amazed at how irrelevant skin color and race are to their self-concepts. When I tried the photo task with Tasha, for example, she said the girl in the photo she picked looked like her "'Cause I'd like to play with her," and Belinda explained her choice with the words "'Cause she's nice." Few three-year-olds will give an appropriate skin-color label for the photo of the child they say looks most like themselves. Rarely, if ever, will they spontaneously use a color word (for example, *brown*) or a racial term (for example, *black* or *African American*) to describe themselves.

Although most three-year-olds can correctly match a color card to their own skin color, they generally do not use an appropriate name (from an adult perspective) to describe the color they choose. When asked "What color are you?" they are just as likely to mention the color of their clothes as the color of their skin. Moreover, children who do have an awareness of their skin color describe it with their own distinctive color words, such as *chocolate, vanilla,* or *peach,* which relate to their experience with food rather than with racial categories.

At age three, children are still in the process of mastering their color recognition and color-labeling skills. No wonder the words they use to describe themselves and their skin color tend to be inconsistent! Consider my conversation with three-year-old Lilly after I showed her a selection of cards ranging in color from dark brown to light pink:

INTERVIEWER: *Which one looks like your skin color?*
LILLY: **[Chooses color.]**
Which color are you?
You know what color. I'm red.
You're red?
No, blue.
What color are you?
Let's see. I'll ask my mommy. Red.
You're red?
Like the fishes. [Points to the fishes in the aquarium.]
You're red like the fishes?
My fishes don't bite.

Like most three-year-olds, Lilly probably doesn't think about her skin color very much. It's obviously of no great importance to her. Consider the remarks of another child, Jetasha:

INTERVIEWER: *Give me the photo of the child that looks the most like you.*
JETASHA: **This one.**
Why does she look like you?
Because she goes to school with me.
She goes to school with you?
Because I got to find her house.

Most three-year-olds can tell you whether they are a boy or a girl. Identification by sex comes earlier and more naturally to the young child than identification by color or by race.

Four-Year-Olds Know Their Color but Not Their Race

Generally, by age four, children are able to identify themselves correctly and consistently using color labels. Many African-American children describe their skin color as "brown." Interestingly, although I've heard some light-complexioned black children refer to their skin color with words like *peach* or *yellow,* some others, especially those who are becoming familiar with the labels adults use to describe skin, will call themselves and others of light complexion "white." Their use of this word seems to be based purely on their perception, on what they see as the similarity of their light skin color to what adults call "white," rather than because of racial awareness or an emotional identification (the infamous "wish to be white").

Some black parents assume that if their children call themselves "white," they must feel inferior and therefore need to be taught that "black is beautiful." Their concern is needless. They are confusing their child's quite accurate *color* identification with an adult's *racial* identification. Typically, when I tell four-year-olds who call themselves "brown" that some people would call them "black," they adamantly reject this word, insisting that they are "brown."

Exceptions exist, however. One was four-year-old Josie, a dark-complexioned child, who said that she was black. In addition to naming her skin color accurately, Josie seemed also to have a rudimentary idea that she is a member of a race—a group of people who are called black. Josie's grandmother, who was her primary caregiver, disclosed that Josie's mother had become obsessed with race, to the point of paranoia, and that she expected and saw racial injustices everywhere. Moreover, the neighborhood where Josie had lived with her mother was predominantly white. Josie's mother had complained to the child's grandmother that a couple of white parents had refused to allow Josie to play with their children and that Josie felt rejected. In talking with Josie, I also learned that she differentiated between her "black" name (she had been given a new "black" name by her mother) and her "white" birth name. (When asked her name, Josie gave her birth name in spite of her mother's exhortations to do otherwise.)

But Josie is unusual. For most preschoolers, skin color is irrelevant to self-image. Preschoolers' sense of identity stems mainly from their name, gender, and familial relationships.

What Their Self-Portraits Tell Us

Preschoolers' lack of attention to skin color is also evident in their self-portraits. When I ask preschoolers to draw pictures of themselves, they seldom give themselves skin tones that resemble their actual skin colors. Indeed, one is far more likely to be able to predict the age than the race of a child from a self-portrait.

Some children do not color their skin even when specifically instructed to do so. Others who color their skin choose colors like green, blue, yellow, and purple, choices that suggest that their actual skin color has little to do with their self-image. By contrast, if you ask most older children and adults to draw themselves and then to color in their drawings, the majority will color their skin an appropriate ("realistic") color.

Of course, many preschoolers cannot draw a reasonable picture of themselves. (Some three-year-olds only manage to draw a bunch of scrambled lines and colors.) But those preschoolers whose self-portraits are discernible tend to focus on similar features of the body, namely, the face (drawn with eyes, usually a mouth, and less often a nose) and sticklike limbs, which may emanate from the face or from some shape representing their idea of a torso. (If you take care of preschoolers, ask them to draw themselves and see for yourself.)

Preschoolers' Understanding Versus Parents' Expectations: A Reality Check

Parents of preschoolers tend to overestimate what their children know about race. I get a kick out of seeing how regularly parents, when they sit in on my interviews with their children, are astonished, amused, and often even embarrassed at the words coming out of their children's mouths. These parents, like many other adults, have difficulty understanding that preschoolers simply do not comprehend the meaning of racial labels even if they occasionally use them.

Developmental psychologists have long known that there are many words to which children do not attribute the same meanings as adults. Child psychologists Ginsberg and Opper explain: "We usually assume that if a child uses a particular word, it automatically conveys the same meaning that it does when an adult uses that word.

Adults often believe that once a child has learned the linguistic label for an object, he has available the underlying concept. But Piaget has shown that this is often not the case. The child does learn his words from the adult, but assimilates them into his own mental structure, which is quite different from the adult's."[2]

In my work as a psychologist, I've met parents who have adamantly insisted that their children are aware of race, only to learn that, if aware of anything, their children are actually aware of skin color. Children do use racial labels that adults try to teach them, but the children do not fully understanding their meaning. *Black* as a racial term is particularly confusing for some adults, so why shouldn't it perplex preschoolers?

Some parents have told me that their light-complexioned children were confused when told that they are really "black." From the perspective of these children, their skin color more resembles white. A few parents were mystified by the "stubbornness" their preschoolers showed when, after being repeatedly taught that they were black, they continued to call themselves "brown" or even "white."

Having just learned their colors, many preschoolers find it confusing to be taught that they are black when their own eyes show them that they are closer to brown or even to white. Children have great difficulty juxtaposing being a shade of brown and belonging to the black race. Not surprisingly, then, they have a frustrating time reconciling the skin color they actually see when they look at their bodies with the label that their parents give it. Parents should realize that it will be years before their preschoolers grow up enough to really understand the difference.

UNDERSTANDING THAT COLOR IS PERMANENT

Before beginning to understand the role that race plays in their identity, young children must first learn that skin color is a permanent attribute. The process children go through to learn about skin color and race is somewhat analogous to learning about gender.

Researchers have found that children's thinking about their gender changes before they come to understand that it is a permanent distinguishing feature of their bodies.[3] Developmental psychologist Lawrence Kohlberg showed that children develop their concept of gender in an invariant, predictable order.[4] Although most children can identify themselves correctly as a boy or a girl by age three, they continue to believe that they can change their gender at will (by wearing different clothes, by changing the length of their hair, or the like). For example, when my little boy was three years old, he would say he was a boy when anyone asked him. Yet he would also tell me that he changed into a girl when he put on his sister's dress and a wig to play dress-up. Only when they are older, around age four or five, do most children begin to understand that gender is an unchanging part of their identity. Similarly, a child reaches a milestone in her understanding of race when she realizes that her skin color is permanent.

So My Skin Color Can't Change?

Given their egocentricity and magical thinking, preschoolers believe that anything is possible. So it is not surprising that most of them do not see their skin color as indelible. To find out whether preschoolers see their skin color as a permanent part of their bodies, I conduct a picture exercise. First, I ask them whether their skin color can change. Then I ask them to look at photos of babies of various races and choose the baby they most looked like when they were little. Finally, I ask them to look at photos of adults of various races and choose the person they will most look like when they grow up.

Preschoolers' responses show that most of them do not see skin color as an immutable characteristic. Even those who say that their own skin color will not change tell me that is so because they do not want it to. They believe that it is possible for other people to change their skin color should they wish to do so.

When I ask preschoolers to choose the photo of the baby they most resembled when they were babies, some of them select photos of babies with skin colors that are obviously different from their own—indeed, sometimes even photos of babies of a different race. When I ask them to explain their choices, these preschoolers do not seem to focus on the difference between their skin color and that of the babies they choose. Skin color is irrelevant to their choices: they choose babies for all kinds of other reasons, like "I want to" or "She's cute."

Sometimes children say that when they were babies, they were a lighter color. If our conversations take place in their homes, some of these preschoolers bring me photos of themselves as babies to support their claim that they were "white" as babies. (Many black children are often lighter-complexioned as infants. Several people have told me stories about their children asking whether their new baby sister or brother belonged to the family because its skin was so different from everyone else's.) If asked about it, these preschoolers attribute the change in their skin color since birth to a magical process. Consider three-year-old Autumn's response:

INTERVIEWER: *Which baby did you look most like when you were a little baby?*
AUTUMN: **[Points to a photo of a light-complexioned black baby.]**
What color is that baby?
White.
Were you white when you were a baby?
Yeah.
How were you white?
'Cause God made me white when I was a little baby.
How do you know that?
'Cause I was down there.
But how do you know you were white when you were a little baby?
'Cause there weren't any more.
What color are you now?
When I come up here I turned brown.
Why did you turn brown?
'Cause there was no more.
No more what?
People down there.

Magical Colors

Four-year-olds are also inclined to believe in the power of magic to change their skin color. Such is the case with Monique:

INTERVIEWER: *When you were a little baby, which baby did you look most like?*
MONIQUE: **[Points to a photo of a white baby.]**

What color is that baby?
Vanilla.
When you were a little baby, were you vanilla?
Yeah.
What color are you now?
Chocolate.
How do you know that you were vanilla when you were a baby?
'Cause my daddy told me. . . . My daddy calls me "Smoky."
How did you come to be that color?
[Laughs.] My mommy and daddy.
How did they make you that color?
They paint me like you paint a house.
When did they paint you that color?
Yesterday.
But suppose your mommy told me she didn't paint you that color.
She *did* paint me though!

As you can see, it is not race that kids are confused about!

When I ask preschoolers to predict what color they will be when they grow up, their responses are just as imaginative and often just as hilarious. Although time, especially future time, is still an evolving concept for most preschoolers, they have some idea of what "the future" means. Just as they do not see the continuity between their past and their present skin color, most of them see little relationship between their present and their future skin color. Consider Rebecca's response:

INTERVIEWER: *When you grow up, which of these ladies will you look most like?*
REBECCA: **[Chooses a photo of a dark-complexioned black woman.]**
Why do you think you will look like this lady?
'Cause.
'Cause why?
'Cause I want to look like that.
Why do you want to?
I'm going to paint myself that color.
Why will you paint yourself that color?
'Cause.

In their initial response, some preschoolers *seem* to be on the right track in predicting their color. For example, four-year-old Dominique mentioned that when she grew up, her skin color would resemble her mother's. Yet a careful reading of her explanation reveals that she, too, relied on the magical thinking so characteristic of other preschoolers:

INTERVIEWER: *When you grow up to be a lady, which one of these ladies will you look most like?*
DOMINIQUE: **Me and my mother look like her. [Points to a photo.]**
What color are you?
Umm. I'm chocolate.

Earlier in our conversation, Dominique had described her mother's complexion as different from her own. She was obviously oblivious to the inconsistencies in her responses:

INTERVIEWER: *What color is your mommy?*
DOMINIQUE: **Vanilla.**
But you told me that your mommy was chocolate.
She vanilla.
How did your mommy come to be vanilla?
He [God] paint her.
He painted her?
He paint her face and all. He paint bubble on her.

When Black Children Say They Want to Be White

Preschoolers' magical ideas carry a critical message: parents and other people who take care of preschoolers should understand that since they do not see skin color as an unchangeable part of their bodies, it is normal for them to talk about wanting to be another color. Some black adults have trouble responding to children who say they want to be white. Naturally, it is frustrating for those parents who have tried to instill a sense of racial identity and pride in their young children to hear them say that they want to be white; these are painful words to any black parent. Many of us can identify with novelist Terry McMillan's poignant tale, published in the

New York Times, of her reaction when her young son told her that he wanted to be white:

> "I want to be white, like Brant," [his white playmate] my 3-year-old said to me the other day. We were on our way home from the Denver Zoo. "Look, Mommy, I'm turning white," he said, pointing to the inside of his palms. We passed through the red mountains. I blinked. Then I said: "The color of your skin is beautiful. Brant just told me yesterday that he wants to be black, but both colors are beautiful. That's why God made people all over the world different."[5]

This is a perfect illustration of preschoolers' whimsical thinking. Children delight in trying on different identities. Trouble arises only when parents and other adults take their remarks seriously, as relating to racial attitudes that preschoolers do not yet comprehend. Some parents overreact when their children say they want to be white by shaming or demeaning them. Others take such remarks as a sign of personal failure. They mistakenly reason that they have somehow been remiss in instilling a positive sense of racial identity in their children; otherwise, why would their children want to be white? Parents need to know the stages children pass through on their way to becoming aware of race so that the parents can understand that children imagining themselves to be different colors is a normal part of their development.

When four-year-old Tony first told his mother that he would like to be white like his playmate, she ignored his remark. When he said it again a few days later, she matter-of-factly told him that he had the perfect color for "my Tony." Then they played a game imagining what an orange would look like if it weren't orange, what color would best suit a banana if it couldn't be yellow, how grass would look if it weren't green, and how Tony would look if he were the color of his buddy. Tony's mother acted in an appropriate manner. She understood that her son's wish was most likely a passing fantasy, so she engaged Tony in conversation that was at his developmental level. She did not scold him or even question him about his wish to be white. Instead, she gave him permission to use his imagination to explore his wish. By not overreacting herself, and by allowing Tony to explore his fantasy imaginatively, she prevented the fantasy of being white from becoming a big deal.

Knowing Their Color Origin

Preschoolers have no interest in categorizing people into different racial groups. This gives young children a cognitive advantage over older children and adults because they are able to appreciate people for who they are as individuals, rather than stereotype them as members of a particular racial group. Once parents recognize this advantage, they have taken the first step in helping their children hold on to it as they mature.

Children say the most fascinating things when you delve into their understanding of how their skin color came to be. Few preschoolers are even aware of where babies come from, much less how their skin color originated. Their thinking about these complicated topics draws us deeper into the magical landscape of their minds.

Since preschoolers regard their skin color as no big deal, it is not surprising that they do not give much thought to its origin. They are still wrestling with the more fundamental question of where babies come from, and they have developed explanations that are as mind-boggling as they are revealing.

To learn what children think about the origin of their skin color, I first look at where they think babies come from. Preschoolers don't know much about procreation. The responses I hear are consistent with those obtained by other researchers.[6] Indeed, preschoolers mingle fragments of adult information on the origin of babies with their own creative notions of babies' origins. Consider the response of four-year-old Andrea:

INTERVIEWER: *When you were a baby, where did you come from?*
ANDREA: **From the hospital.**
Really? . . . Where did you come from?
From out of my mother's stomach, with the food.
How did you get out of your mother's stomach, I wonder.
Don't tell.
OK, I won't tell. How did you get out?
And don't tell my father either.
I won't tell your father.

Don't tell anybody.
I won't tell anybody. How did you get out of your mother's stomach?
I just took the key out of her hand and sloped it out of her throat.
How did you get into her stomach?
I broke her stomach and I fixed it back with some glue.

Similarly, preschoolers have intriguing ideas of how they came to have their own skin color. Some children say that God is responsible for their color. When I asked four-year-old Jasmine how she came to be the color she is, she quickly responded: "My Heavenly Father made me this color." But like other children, Jasmine believed that God used a magical process involving paints, wands, and the like, to give her her skin color. I've heard of another child who thought that drinking chocolate milk had made him brown. Regardless of whether preschoolers believe that a deity, a parent, or their own actions are responsible for their skin color, their explanations are a mixture of mostly fantasy and sometimes a sprinkling of fact. At this early stage of their cognitive development, preschoolers don't perceive skin color as a fact of their bodies and biology. Rather, they see it as something they themselves choose—and can change at will.

Family Colors

Some three-year-olds have difficulty identifying the members of their own family when asked to do so. During these early years, their concept of family is still emerging. They will, for example, include in their family friends who regularly visit their homes. Since preschoolers don't understand the genetic and marriage ties that bind family members together, it should not be a surprise that they have trouble understanding that families are generally racially homogeneous or that there is a logical genetic connection between their own skin color and their parents' skin color.

I notice sharp differences in the color consciousness of three- and four-year-olds when I show them a set of photos of children of various races and ask them to choose the children who belong to three pairs of parents: one white, one black, and one Chinese. The three-year-olds tend to assemble mixed-race families. They obviously have little idea that family members are racially homogeneous. Not yet aware of the genetic connection among family members, they put families together for their own reasons, such as "they like each other" and "they go together." Interestingly, most three-year-olds do not see any incongruity regarding an interracial couple (black and white) being parents of the same children. By contrast, most four-year-olds express disbelief when asked to find the children of an interracial couple; they do not accept that such couples have children.

Four-year-olds usually choose members of a family based on their skin-color similarity, as they put it, "because they match each other." But they are just as likely to put light-skinned black and Asian children in the same family as they are to select white children. As long as their skin colors match, it does not make a different whether they belong to different races. I have found that even children who themselves are from families where there are pronounced skin-color variations between parents and children insist that the photos of the children they choose to "go with" a specific pair of parents should be a similar skin color. Consider the response of four-year-old Aria, who is from a family with pronounced skin-color variations:

INTERVIEWER: *Why do these children belong to them? [Referring to the photos of children chosen as belonging to medium-complexioned black parents.]*

ARIA: **'Cause they look the same. . . . 'Cause the mommy and the daddy and the kids look the same.**

What looks the same?

Their face . . . the color.

Most four-year-olds reject the interracial couple as a "mommy" and "daddy" and as members of the same family because of their skin-color difference. These children often search the interview table, looking for other, more appropriate, photos, or pointedly ask me whether I have misplaced the appropriately colored parent. Latoya's puzzled reaction illustrates the typical four-year-old's response:

INTERVIEWER: *This is another mommy and daddy. [Shows photos of a black man and a white woman.]*

LATOYA: Where is her other daddy?

Uh . . .

She had a other one.

What do you mean?

She had a other one like her. . . . She don't look like him.

She doesn't look like him?

Nope.

Although some preschoolers are aware that their family members' skin colors are similar, none of them understand that skin color is genetically transmitted. The idea that family members usually belong to the same race is beyond them.

UNDERSTANDING RACIAL GROUPS

Are preschoolers aware of the physical cues that adults use to classify people into different racial groups? Preschoolers, according to experts in child development, have rudimentary classification skills, that is, the ability to correctly group things that belong together. For example, if you ask a four-year-old to sort a pile of various shapes (for instance, circles, triangles, and squares) into different groups of similar shapes, most of them can do it, especially if you show them how first. However, even with considerable instruction, children do not develop the kind of advanced classification skills needed to categorize people into different racial groups until around age seven. They are not naturally inclined to perceive people as belonging to different skin-color or racial groups. So it is not surprising that when they are forced by a researcher to look at people in this manner, they become resistant and are more likely to return to their own unique way of seeing people.

Preschoolers cannot comprehend the basis for putting people into different groups by race (for example, white, black) or ethnicity (for instance, Chinese, Mexican). To determine which people belong in what racial group, adults use a complex set of cues, including physical characteristics (skin color, hair color and texture, nose and lip shapes, and the like) and social cues. But even with all this knowledge to draw on, adults still have trouble guessing some people's races. I wish I had a dime for every time I was asked, "What is she?" or "Is he really ______?"

The nuances involved in determining an individual's race are well beyond the cognitive skills of most preschoolers. When I show preschoolers a pile of photos of children from various races and ask them to group children who belong together, they do not spontaneously sort children by skin color. Three-year-olds are more likely to divide the children into groups they call "brothers and sisters" or "friends." By contrast, four-year-olds are more likely to group children into boy piles and girl piles, grouping by gender and not race.

Only after additional prompting do children use skin color as the basis for sorting people into different groups. Children usually group the photos of black, Chinese, and white children into three skin color groups comprised of dark-, brown-, and light-skinned children. Interestingly, most of the preschoolers do not spontaneously use a color or racial word to describe their groups.

If you explicitly ask preschoolers to sort photos of the children of different races, all wearing identical clothes, into "black," "white," and "Chinese," it is a sure bet that they will not sort all of them accurately without coaching. Most preschoolers interpret the term "black" literally and put only the darkest-complexioned people into the "black" group. Some will say that "black" refers to people with black hair.

Preschoolers usually put all light-complexioned children (whites, Chinese, and light-complexioned blacks) into the "white" group. Children who have had some exposure to Chinese people (whether in person or on television) are more likely to accurately sort people into the "Chinese" group than children who have had limited familiarity with people of this race. But these children also see Chinese as belonging to both the "white" and "Chinese" groups.

Sometimes I feel a little guilty asking children to do some of these exercises—for example, prompting them to sort people by skin color—because I'm encouraging them to look at people in a way that doesn't come naturally to them. In real life, when I hear preschoolers describe people by a color name, I find they are likely to be describing any one of several things about them, for example, the color of their clothes, their hair, or even their hats. The children don't always, or even usually, mean skin color.

Just the other day, I heard my six-year-old telling his ten-year-old brother about the "white men" in a *Star Wars* book. My ears pricked up because I'd never heard my younger son talking about people in terms of their skin color. Later that evening, I learned that he was calling the men "white" because they were dressed in white masks and suits. Even with all my experience in the field, I cannot escape the race consciousness of my culture. I still occasionally fall into the trap of thinking children are talking race when they are really talking color.

Confusion About Racial Labels

Preschoolers are not naturally inclined to describe people by skin color, but when they do, they rely on their limited experience to come up with words to do so. Food is something with which they are familiar, and so it is not surprising that many of them use words related to food to describe people's skin color. For example, some preschoolers call dark-complexioned people "chocolate" and light-complexioned people "vanilla," "peach," and, less often, "lemon-colored" or "banana-colored." One black preschooler referred to a white friend as "the cherry-colored girl"; I initially assumed she was describing the girl in terms of skin color, but I later learned from her grandmother that she was describing the girl by her hair color. As preschoolers learn their colors, they gradually switch to using simple color words like *brown, pink, black,* or *white* to describe skin color. However, it takes a while before they use these color words to describe people's races in the way that adults do.

Parents often tell me that their preschoolers are confused about how to use racial labels. The mother of a four-year-old repeatedly tried to teach her daughter to differentiate white people from light-complexioned black people. Even after several months, her daughter remained baffled: "When she sees a white person, she'll say that person is white—that's a 'white girl' or a 'white boy.' . . . Sometimes she gets confused. If she sees someone that's real light, she thinks they're white."

Some parents say that their children are not even interested in learning racial labels and cannot be persuaded to talk about people in terms of skin color. For example, a mother recalled the following reaction when she asked her four-year-old daughter about the color of a white neighborhood playmate: "My daughter was telling me a whole lot about him. And I said to her, 'What color is he?' And she looked at me real hard, you know, but she wouldn't tell me his color."

Young children's cognitive advantage in seeing people as individuals allows them to appreciate people for who they are rather than pigeonholing them according to racial stereotypes. When parents recognize this benefit, they take the first step in helping their children hold on to this precious gift for as long as they can.

How Biracial Children Learn About Their Race

Compared with children of black parents, children of mixed-race (for example, black and white) parents have to process information about two parts of their identities that in our society are often in conflict with one another. Fair-skinned biracial children seem to become aware of their race later than black children but earlier than white children. Like parents of black children, parents of mixed-race children may conclude that a child is aware she is biracial because she uses the appropriate terms to refer to herself early on, while she is still learning her racial identity. However, like the black child, she may pick up on the feelings behind the racial names she is called long before she understands what these terms really mean.

Consider the following account, from a story in the *San Francisco Chronicle,* of Katherine, a light-complexioned biracial (white and black) four-year-old, who had a sandbox conflict with her classmate. As Katherine's adoptive father remembered it, "A little black boy grabbed her shovel and said, 'Give it here, whitey.' Katherine said, 'I'm not whitey. I'm not white. I'm Katherine.' " But Katherine's memories of her sandbox conflict differed from those of her father: "I said, 'I'm not white.' He said, 'Yes you are.' I said, 'I'm Katherine, and I'm half white and I'm half black.' My parents were really proud of me, but I didn't know what it meant. I just knew that I didn't want to be associated with the negative, and in this case, being white was the negative."[7]

WHITE PRESCHOOLERS' DIFFERENT LESSONS ABOUT RACE

Black children seem to become aware of their race at a younger age than their white peers. Limited research and anecdotal evidence suggest that race is not as salient an issue for white children as it is for black ones.[8] This makes sense because of the continuing stigma associated with darker skin in our society. Until the United States puts race prejudice behind it for good and all, black children will eventually have to confront negative stereotypes about their race as they grow up.

Over years of observing young children draw their self-portraits, I've noticed that black children, particularly those who attend school with white children, begin coloring in their skin color in their self-portraits at an earlier age than white children. Black children begin to do so as early as kindergarten, while white children generally do not focus on skin color until they are a little older.

Most young white children are as ignorant as black children regarding the meanings adults attach to skin color. White children, like their black peers, are not developmentally inclined to categorize people by color, much less by race. A white mother told a story that her three-year-old son had told her. He was surrounded by many of the older children at a predominantly black preschool a short while after he started attending. They told him that he was white. He didn't understand why the other children were telling him about his color. He responded, "So?" When he arrived home he asked his mother why some of the other children told him he was white.

From the other side of the fence, a black columnist wrote of her surprise when she heard about a negative comment made by Jacob, her son Darrell's white four-year-old next-door neighbor and best friend. She admitted being "confounded" when she learned that Jacob told his day-care provider that he "didn't like black people." Jacob's mother said that her son "looked puzzled" when she questioned him about whether he was also talking about Darrell: "'But Darrell isn't black,' Jacob insisted. 'Darrell and his family are nice,' he said, 'not like those scary strangers on TV that hurt people.'"[9]

Jacob's comments suggest his literal interpretation of the term *black.* Chances are that, like his black peers, he has not yet learned to include people of various shades of brown into his concept of "black" people. When Jacob heard a TV anchorperson report that blacks committed certain crimes, he most likely imagined the "bad guys" to be literally black. Adults automatically assume that when a child describes a person by color, the child is referring to race. However, it is alarming when such a young child associates "black" people with fear, especially when he himself has never had any personal experiences with scary "black" people and does not even recognize a black person when he sees one.

Perhaps the major difference between how black and white children learn about each other's race is that many whites learn early to be fearful of people called "black," whereas many black children learn to be distrustful of people called "white." Sadly, children of both races often learn about negative attitudes attached to other people's skin colors long before they can identify who these black and white people really are.

White preschoolers share with their black peers an innocence about racial differences. A black family day-care manager, Mrs. Scott, related an incident that conveys the hilarious naïveté of two children, Owen and Adam (one black and the other white), about skin-color differences.

One day, after Owen, a four-year-old white boy, had been in her care for several months, his father telephoned her. He said that the first thing his son told him excitedly after leaving her center that day was, "Dad, Adam's penis is a different color from mine!" He had noticed the difference when he and his buddy went to the bathroom together that day.

The father and Mrs. Scott shared a few belly laughs over the incident. But Mrs. Scott was perplexed. She wondered why Owen was surprised. He had met children from other races at the child-care center. Moreover, Adam and Owen spent considerable time together, so they had ample opportunity to observe each other's physical differences. She didn't realize that children do not see things, even things that adults consider obvious and important, until they are ready to see them.

Mrs. Scott heard nothing further about the incident until about two weeks later during nap time when she overheard Owen say to Adam: "Since we're a different color down there, let's see where else we're different." They both eagerly lifted their clothes and displayed different parts of their bodies to each other. As the boys strained beneath the various layers of their clothes to peek at each other's derrieres, she heard one of them say, "I can't see it. Is it a different color too?"

Some young white children (and even some light-complexioned blacks and Latinos) think that people with dark skin are "dirty." They believe that dark people only need a good wash to be restored to a "normal" (that is, white) skin color. At this early stage of race awareness, children do not understand that skin color is permanent. They genuinely believe dark people can wash away their dark skin color. Some adults, blacks as well as whites, misinterpret young white children's innocent remarks like "He's got dirt on his face because his mama didn't wash him" or "She looks dirty." Such comments are taken as proof that these children have negative stereotypes of blacks.

People who interpret such naïve remarks to mean that these children see blacks as dirty are themselves guilty of naïveté. A preschooler who says that a dark person is dirty sees skin color very differently from a teenager who might make a similar statement. They are simply at two developmentally different stages of race awareness. The preschooler sees skin color as a temporary condition of the skin of others presumed to be like himself. The teenager sees skin color as a signal of a permanent difference to identify targets he can harass.

A white preschooler who has had little or no contact with blacks has a different concept of people than a child who has had more exposure. It is understandable that such a child would think that the world is composed only of whites. If he sees people of a different color, then he naturally and not altogether illogically assumes that they must actually be white people whose "whiteness" is hidden by a different surface color. This child uses as his reference point his own experience of becoming brownish when he plays in dirt. So in his experience, people who are brown are "dirty" and can wash themselves and become white again.

Unfortunately, some adults are not aware that children do not attach the same meaning to skin color that adults do. I heard of a white teacher who complained to a white preschooler's mother that her daughter had called a black classmate "dirty." The adult interpreted a minor misunderstanding between the two preschoolers as racist in origin. But in truth, the white child, who prior to entering nursery school had only limited contact with blacks, simply did not understand that people came in different colors. And while the children went back to playing together and seemed to have forgotten the incident, the adults, unaware that children have not yet learned racial stereotypes, were left with the impression that the little white girl was a budding racist.

In a similar situation, Marcia, an engaging black four-year-old and the darkest child in her preschool class, meekly told me that another little girl (whom I later learned was a light-complexioned Puerto Rican) had repeatedly refused to hold her hand during circle times because her classmate said that Marcia's arms and hands were dirty. Marcia insisted to the girl that they were clean while her classmate adamantly demanded that Marcia wash them. Marcia felt rejected and puzzled by her classmate's behavior. The teacher was oblivious to the conflict, and Marcia suffered in silence.

Teachers need to be particularly aware how children from different backgrounds are relating to each other. For most preschoolers, skin color is not a big deal: they'll play with any other children who are nice to them and interested in doing the things they enjoy doing. But some children who have different temperaments or backgrounds may be particularly sensitive to differences between themselves and others. If Marcia's preschool teacher had been more observant about how the children in her class were interacting, she would have noticed that the classmate repeatedly avoided holding Marcia's hand. Then the teacher could have dealt sensitively with the situation by holding Marcia's hand herself and conducting a little lesson showing the class that people come in all colors and that skin colors do not rub off. It takes time for preschoolers to grasp certain concepts, but if the teacher had discussed the topic of skin color, the child who felt uncomfortable touching her classmate's hand would have gradually learned that she had nothing to fear. But I can't completely blame the teacher. Marcia had not even told her mother about the distress she had experienced by the rejection of this classmate. I learned of the incident while I was interviewing the youngster for my research.

Preschoolers are at a wonderful time of life that provides parents and educators with an exceptional opportunity to nurture their natural inclination to see people as individuals, not as stereotypes. As we'll see in the next chapter, these early years can be a hazardous time for children whose caregivers teach racial bigotry. Since earliest learning is hardest to change, the racist talk they hear and the bigoted behavior they observe become entrenched and more difficult to unlearn when they are older. They are placed at considerable risk of being unable to relate to people who do not look like them. When they learn to see people in terms of racial stereotypes, their expectations for the kinds of relationships they can have with these people become distorted. Fortunately, given their natural lack of preconceptions, it takes a great deal of negative input to turn preschoolers into bigots.

CHAPTER TWO

How Preschoolers Begin to Learn Racial Attitudes

The four-year-old's skin color was considerably lighter than his mother's. He never seemed to notice the difference until one day, out of the blue, he pointed to her arm and remarked, "You brown, Mommy," as if to reassure himself that he was correct in his observations. A few days later, he elaborated on his developing awareness of his mother's skin color. As he hugged her, he observed, "You're chocolate. You're yummy, Mommy, like a chocolate cookie." (Around the same time, he made the observation that a very obese man on TV was "fat.") He was making simple observations of people's physical characteristics—nothing more.

Clearly, this boy had not yet grasped the societal meanings attached to people of color (or obese people): he innocently spoke what he saw and felt. He loved his mommy, and her color was a very positive, "yummy" feature. Yet some people would predict that in a few years, his delighted association of his mother's color with a favorite treat would be transformed into an interpretation of brown skin as a label marked "black" with a lot of heavy baggage attached. How could it happen?

In this chapter, we will look at how children begin to form racial attitudes. We'll see a myriad of influences in everyday life that contribute to preschoolers' growing sense that there is something more to skin color than mere color. Children begin to notice that those who are important in their lives—relatives, friends, and others—feel negatively or positively about people of different colors. We will look at several of these influences—language, cultural standards of beauty, books, toys, and cultural images—and explore how they affect the preschooler's developing awareness of the meaning of skin-color differences. Often the greatest impact comes through the reactions these influences trigger in the child's caregivers.

Conventional wisdom holds that most black children dislike themselves because of their race. In their best-seller *Different and Wonderful,* black psychologists Darlene and Derek Hopson wrote, "Black people think of themselves as lacking in self-worth. And nowhere is this problem of low self-esteem more widespread or more critical than among children."[1] Some blacks blame "society," specifically white society, when young black children display negative feelings about their color and race, but *if a preschooler has negative feelings about her color, the most likely source of those feelings are the people close to her,* her family members and friends.

Considerable misinformation exists about children's negative racial attitudes. Parallels can be found between sexual abuse and racial abuse. Children are warned by their elders to be wary of "strangers" who may sexually molest them. But only a small number of children are sexually abused by strangers. Studies show that the sexual abuse of children is usually perpetrated by family members or people in the family's circle of acquaintances—in other words, children are usually victimized not by strangers but by people they trust. Similarly, some blacks believe it is whites who make their children feel inferior. But in reality, many young black children are racially abused by their own family and friends—perhaps because their skin color is not light enough or dark enough, because their hair is not "good" enough, or because their features are not "right." For these physical "deficits," racial victims pay dearly: they are ridiculed, demeaned, even rejected. Young children, because of their cognitive and emotional immaturity, are predisposed to pick up on these negative values and internalize them.

VIEWING COLOR THROUGH INDIVIDUALS

Preschoolers are developmentally inclined to view people as individuals. They tend to relate to people according to how people treat them. They view people in extremes: nice or mean, good or bad. In a sense, preschoolers are at a developmental advantage in that they see people as individuals rather than as members of groups. Unless children have been sensitized by others around them either to feel inferior or superior to people who have a different skin color, they are generally ignorant of the social connotations of skin color.

Preschoolers, whatever their race, who are taught by their caregivers' words, behaviors, or attitudes to fear or dislike people who are of a different color are more likely to become prematurely sensitized to color issues and to regard people of different colors as enemies without ever having any personal experience with them. Interestingly, these children will still be unable to comprehend what race means, but they begin to acquire the societal meaning attached to different skin colors. A prime channel of this information is other people's language.

From Color to Connotations

When skin color or race is frequently discussed in the family, children will learn at a young age that there is some meaning beyond mere color associated with such color words as *black* and *white*. Depending on his or her family's attitudes, the child will learn that there are positive or negative connotations to *black* or *white*, to dark skin or light skin. Though they may not be able to understand these differences, children do *feel* them. A child will be able to sense from subtle messages that being lighter or darker is better or worse.

Many black children grow up hearing the word *black* being used in a negative fashion by family members or friends. For example, a frustrated mother might say to her child, "Get your black behind up to your room and pick up your toys!" An angry father might say to a friend, in his child's presence, "Get out of my face, you black bastard!"

In informal interviews I've had with white people, I've asked if they remember whether their parents and caregivers included derogatory references to their skin color when they were being scolded or disciplined for misbehaving as children. Invariably, they tell me no. Many blacks, by contrast, have painful memories of their skin color being demeaned when someone, usually a close relative or friend, reprimanded or criticized them. The caregiver's tone of voice and the emotions they convey when they use skin-color words undoubtedly have a powerful impact on the child's feelings about these words. Too often, young black children learn early in their lives to associate being black with a negative feeling. Why else would their daddy or mommy use the word *black* to put them or other people down?

Racial Epithets: Language as a Weapon

Once, while I was waiting in a checkout line at a children's clothing store, I witnessed a distressing scene involving a black teenage girl and a small solemn-faced black boy, about three years old. The girl repeatedly asked the little boy to do something, and he repeatedly refused. Then she said something else, and the boy answered her in a voice so soft I couldn't hear. I could see that she was startled by whatever he had said, so startled that she called out loudly to a friend, who was in another section of the store, "Did you just hear what this little nigger called me? 'Bitch!'" She seemed at once amused and perturbed by what she perceived as the boy's insolence. She summoned her friend to her and tried to provoke the boy into repeating his use of *bitch* for her friend's amusement. While trying to elicit the grown-up word from the little boy's mouth, the teenage girl repeatedly addressed the little boy as "nigger."

I cringed at the lesson this little boy and the other children in the checkout line were learning: that a mean little word—one that they would eventually learn is a racial epithet—could be used so easily to hurt.

I hear that preschool teachers have noticed a sharp increase in the use of racial epithets among their students as young as three years old. These little tykes are using racial epithets to attack each other. What's happening to make their speech so seemingly racist?

It's easy to point the finger at the usual suspects: TV, pop music (especially rap), and other people's brats. In truth, when you hear a preschooler making frequent use of this kind of objectionable language, you should look to the child's parents or other caregivers, including older siblings, other relatives, and family friends: they are almost certainly the source of the abusive language.

A frustrated father, though in the presence of his three young children, didn't think twice about telling a difficult friend, "Kiss my black ass, nigger!" What happens in a child's mind when she repeatedly witnesses similar scenes in which black skin color is associated with such anger and such demands? It is easy to guess what happens: the child quickly learns that skin color can be used as a weapon to inflict pain.

Children often grasp the abusive connotations long before they can comprehend the racial bias involved in using such offensive words. Take the case of a preschooler I met. This little boy frequently overheard his father and his buddies complaining about the "white trash" and "honkies" and "crackers" who made their lives difficult. The child, even after repeatedly being told that the words referred to whites, did not quite grasp the racial connection. But he did understand that the words had something to do with anger and frustration, so he used them liberally whenever he had conflicts with his playmates, although most of them were black.

I know a psychologist who, while visiting a home to give a black mother parenting guidance, was greeted with the word *nigger* on the lips of the woman's four-year-old son. This little boy lived in a very dysfunctional home with several siblings and his mother, who had a history of abusing her children. Early in his young life, this little boy had already learned that certain words created a stir among adults and that if he used these words, he could attract the adult attention he so desperately craved. When the psychologist did not react, the boy eventually realized that the shock word *nigger* had no effect on her, and he stopped using it (at least in her presence).

Indeed, young children do learn that some racial words—like other profanities—are "bad" and have a naughty punch to them. Such words convey a kind of power. They make people flinch or sit up and take notice. Preschoolers do not know precisely what it is about these words that give them such power, but they do know that using them works wonders in attracting attention.

Racial epithets usually arise as part of a larger repertoire of profanity and abusive language in the child's home environment. Invariably, children who regularly use racial epithets at an early age also have at least a sprinkling of other profanities in their vocabulary. I have never met a preschooler who habitually used profanities whose parents or primary caregivers did not regularly use them as well.

Stopping Hate Language Starts at Home

If you want to raise children who are not prejudiced against blacks, whites, or anyone of a different race, you must avoid using racial epithets or allowing others to do so in your children's presence. There's no getting around it. Using derogatory racial epithets to refer to people of other races makes the user no better than a bigot.

If it is not permissible for blacks to employ racial epithets when speaking about people of other races, it is surely almost blasphemous for them to use racial epithets to refer to fellow blacks. No matter how some people may rationalize, *nigger* is a word that causes pain to many blacks, no matter who brandishes it. To claim, as some African Americans do, that it is permissible for blacks to refer to one another as "niggers" dishonors our heritage.

Richard Pryor, the popular comedian, was fond of using the word *nigger* in his monologues: it had shock value; its use made people uncomfortable, but it also made people laugh. But when he visited Africa for the first time, he experienced an epiphany in which he came to see the word for what it truly is: a profoundly dehumanizing term. He vowed never to use the word again. Surely, it is one word that we should not pass on to our children.

Just as children learn from observing and modeling the behavior of significant others in their environment, they memorize and mimic the language they hear. The implications are obvious: if you want to minimize the likelihood that your child will use racial epithets, don't use them yourself, and carefully monitor other sources, like television programs and music, that may influence your child's vocabulary.

THE EFFECTS OF BEAUTY STANDARDS AND GROOMING

In addition to the language that they hear, other experiences will sensitize preschoolers to the meaning skin color and race have for important people in their lives. Since their cognitive abilities are limited, young children come to know much of the world through their feelings. Early on, children pick up the messages broadcast by family members and others regarding their own worth relative to that of other members of their immediate social circle. Jean Piaget, the noted child psychologist, showed that children, like little scientists, try to figure out the reason others are loved more or less in comparison to them.[2]

So the key to understanding the roots of a child's racial attitudes, both regarding her own race and regarding other races, is to learn how she is treated by members of her family and how they view people of other races. Look to the skin-color, hair, and facial-features preferences of parents and others close to the child. As the child grows older, she may come to understand that her brother is valued more because he is lighter, or a sister is considered prettier because she has "better" (that is, straighter) hair, or a cousin is seen as "cuter" because he has a narrower nose.

Children not only listen attentively but observe carefully how family members and friends respond to their own physical characteristics and those of others and what comparisons they make. They note the labels attached to these descriptions—"good," "bad," "nice," "ugly," "dumb," "smart." Whatever a child's race, some adults will make observations about her appearance, observations that reflect their own preferences and prejudices. When people verbalize these observations or reveal them in action by favoring one child over another, children become sensitized to the messages, however subtle, they receive. Preschoolers may not yet be able to articulate their awareness that a person is treating them differently because of their physical appearance, but they *feel* it.

Skin-Color Preferences

As far back as the era of slavery, light-complexioned blacks, the offspring of the white owners and slaves, were given preferential treatment compared to darker-skinned blacks: they usually worked as house servants, while dark-complexioned blacks were assigned to the fields, stables, mills, and other places of hard labor. Through the generations, the slaveholders' preference for light skin has persisted in the values handed down by those they oppressed. There was a popular children's rhyme that went

> If you're light, you're right.
> If you're brown, stick around.
> If you're black, stay back.

The "black is beautiful" movement of the early 1960s, though it caused a revolution in the way blacks looked at themselves, was not entirely successful in erasing the stigma of being dark-skinned. Many blacks will tell you that although standards have changed a lot, light skin, especially for girls, is still an advantage. (Look at most of the models in black magazines or the wives of rich and famous black men.) As columnist Brenda Payton wrote in *Thinking Black*, "Just as blondes define beauty in the general society, light skins with straight hair define it within the African American community. It's become our own standard of beauty, independent of the white standard."[3] It is only a matter of time before children become aware, primarily from family and friends, that if you are lighter, you are regarded as "better."

Most of the preschoolers I've interviewed about skin color don't seem to have a clear preference for a certain color skin. However, I have met a few preschoolers, usually of dark complexion, who reported that they would like to be lighter. In practically every instance in which children expressed a wish to be lighter, it was because they felt that other children were favored because of their lighter color.

In the documentary film *Black Is, Black Ain't,* a young black woman discussed her painful memories of the overwhelmingly negative comments that she received about her physical appearance when she was a child.[4] As she grew older, it slowly dawned on her that the people making the negative comments about her dark skin (and her full lips and broad nose) were almost always other blacks. She felt that their negative remarks about her reflected their own insecurities and pain.

Of course, within every race, there are people who are considered more or less attractive because of certain physical features that others of that race may or may not find appealing. But emotional or verbal abuse because of skin color or any other physical characteristics (racial or otherwise) is most reprehensible when it is perpetrated by loved ones or people of one's own race.

Many children grow up in an atmosphere where they are demeaned because they are too dark or their hair is too nappy or their noses are too broad. (Full lips used to be a problem, too, until the last few years, when the fashion world began to regard them as an asset.) Other children are belittled because they don't look "black enough": they are light-complexioned or their hair is too straight and long. There are depressing stories on both sides of the color line.

Hair Preferences

The messages children, especially girls, pick up about their hair exert a powerful impact on their developing self-concept. The hair-care ritual sensitizes young children to the meaning of color and race. This ritual plays a central role in black children's discovery of the lengths they have to go to in order to "look good." For girls, especially, the hair-care ritual can be particularly traumatic. The tugging, yanking, and pulling involved in transforming their hair is often time-consuming and painful. Some children are forced to endure long hours of hair straightening, either chemically or with a hot comb, a grueling experience for a young child.

What the "Afro" was to the 1960s, hair extensions are to the 1990s. Now black children who desire long hair can have it. Hairpieces, once mostly the province of adults, have invaded the child's world. Today, with the popularity of hair extensions, the hair ritual can be even more daunting for young children. Preschoolers are sometimes required to sit quietly for hours while hair extensions are woven into their hair and then styled into elaborate braids. This ritual is a challenge to young children with limited attention spans.

Whether it is extending, straightening, or the old-fashioned pressing with a hot comb, the pain—yanking, tugging, pulling, twisting, weaving—that is involved in transforming hair is an ordeal for young children. While they are enduring this ritual, children may also hear negative comments about how kinky and unmanageable their hair is. What is the effect on children's developing self-image when so much time and effort is put into hair grooming? What message does it send about their own hair?

Attractive hairstyles that allow children's hair to remain in its natural state seem preferable to painful and lengthy hair-altering processes. Take the time to regard the hair-care ritual from the child's viewpoint. Aliona Gibson, in *Nappy: Growing Up Black and Female in America,* offers such a viewpoint; she remembers having "a massive head of long, thick, uncontrollable hair that was more than a notion to comb and, God forbid, to wash. At the age of four, I got my hair pressed for the first time, which made combing my hair an act of grooming and less one of abuse."[5]

Parents of any race who find it an ordeal to manage their children's hair should look for an alternative that will make washing and styling their children's hair a pleasant experience for both children and parents. For some children, it is easy to keep their hair "natural"; others may need a little help in managing their hair. In recent years, products have come on the market that make hair care much easier for blacks. Conditioners and mild relaxers are now readily available, so there is no reason children should have to endure the torture that was the hair-grooming ritual of yesteryear.

Dealing with the Blonde Myth

"Blondes have more fun" and "gentlemen prefer blondes" are more than seductive advertising lines; to some blacks, they are put-downs. In addition to young children learning that there is a societal preference for a certain kind of hair texture (straight), they will also eventually become aware that there is a preferred hair color.

Some black parents become very concerned when their young daughters express a preference for blonde hair. They wonder where they went wrong in influencing their daughter to embrace a white standard of beauty. These parents need not torture themselves. Children express a preference for blonde hair when they sense, without necessarily being able to articulate it, that people value it more highly than other hair colors. These children are simply picking up on the culturally prevalent value that this color hair is the most desirable. Isn't it most often depicted as the hair color of fairy-tale princesses and of television and movie "stars"? (Interestingly, many of the stars who embody the blonde ideal, like Marilyn Monroe and Madonna, were born brunettes.) This is a bias other racial groups, including whites, have to deal with.

A poignant example of this occurred in a Little Miss of America Pageant, Tiny Division, where girls as young as three compete. In an article in *People,* a white mother expressed the sentiments of many white parents of contestants who are not blondes: her dark-haired daughter, she said, "is getting very leery of blonde children because they always beat her out."[6]

Black parents, concerned because their daughters prefer blonde hair, should be aware that many white parents with dark-haired or red-headed daughters confront a similar problem. Hair-color preference is not simply a racial issue. For example, the actress Cybill Shepherd told an interviewer that her mother became upset when Cybill's blonde hair began to darken; she then described the lengths to which her mother went to restore her young daughter's original hair color. A representative of a major hair-coloring company said that one of the questions that is most frequently asked comes from white mothers who are seeking information about how to lighten their young daughters' hair.

Indeed, it is the exceptional child or adult who does not want to change *something* about his or her physical appearance, if only temporarily. I'm reminded of this by a parent's letter to prominent pediatrician and parenting columnist T. Berry Brazelton. A white mother of two preschool biracial daughters (their father is black) wrote to seek his advice on whether she had responded appropriately to her four-year-old daughter, who "has begun to express her desire to be white, have a 'pinchy nose' and blond hair and blue eyes. My husband and I try to reassure her that she's beautiful and we love her just the way she is. Part of me feels this may be normal, as I remember wishing I had straight hair when I was a child." Brazelton's advice was right on the mark. He answered that "almost all young children want to be what they aren't. Continue to assure your daughters that they are beautiful just as they are."[7]

Black children's ideas of physical attractiveness are similar to those of children of other races who are influenced by the same cultural values. Why expect them to be immune from the cultural forces that shape everyone's attitudes simply because they are black? Since children's notion of race during the preschool years is at best rudimentary, they are oblivious to the ethnic significance of skin and hair colors unless the older people in their world make too much of their ever-changing preferences.

If we raise our children to believe in themselves and to develop their abilities, they are less likely to be negatively affected by advertisers' hyped standards of beauty. As my daughter said to her father as she was happily skipping to school one morning when she was nine, "They say blondes have more fun, but I can't see how anyone can have more fun than I'm having."

LOOKING AT RACE IN CHILDREN'S BOOKS AND PLAYTHINGS

Some parents worry needlessly about the race of the characters in their children's books. In the past, blacks had considerable difficulty finding *any* children's books with positive black characters. Now, however, there are *plenty* of books in all genres that feature positive black figures.

Black parents understandably become upset when their children are exposed primarily to books about whites in their preschools. But concerned parents should realize that preschool children do not see characters in books the way some race-conscious adults see them. Children are drawn to fantasy. Whatever their skin color, children are able to identify with and even become all kinds of characters in their fantasy. Young children's imaginations simply do not recognize the boundaries of race. In fact, the scope of their fantasies is vast. I still remember how disappointed my preschool daughter was when she learned she could not marry Mickey Mouse!

Some parents are so offended by the domination of white characters in books that they want to do something about it. Some even go so far as coloring white characters brown or black to counteract the dominance of white characters in books. However, this approach may backfire: race becomes even more of an issue when books are tampered with. (Furthermore, this kind of activity conveys the negative message that it is all right to damage books if you dislike something about them.) Parents and other caregivers who obsess about the colors of the characters in books (and elsewhere) may cause children to become overly sensitive to skin color and may actually harm their development of healthy self-concepts.

Some people have demanded that books that portray blacks negatively be removed from circulation, and that's putting it mildly. But censorship is not the answer, either. More often than not, children do not see the biases that adults become so worked up over. The more constructive response is for parents to start early to teach their children to read critically. Educator Herbert Kohl has shown how one can allow children to enjoy the pleasures of books that may have certain biases while guiding them in understanding these books' limitations.[8]

Although more books today deal with the lives of black children and their families, there is still a paucity of books that present the rich diversity of blacks' everyday lives. Parents and caregivers need to seek out books whose range of characters is not restricted to the ghetto, the inner city, or dysfunctional homes. It is important that preschoolers, though unaware of race, recognize people like themselves in the stories that are read to them and that they are learning to read. But it is equally important that books include people of other races. The most treasured stories represent a shared cultural heritage that transcends the boundaries of race, geography, and even time.

Choosing Toys

Parents (especially new parents) treat toy selection as a serious matter. But regardless of what parents want their children to play with, even very young children have their own ideas about what toys they want. Several black parents have told me that they want toys that will promote their children's ethnic identity. However, it is important, even in our race-obsessed society, not to forget that the main purpose of toys is to give children the opportunity to have fun.

A black entrepreneur revealed that she was inspired to found a company manufacturing black fantasy hero toys for black children when she became distressed by the remarks of her four-year-old son: "'I want to be like He-Man,' he said, referring to a popular toy, a blond, blue-eyed action figure. 'But I can't, because he is white.'"[9] This boy's remarks were unusual for a child of his age.

Most children his age are so highly imaginative that they think they can be anything they want to be.

I believe that it is important for children to have toy figures that are representative of people who look like them *and* representative of people who look different: this holds true for white as well as black children. But selecting "appropriately" colored toys is only a small part of fostering a child's racial identity. The skin color of his toys is simply not a meaningful distinction to a preschooler. Parents and others who emphasize obtaining the "right" colors for the toys their children play with may be setting their children up to be racially sensitive, if not race-obsessive.

It is interesting that some of the most sought-after toys have been race-neutral. Consider "My Little Pony," a toy that was hugely popular several years back. The developers of this toy learned that children, particularly girls, liked combing the ponies' long, flowing manes and tails (which came in an array of colors, including purple, pink, and green), and so they were able to profit handsomely by creating an extensive line of ponies and their accouterments. My eldest daughter and her friends, who were black, Chinese, and white, simply adored collecting the various little ponies and their limitless accessories.

Barney, that lovable purple dinosaur on TV who so enraptures children, regardless of their ethnicity, spawned the creation of a hot series of toys. Several times in stores I've witnessed similar exchanges between preschoolers and their parents regarding their children's demands for a Barney or a Barney-themed item. Some parents admitted that they have had their fill of Barney. Although Barney is one of my favorite characters because of the prosocial lessons he teaches, I must admit that once I too became exasperated with him when my younger son threw a tantrum in a store after I refused to buy him yet another Barney item. I was feeling somewhat embarrassed until three parents, one black and two white, individually offered their sympathy. They all told me that they had had similar experiences with their children in stores after they refused their requests to purchase something else from the Barney collection of toys.

Some of the most sought-after toys a few years ago were the Power Rangers, figures based on the TV action heroes who morph (change) into dinosaurs and other powerful creatures to fight evil.

(Remember that the belief in their ability to change their identity is very consistent with preschoolers' developmental stage.) These characters are of different genders and races.

Critics have charged the Power Rangers' television show with promoting gratuitous violence. But such critics may be overreacting to a show that does have prosocial value. Preschoolers and older children can see that these characters, of different ethnic backgrounds and genders, share common values and are able to cooperate to combat evil. Children, who sometimes feel powerless, become powerful when they identify with these characters. In so doing, they not only triumph over evil but transcend gender and skin color as well.

At age four, my younger son had his heart set on collecting all the Power Rangers figures. He enjoyed spending time making up endless stories about their adventures. When he referred to their colors, he meant their uniforms, not their skin. In his imaginary world, girls are as courageous as boys, and blacks are as heroic as Asians and whites.

The toys that are most popular with children are heavily influenced by television, either by being offshoots of shows or being heavily promoted on television. In the final analysis, most young children are attracted to qualities in toys that have little, if anything, to do with race.

Selecting Dolls

Many girls, regardless of their race, like the perennial favorite Barbie, who is now manufactured in many skin colors. It's understandable that many black parents prefer their daughters to have black dolls because they believe that owning white dolls symbolizes a rejection of one's racial identity and a striving for whiteness. Poppycock! For the "normal" preschooler, skin color is simply not as important as adults make it out to be and so is irrelevant to their doll preferences.

A white friend told me that when she was growing up in Australia in the 1950s, she and several of her friends were very attached to their "golliwogs," black dolls made of wool. The girls took the dolls with them everywhere and even slept with them. Their parents never expressed a worry that such attachment to black dolls would lead to confusion in the girls' racial identity or that it symbolized a rejection of their whiteness. Of course, because of history, and especially the history of white-black power dynamics, a white child owning a black doll symbolizes something different for white adults than a black child owning a white doll does for black adults. But not for children. A favorite doll becomes a cherished friend.

In her best-seller, *Waiting to Exhale,* Terry McMillan expresses some black parents' fears about the effect of owning white dolls on their children's developing self-concept:

> Onika's dolls were sitting stiffly on her bed, lined up in front of her pillow. Bernadine [her mother] picked one up and looked at it. All except one was black. That stupid Barbie. The first doll Bernadine bought Onika was black. She explained to her daughter a long time ago that she wasn't buying any blond-haired, blue-eyed dolls so Onika would grow up believing that Barbie set the standard for beauty. But last Christmas, Onika pleaded with her for a Barbie, because all her friends had at least one Barbie. Couldn't she have just one white doll? Bernadine gave in.[10]

Realizing Your Preferences

Parents' insistence that their children have only politically correct dolls sends a powerful message to their children about the importance of skin color. Some years ago, the "Cabbage Patch Kid" was the "hot" doll. There were literally riots as parents competed to obtain them for their daughters. These dolls, designed to look like newborns, came in different skin colors. Blacks in some areas had a better chance of obtaining dolls for their children because some whites refused to purchase the dark-skinned dolls. I knew a couple of young white girls who became furious at their mothers when they learned that they had not purchased the dark-skinned dolls because they were the "wrong" color. The color of the doll's skin was, not surprisingly, more important to these parents than to their daughters.

Most of the children I interviewed for this book had at least one black doll. Some parents reported that when a relative, usually a grandmother or an aunt, noticed that their granddaughter or niece did not have a black doll, the relative took it upon herself to rectify the situation. However, the parents interviewed for this book expressed varying opinions on the importance they attached to their daughters' having a black doll. Some felt it was not very important, while others felt is was crucial to their daughters' self-esteem. Among the latter was this mother of a three-year-old, who explained, "When I was a child, all the dolls were white, and how are you going to have a doll baby—something you like to hold and love—if it's not like you? I won't say that you can't go out and adopt a child and have it be white and love it. You can love anybody's child, but when you think in terms of a little girl with her own child, you don't always think of it as a white child with blonde hair."

Generally, the mothers interviewed for this book agreed that it was more important to them than to their daughters that they have a black doll, as illustrated by a three-year-old's mother's remarks: "When she picked the white Barbie doll, I wondered why she picked that one and why she didn't pick the black one. I did say to her, 'Would you like to have the black one?' . . . So I think I look for it more so than she."

Unfortunately, one of the cues some blacks use to judge other black parents' racial allegiance is their children's toys, especially their dolls. Black tennis great Arthur Ashe poignantly reported that he panicked when, at a televised charity event, his young daughter, Camera, and a white friend were playing with twin dolls, which a white friend had just given her:

> I noticed that Camera was playing with her doll . . . in full view of the attentive network television cameras. The doll was the problem; or rather, the fact that the doll was conspicuously a blond. Suddenly, I heard voices in my head, the voices of irate listeners to a call-in show on some "black-format" radio station. I imagined insistent, clamoring callers attacking . . .
>
> *"Can you believe the doll Arthur Ashe's daughter was holding up at the AIDS benefit? Wasn't that a shame?"*
>
> *"Is that brother sick or what? Somebody ought to teach that poor child about her true black self!"*[11]

Ashe felt tremendous mental pressure to interrupt his daughter's innocent play with her white doll, even though he knew that he should not succumb to the ignorance and prejudice of others. His daughter owned several dolls of different ethnicities and had shown no sign of racial preference, but he knew that would not matter to people who believe that black children must play only with black dolls lest they be psychologically damaged. Ashe sadly concluded that white racism had boomeranged and "created defensiveness and intolerance among the very people harmed by racism."[12]

However, regardless of what adults think about the significance of dolls' skin color, most preschool girls simply do not assign it much importance. Indeed, they place much more emphasis on their dolls' hair. Most girls like dolls with long, luxuriant hair that can be groomed in a variety of styles. It is understandable that parents, both blacks and whites, want their children to have dolls that resemble them. But it is more important that children have a choice, that they be allowed to select their own dolls. I believe that it is but a short step from pressuring young children to choose only dolls that share their skin color to pressuring older children to choose only friends who are of their skin color. As we shall see when I discuss older children's racial issues, choosing friends across racial lines can become a challenge for some children as they advance to the higher grades in school. So emphasizing a doll's skin tone may create a mind-set that might have ramifications for children later on.

DEALING WITH THE PROBLEM OF SANTA CLAUS

Some people think that black children's self-esteem is so fragile that exposure to white images will irrevocably damage it. A representative of a national civil rights organization complained in a newspaper interview a few years ago that "white Christmas images have a very negative effect on children of color. . . . The absence of Christmas role models undermines a black child's sense of self-worth and confidence."[13] Images ranging from secular heroes to divine beings are depicted as white, and as a consequence, white is associated with perfection, goodness, beauty, and a host of other positive attributes.

Even Santa Claus, the universal cultural icon of generosity, is considered by some a threat to black children's healthy self-image. One civil rights advocate called for a boycott of stores with white Santas because he was convinced of their harmful effects on black children.[14] Such views reveal an ignorance of child development and of the relative insignificance of skin color to young children.

Children do seem to become aware of Santa's skin color much earlier than they can verbalize it. When confronted with the image of a Santa whose skin color clashes with their internal image of him, some children will let you know that they are aware of the incongruity. However, children who are aware of the difference between their internalized image of the "real" Santa and the image of the "fake" Santa must be at the appropriate developmental stage in order to recognize the difference.

When I showed my son, then four years old, a snapshot I had taken of him sitting on Santa's lap, he remarked, "That's not the *real* Santa. *He's brown!*" Although my husband and I make a point of not discussing people in terms of their skin color or race, Santa's skin color became an issue for my son because of the contrast between his internalized image of Santa and the Santa on whose lap he sat in the photo. This was during a time when he was still learning his colors. He occasionally showed off his knowledge by spontaneously naming the color of an item to any family member that was around to be impressed by his knowledge. During this same time period, he had begun to verbalize his observations about skin-color differences among family members.

For most preschoolers, people's skin color, even Santa's, is simply a physical fact; it carries no social baggage of the kind adults bring to it. For them, the meaning of Santa transcends his skin color. Many adults have difficulty understanding that children make much less of Santa's skin color than they do. In response to adults' concerns, ethnic Santas (black, Hispanic, Asian) are increasingly becoming a part of Christmas celebrations. Although it may be important to broaden the image of Santa for adults, it may not be as important for children.

"A child would sit on Santa's lap and not give a hoot if Santa's skin is red, brown or whatever," a representative of a company that trains Santas said. "The only things kids regularly notice are things like body odor or bad breath."[15] "The single most important thing is that he [Santa] means love and he means happiness."[16]

Some black parents refuse to allow their children to visit a white Santa; they prefer a black Santa or "Kente Claus." Similarly, some white parents are "less than accepting of a nonwhite Santa." But those who have extensive experience in observing children's interactions with Santas of different races recognize the situation for what it is: children "don't seem to have a problem with it. They do see Santa in their own eyes."[17] They see his color but not the baggage of race that adults attach to color.

The prevalence of white images is an unavoidable issue for many black parents. What does it mean in a child's world when practically all the people, ethereal and earthly, considered "good," courageous, and beautiful, are depicted as white? What happens to a child's emerging race consciousness when God, angels, Santa Claus, presidents, inventors, artists, and authors are predominantly white? Some people argue that to preserve the young black child's sense of self-worth, it is best either to reject these images outright, or at least to limit a child's exposure to them. That would be very difficult! But in denigrating or rejecting popular images people consider as harmful to their racial identity, they foster in their children a hypersensitivity to race that is just as crippling as the racism they fear.

I've observed the extraordinary lengths that some parents have taken in order to deny that any goodness exists in whites. They perceive whites as "devils," exploiters, and enslavers and in so doing demonize whites, reciprocating the kind of treatment blacks have suffered for generations. But this approach is likely to backfire. In countering the white racism that they fear, they perpetuate the very racism that they have tried to escape.

A more constructive approach to combating the perpetuation of racial animosity is to educate children about the diversity that does exist in divine and earthly role models. Don't angels, saints, holy leaders, secular heroes, and achievers come in different colors? Increasingly, blacks (for example, Nelson Mandela, Rosa Parks, Colin Powell, Oprah Winfrey) are embraced by people of all races as role models. Much has been written about the media's focus on blacks who are athletes and entertainers, but all children need to know about the accomplishments of blacks in other fields. Black children, before they come to understand the role that skin color plays in our society, should be exposed to a variety of images of black achievers, just as they should be exposed to the images of people of other races who have contributed to the advancement of humankind.

PROVIDING EARLY CONTACT WITH OTHER RACES

It is as difficult for black children who live in segregated communities to develop an objective view of whites as it is for whites who live in homogeneous environments to develop an objective view of blacks. Children who do not have ample opportunities to interact with people of other races are more likely to be influenced by the cultural stereotypes concerning those people later on simply because they have few, if any, personal experiences to counteract them. Fortunately, preschoolers, given their developmental immaturity, are not as likely to be affected by racial stereotypes as older children are. A preschooler can hear all sorts of negative things about white people, but when he meets a white person, he will have trouble recognizing that this person is a member of the group "white." If the white person is a nice person, nothing else matters to the preschooler: they'll be fast friends.

Having little or no contact with people of other races is less a problem for what it does during the preschool years and more a problem of how it affects children's developing view of the world. Without yet registering it, children become accustomed to a world where blacks, whites, Latinos, Asians, and others have little to do with each other. Sure, they may bump into each other now and then at the supermarket or at the mall or in other public places, but these contacts are superficial. Preschoolers learn that the world is organized into "them" and "us." Who they habitually see as "us" and "them" is what they think ought to be. If they continue to have little contact with people of other races and only observe them in certain roles (for example, as landlords, as police officers, as store managers, as teachers) and seldom as equals (as playmates, as neighbors, as friends), they think that's the way things should be. The older the child becomes, the firmer this mind-set becomes, making it increasingly difficult to combat racial stereotypes that thrive in the absence of personal contact.

People complain that black and white students self-segregate at high school and in college. What's the big surprise? If from an early age, children are socialized to hanging out *only* with people who look like them, that is how they will behave when they grow up. Familiarity is comfortable. But I have met children, of various races, who have lived most of their lives in racially mixed neighborhoods or have attended integrated schools. What strikes me about many of these children, and adults with similar backgrounds, is their acknowledgment that they are more comfortable in mixed settings. Often in their own lives they seek out environments with which they are familiar—they are more likely to live, study, and work in integrated environments.

Children who are accustomed to interacting with people of other races from an early age are undoubtedly at a social advantage because they can fit in anywhere. They also have a cognitive advantage because they are less likely to see people in racially stereotypical ways. Exposure to people of other races during early childhood is especially important for white children. They, too, gain a sense of how the world is organized by what they become accustomed to seeing as children. If during their childhood they do not have contact with blacks and others as playmates, neighbors, and professionals, later they are more likely to find it a challenge to make the adult transition to having blacks as classmates, neighbors, or professional peers.

Even if they live in segregated communities, young black children can have significant, life-enhancing contact with whites and other ethnicities via preschool programs, library visits, boys' and girls' clubs, community sports, after-school programs, and the like. Admittedly, this kind of exposure is limited, but at the very least, it offers black children a chance to interact with people of different skin colors and races *before* they become aware of racial stereotypes. It is important that black children interact with people who look different from them as early as possible so that they will develop positive regard for people of other races. Positive early exposure predisposes children to regard people as individuals before they see these others as members of a particular group.

Interacting with diverse people allows children to view these people as a normal part of their environment and minimizes racial stereotyping, even if the children later encounter racial bigotry from people who are racially different from them. Ralph Ellison, author of *Invisible Man,* the 1952 classic that depicts how whites' racism relegated blacks to nonentities,[18] remembered the lingering effect that positive early exposure to whites had on his concept of whites. Ellison grew up in an integrated community in Oklahoma, where his parents "had many white friends who came to the house when I was quite small, so that any feelings of distrust I was to develop toward whites later on were modified by those with whom I had warm relations."[19]

~

Many things influence the black preschooler's developing self-concept and attitudes toward people of other races. Parents and other caregivers play a crucial role in contributing to the child's early self-concept and in modulating influences that can affect his perceptions of people of different skin colors and races. Often it is not what the child experiences that matters most but how the important people in the child's life interpret and react to those influences. The child looks to those close to him for direction; thus it is crucial that he be given the right kind of direction. As the next chapter explains, there are certain experiences that predispose preschoolers to learning negative things about their own and others' skin color and race. When preschoolers face these perceived or actual racially charged situations, it is important that they receive enlightened guidance from parents, teachers, social workers, and others who want them to grow up with healthy racial attitudes.

CHAPTER THREE

When to Be Concerned That Race Is a Problem for Preschoolers

As young children's protectors and as the gatekeepers of race-related information, black parents work hard to shield their offspring from the negative effects of racism. Sensitive to the harmful effects of racial bigotry on children's developing self-concept, teachers and other caregivers often go to great lengths to ensure that the children in their care feel good about being black. Unfortunately, some well-meaning adults go too far. In their efforts to protect children from racism, they perpetuate the very racism they decry and put children at considerable risk for later emotional and social problems.

I have found that a preschooler who is preoccupied with skin color or other racial attributes is likely to have been unduly sensitized about color or race by information provided in the home or elsewhere. She may even have been traumatized by experiences of racism, and have become developmentally incapable of coping with the distress such awareness engenders. Parents, teachers, and others who are interested in the child's well-being should view such a preoccupation as a red flag that the preschooler is at risk for identity as well as other psychosocial problems. I have observed three types of situations that predispose children to become aware of the negative connotation of skin color before they are able to cope adequately with this information.

The first is witnessing racist maltreatment of parents, siblings, or other loved ones, for example, in the form of racist taunts or physical abuse, or experiencing racism themselves, perhaps in the form of rejection by white adults or white playmates. When these situations occur, the child may feel angry or puzzled but usually does not understand the racial meaning of the incident until it is repeatedly explained to him.

The second predisposing situation is being under the influence of people, such as parents or teachers, who are obsessed with race. This obsession may take the form of an anti-white and pro-black bias that results in blaming all black people's problems on whites or even in "demonizing" whites as evil enemies; or it may take the form of a pro-white and anti-black bias that results in favoring people who are light-complexioned and have "good" hair and rejecting people who are "too black." When children spend a considerable amount of time around racially obsessed people, they gradually become sensitive to the negative feelings such people broadcast. Children in such situations absorb the lesson that skin color is very important, although they are unable to understand why it is so important. (Fortunately, a negative imprint need not be permanent. Positive interactions with people of their own or other races can counteract the poison of environmental racial bias. After all, the children of bigots sometimes grow up to be open-minded.)

The third situation that prematurely sensitizes children to skin color is falling victim to a misguided government policy, euphemistically called "racial matching," that until recently made race the primary consideration in foster and adoptive placements. I worked in a system in which children, black and white, were sometimes snatched away from foster parents of the "wrong" race who loved them enough to want to adopt them. In this situation, the young child is forced to become painfully aware that skin color is more important than anything else in determining whom he considers "family" and is allowed to love.

EARLY EXPERIENCE WITH RACIAL PREJUDICE

Preschoolers have difficulty recognizing racial bigotry even when it hits them full in the face, as when they are subjected to name-calling, rejection, or other mistreatment because of their skin color. Such experiences make preschoolers uncomfortable, upset them, even make them aware that something is not right with the world. These kinds of situations, even when carefully explained by concerned adults, remain puzzling to small children. Children can't really understand racial bigotry until they mature cognitively and can process the relevant information. In an article in the *New York Times Magazine,* Karen Russell, an attorney and the daughter of the legendary basketball player Bill Russell, recalled a distressing incident that she experienced as a young child, which only in hindsight, several years later, became clear:

> I was afraid to come back to Boston. My first memory of the place is of a day spent in Marblehead, walking along the ocean shore with a white friend of my parents. I must have been 3 or 4 years old. A white man walking past us looked at me and said, "You little nigger." I am told that I smiled up at him as he went on: "They should send all you black baboons back to Africa." It was only when I turned to looked at Kay [the adult friend accompanying her] that I realized something was wrong.[1]

This young child was oblivious to the negative meaning of the words spoken to her until she turned to her adult friend and observed her reaction to the bigot's words. The child in turn became distressed, although she still did not understand the meaning of the man's words. As this report indicates, children, in times of confusion, rely on adults to interpret their world. They take their emotional cues from adults.

Imagine, now, what would have happened if the adult in this situation had reacted in a different way, one that indicated to the child that the man on the beach was ill or deranged and that his words were nonsense. The child's reaction would have been different had the adult regarded the intruder with pity or even indifference. Who else but an irrational person would walk up to a complete stranger and an innocent child and spout such garbage?

Many of us encounter people on the streets and in other public places who say bizarre things. We tend to assume that such people are high on drugs or alcohol or mentally incompetent and recognize their words as meaningless. However, when such people say bizarre things about race, those they accost have a tendency to give their words an importance they do not merit. Just because some people express their paranoia in the form of racist remarks does not make their utterances any less irrational. Parents and others are more helpful to a child in such stressful situations if they react to crazy or even malevolent words with the same dismissive attitude that they give to any other uninvited weird talk, thereby denying such words their ill-gained potency.

A wonderful story suggests a more constructive way to handle a similar situation. William H. Gray III, president of the United College Negro Fund and former majority whip of the U.S. House of Representatives, recalls an incident that he describes as the "watershed" experience of his life. When he was five years old, he accompanied his grandmother and sister on a shopping trip in downtown Baton Rouge, Louisiana. He was headed for a water fountain when he was abruptly halted by an insistent voice: "Nigger, you can't drink here." He was directed to the "colored only" fountain.

His grandmother handled what could have been a painful situation brilliantly: "She told me I was so important and so powerful that it took the mayor, the State Legislature, the governor and all the courts to keep me from drinking at the water fountain. . . . She made the people who discriminated against me seem sick, petty and small. I came from the experience not scarred and scared, but strengthened."[2]

THE EFFECTS OF ADULTS' REACTIONS TO RACIAL SITUATIONS

As I have suggested, how adults respond to a situation they perceive as racist can mitigate or intensify the situation's effects on the child's developing concept of race. Consider the following case of a black mother facing a choice of how to react in a situation that she perceived as blatantly racist and humiliating.

This mother and her three young children were standing in the express line of a supermarket waiting their turn to pay for the few items in their grocery cart. The cashier, a white woman in her early twenties, while waiting for a white customer to finish writing his check, loudly inquired of the black woman, who was next in line, whether she was going to pay for her purchases with WIC coupons (Women, Infants and Children is a federal program that provides nutritional assistance to mothers and their young children). The mother felt embarrassed to be asked this question in front of a suddenly curious group of white strangers who were also in the line. She had been in line long enough to realize that no one else had been asked how they were going to pay for their groceries, and she suspected that she was being singled out because she was black. When it came her turn to pay, the mother could barely control her anger as she asked the cashier to explain the reason for her question. The cashier, surprised by the mother's question, feebly responded that she had assumed that since the mother's purchases included milk, bread, and eggs and because she had young children with her, she would probably be paying with WIC coupons. Left unsaid, of course, was the third reason: "and you're black . . . and therefore poor."

The mother, a professional, became increasingly angry as she realized that this cashier did not have the remotest clue as to why the question had upset her. So she demanded to see the store manager. Only then did the mother suddenly become aware of the eyes of her three young children staring at her. She realized in a moment of clarity that what she said next might be imprinted on their memories and influence the way they viewed the world. It was then that she decided that she would not present her complaint as racial but simply as a matter of embarrassing rudeness.

The manager, an Asian American (and perhaps himself sensitive to racial issues), immediately understood why the mother was upset and reprimanded the clerk. The clerk offered an unconvincing apology, but the mother now felt partially vindicated and gracefully accepted the halfhearted apology. By refusing to present the complaint as racial, the mother acted wisely. She set a better example by remaining calm and offering a reasoned response to the embarrassing situation. Thus she taught her children a model style of handling conflicts. She also taught them to give the perpetrator the benefit of the doubt.

Many young whites know little about the not-so-long-ago past when U.S. blacks were denied equal rights. What they hear about and what they selectively observe is the "special privileges" blacks receive today. Many whites believe that blacks are now accorded equal, or even preferential, treatment in such venues as schools, the workplace, and government. These same whites are not aware of continuing discrimination in housing, banking, employment, and other areas. They do not understand that a black complexion continues to be a liability in this country or that blacks, just by virtue of their skin color, are subjected to negative assumptions by people of other races. The white cashier, though she may not have considered herself a racist, had made a racist assumption about the black mother in line. By questioning the cashier's assumption, the mother not only began to educate the cashier but also taught her children a lesson about a healthy way to handle conflict.

In response to her children's questions about why she was upset with the clerk, the mother told them, truthfully, that the clerk had been rude. That the rudeness was bound up with a racist attitude was something the children were too young to understand and didn't need to know. By focusing on rudeness, not race, the mother did the right thing: she taught her children that one can do something about unsatisfactory service in a dignified manner. The mother and her children left the situation with their sense of self-worth intact.

This anecdote teaches us that it is not a racial incident per se, but how the incident is handled, that determines what is stored in a child's mental data bank and remains there to be retrieved and reprocessed at a later time. One has to be careful in interpreting another person's behavior as "racist." Sometimes even people who are not racists can act in ways that give offense to others. To call such people "racist" is itself offensive.

Blacks are also sometimes treated rudely by black service workers. But rudeness takes on a different meaning when the mistreatment crosses racial lines. It can be traumatizing for young children to be exposed to racial prejudice that is given more significance than it deserves. They are placed in the position of having to confront a situation they are ill-equipped to cope with since they lack the necessary cognitive and emotional resources. Preschoolers may not know that their race is the reason for all the fuss, but they sense that something is amiss. As the famous linguist Noam Chomsky puts it, they know before they can articulate what they know.

Too many parents of black and biracial children unnecessarily burden them with knowledge of society's pervasive racism. These parents believe that they are preparing their children to deal with reality, but for young children, knowledge that is thrust upon them too soon may have the opposite effect: it may make them feel that their skin color is such an overwhelming handicap that they can never transcend it. At an early age, children need protection from the racism maelstrom.

THE EFFECTS OF RACIAL OBSESSION ON THE CHILD'S DEVELOPING AWARENESS OF RACE

One of the only preschoolers interviewed for this book who expressed negative feelings toward whites came from a family where her mother and her mother's siblings seemed obsessed with race. According to this child's maternal grandmother, her granddaughter, Josie, was frequently told by her mother and other young adult relatives that white people were "evil, blue-eyed devils" intent on mistreating blacks. The grandmother disclosed that Josie had begun to imitate her mother's animosity toward whites: "Certain things she hears from her mother; she doesn't get it from me. One day, we saw a little girl standing outside of a store. Josie looked at her and said, "I don't like white people." I said, "Josie, you should never say that. You don't know anything about her. It is not nice to say you don't like people just because of their color."

Josie's hostile feelings toward whites (including light-complexioned blacks, whom she regards as white) show that she is reacting to negative color tags that reflect her mother's attitudes. As explained in Chapter Two, it is unusual for skin color to be so salient an issue for a preschooler. It is telling that Josie's prejudice is based on color, not race. She is too young to understand racial categories; that is why she groups whites and light-skinned blacks together.

When children are not allowed to develop at a normal pace in their perceptions of people of other races, the results can be disturbing. One of the most distressing cases that I have been asked to evaluate was that of a five-year-old black girl, Breanna, a foster child, who was raised for most of her life in the home of Black Muslims. Indeed, one of the reasons that I was selected to assess Breanna was because I am a black psychologist. Her white caseworker told me during our initial discussion that Breanna was very uncomfortable around whites. (The caseworker acknowledged that the child often left the room when she made home visits.) I had never met a child so young who was so virulently anti-white. Breanna was immediately suspicious of any whites with whom she came in contact, and she openly expressed her distrust of them. This was particularly surprising to me because she had had practically no contact with whites. Then I discovered, from the report of someone who was acquainted with Breanna's foster parents, that she had been indoctrinated by them to regard whites as the enemy, as devils.

Breanna's psychological evaluation was requested after a relative petitioned for custody. When Breanna visited her, the relative was shocked to discover Breanna's animosity toward whites. The relative had a close white friend whom Breanna initially refused to meet. So this relative devised an elaborate plan to convince Breanna that her friend was really black. This took some doing. However, over a period of months, Breanna and the white woman became friends. When the friendship seemed firmly established, the relative disclosed to Breanna that her friend was really white. But the little girl had difficulty dealing with the disclosure, feeling alternately betrayed and confused. Breanna didn't know what to believe. It was hard for her to reconcile two conflicting ideas, that all white people were evil and that this one white person was good.

The harm that the foster parents did to this child is inestimable. No mistaking it, this is child abuse.

It is not just parents who may instill in children a dislike of whites; some preschool teachers who hold a distorted Afrocentric perspective may also do so. Understandably, many of these teachers consider one of their most important responsibilities to be instilling a sense of self-worth and cultural pride in black children, whom they view as having been psychically harmed by a racist society. But at what cost do they build up black children's self-esteem by teaching the very racism that they regard as contemptible? Black preschoolers who are taught that whites are the enemy are as much at a disadvantage as white children who are taught that blacks are inferior. Neither group is being prepared to function in a world that increasingly requires interracial interaction and cooperation.

Parents, teachers, and other caregivers who set up preschoolers to have negative expectations concerning whites or people of other races steer children down a perilous path. These expectations distort children's experiences and can be detrimental to their quality of life. They also play into the worldview of racists. What happens to children who expect their white teachers to dislike them, white children to think they are superior to them, white service workers to be rude to them? These children's lives will be dominated and diminished by their expectations as they live out a self-fulfilling prophecy.

I am also aware of situations in which black preschoolers developed a pro-white bias that was not the result of the teaching of their parents or other caregivers. These children were all in foster care, following their removal from neglectful or abusive parents. Cared for primarily by whites—caseworkers, foster parents, and therapists—they developed a pro-white bias. These children came to regard whites as their rescuers and protectors. Whenever they saw white people, they were favorably disposed to them because they had positive associations with people who looked white and so generalized that all whites are good. (A few preschoolers also developed an anti-black bias, particularly toward black males, a bias perhaps explained by their association of black males with the abuse they suffered at the hands of their birth fathers or their mothers' boyfriends.) After experiencing traumas, children are forced to develop constructs, immature though they may be at such young ages, that allow them to distinguish between people who are threatening and those who are protective.

Fortunately, experiencing trauma is an atypical occurrence for most young children, even if they come from a socially or economically disadvantaged background. Preschoolers who have not been traumatized tend to regard all people as potential friends. Young children are generally quick to smile and greet total strangers, regardless of their race, in spite of their parents' admonitions to be wary of "strangers" or people who are of a different color. Children who are allowed to develop normally are inclined to base their perceptions of people on their own experiences with them. That is why children, left to their own devices, form mixed-race play groups and develop attachments to adults of different races (for example, teachers, baby-sitters, housekeepers, doctors, recreational personnel) that transcend the superficialities of skin color and race.

THE EFFECTS OF RACIAL MATCHING

Unfortunately, certain children's lives have been disrupted by the racial obsession of some "experts" who force preschoolers, when they are most vulnerable, to confront racial bigotry head on. Until recently, a high proportion of the placements of the children in the foster care system was determined by the availability of "ethnically matched" foster and adoptive parents. In my work, I came into contact with children, black and white, who were forcibly removed from the care of their foster parents simply because they were of a different race. The traumas that result from these separations have significant consequences not only for the children's developing concept of race but for their psychological health as well.

Racial matching is a well-meaning but misguided policy. It makes race the primary criterion in foster placements and adoptions. In theory, the policy seems logical, but theory clashes with reality when there are more black children in the foster care system than black parents available to adopt them.

Advocates of the policy of racial matching claim that black children reared in white homes will be deprived of their racial heritage and prone to develop a poor self-image. Indeed, adoptive families who are not sensitive to and supportive of their children's racial heritage can have a detrimental impact on these children's development of a healthy identity. Consider the case of Nathan, a black child adopted by white parents: "Nathan was only a few years old when he began trying to look white, spending hours in the bathroom plastering down his hair. He would get down on all fours and drag his head on the living-room carpet, straining to straighten the kinks."[3]

If we examine the available details of Nathan's early life, we learn that the white grandfather in his adoptive family played with Nathan's white siblings "but left the room when Nathan entered." Moreover, his adoptive family had a racist neighbor who was frequently verbally abusive to Nathan. One wonders what else may have occurred in this young child's early life that contributed to his negative feelings about his physical appearance. No matter how much his adoptive parents loved Nathan, unless they could protect him from the bigotry in his immediate environment (especially within their own family), the likelihood of his developing a healthy identity, racial or otherwise, was remote.

However, if prospective foster or adoptive families are loving, supportive, and sensitive to (but not obsessed by) the role race plays in shaping their children's lives and are committed to working in the best interest of their children, race should not be allowed to be an obstacle to their ability to foster or adopt children. Indeed, the preponderance of the empirical research literature, including longitudinal studies, on transracial adoptions, specifically of black children adopted by white parents, have demonstrated that these children are as well adjusted as blacks who are raised in black families.[4] Is it humane or even logical to condemn already victimized children to lives without families simply because the families who want them are not the "right" color?

A Primal Trauma: Separating "Mismatched" Children and Parents

The policy of racial matching has wreaked havoc in the lives of too many children. There has been needless heartbreak for both children and families who are denied each other simply because of their skin color. Children, some of whom were placed with these families in their infancy, are literally snatched from the bosom of the only families they have known and loved and moved to homes that are deemed more "appropriate" because the new parents are the same race as the child. Decisions to remove these children from their psychological families make race more important than anything else, including the emotional bond between the child and the original foster parents. This unnecessarily places these young children at high risk for later psychological problems. Children are forced before their time to confront the harsh realities of a racism imposed by well-meaning bureaucrats.

Consider three-and-a-half-year-old Christopher, a black foster child whose case attracted national attention.[5] The only parents he had known were a white couple, Lena and Phillip Jenkins of San Antonio, Texas, who raised him from the time he left the hospital as a five-week-old, drug-exposed preemie. After allowing him to remain in their home for three years, the social service agency threatened to remove him when his foster parents petitioned to adopt him.

And what was the compelling reason for yanking this child from the bosom of a family who even the agency acknowledged loved and was devoted to him? It wasn't one of the usual powerful reasons for removing a child from his home: his foster parents were not abusive or neglectful. What they weren't, however, was politically more potent: they were not "racially compatible" with Christopher.

For this sole "transgression," Christopher and his family paid a very high price. The consequences to his emotional health as the result of being separated from the only parents he had ever known were drastically underestimated. Christopher, on learning that he was to be removed from his foster parents' care, became a very sad child. It was not surprising that he could not understand the reason he was being separated from his parents. Given his developmental level, he reacted in the only way he knew. One day, he approached his foster parents, proudly showing off his "new" self. He had rubbed white toothpaste all over his body: "I'm white now. . . . I don't have to go over there and live with them" (the black couple, whom he had been visiting and who were approved as his "appropriate" prospective adoptive parents).

Christopher's actions exemplified the level of race awareness of preschoolers I discussed earlier. He had not yet achieved an awareness of skin-color constancy, much less racial constancy. He had no understanding about the reason for all the fuss about color. All he knew was that he wanted to remain with his parents and that by changing his color to white maybe he could make that possible. Whatever logic policymakers use to justify it, racial matching comes across in this case as an act of extreme cruelty. But what is worse is that it has been condoned by "the system" in our supposedly enlightened age.

There are many other cases like Christopher's that are not as high-profile. As an expert witness in a few of them, I have had to confront the devastating consequences the racial-matching policy has had on children and their foster parents. Placement and removal decisions regarding foster care or adoption should be based on the child's best interest, as is fortunately becoming the standard practice in the field. There are more important considerations than race or ethnicity when deciding who should be a child's foster or adoptive parents.

Patricia and William Mandel, who are white, became the foster parents of five-day-old Robyn, a black child who at birth tested positive for cocaine and barbiturates. When she was thirty-two months old, they were involved in an emotionally and financially costly legal fight with the San Francisco Department of Social Services, which had denied their petition to adopt Robyn because they were not racially appropriate. A black friend of the Mandels disagreed with the department's position:

> [The Mandels] love that little girl so much. That should be enough to stop people focusing on other issues, because she'll never find this kind of love anywhere else.
>
> Bill and Pat are worrying that they can give Robyn proper awareness of her culture. I raised my own black child and I'm not sure I gave her the proper cultural awareness. Even in an all-black home, my daughter has all sorts of issues. When I look at Robyn, Pat and Bill, I see that love is what counts most.[6]

Public opinion is on the side of the Mandels' friend. Opinion polls on this issue generally show that the majority of blacks, the group most affected by this issue, approve of transracial adoptions when it is the best alternative available to children for being placed in an adequate adoptive home.[7] Interestingly, blacks who are acquainted with white couples and can see close up how much these families love and care for their foster and adoptive children almost always support these placements whether or not alternative racially matched homes are available.

Ethnic matching, whatever its original good intentions, has made it harder for black children to find permanent homes. The National Adoption and Information Clearinghouse reported that black children in foster care average a one-third longer wait for adoption than nonblack children.[8]

Promise of Change in the Placement of Children in Foster and Adoptive Homes

Fortunately, in the past few years, Congress has passed legislation to address this wrong. The Multiethnic Placement Act of 1994 and the Adoption Anti-Discrimination Act of 1996 prohibit social service agencies from denying any person the opportunity to become an adoptive or foster parent solely on the basis of the race, color, or national origin of the potential adoptive or foster parent. Only time will tell whether these laws will be effective in reversing the cruel race-obsessed trend that snatches children away from families or stops them from ever finding families who, although racially different, love them.

~

Certain experiences in the early years can prematurely sensitize children to skin-color differences or traumatize them as they are forced to deal with adults' racism. In this chapter, we looked at several such situations that pose risks to the children's development of a healthy self-concept and positive racial attitudes. Even in the worst cases, adults, if they respond appropriately, can do much to minimize the risks to the child. Fortunately, most preschoolers do not experience or even recognize racial discrimination. When I interview "successful" black adults or read biographies of blacks, some who grew up in the pre–civil rights era, most of them say that they do not remember being routinely discriminated against as children. Many of them see now that they were shielded from knowledge of racism by their families and communities and allowed to experience a normal childhood.

The preschool years are a time of innocence and wonder when every child's possibilities seem limitless. It is important to seize the opportunity this stage of a child's life presents and lay a strong foundation for the years ahead, when there is a high likelihood that personal and societal forces will assail the black person's very sense of being.

Chapter Four begins with pointers for parents concerned with raising racially healthy black children. It then presents suggestions for preschool teachers on laying the foundations for healthy racial attitudes in the classroom. Finally, it offers a quiz to help parents evaluate their pattern of responding when their preschoolers are being affected by colorism or racism. The quiz should be used to determine whether the parents' approach to dealing with issues of skin color and race is having a negative or positive effect on their children's developing self-concept and racial attitudes.

CHAPTER FOUR

Raising the Racially Healthy Preschooler

My parents had me absolutely convinced that even though I couldn't get a hamburger at Woolworth's, I could be president of the United States.
—CONDOLEEZZA RICE, *provost, Stanford University*

The mind-set of young children regarding the roles skin color and race play in determining the quality of life is shaped by their earliest teachers: parents, other members of their families, and friends. Much can be done to make black children's early years as normal as possible and thereby counteract the power of racism to adversely affect their lives.

Remember the story of Sleeping Beauty? An evil witch cast a spell on a princess that would kill her when she pricked her finger on a spinning wheel. Her fate seemed sealed until the good fairy came along. She couldn't remove the witch's curse, but she modified it. With the appropriate intervention (the prince's kiss), the curse would lose its power to kill the princess and allow her to enjoy a happy life. In a way, combating the effects of racism on black children's lives is like that. It is impossible to undo the curse of racism overnight, but there are many things parents and others can do now to reduce its negative impact. A child who is lovingly cared for, who is shielded as much as possible from racism, and who learns about race in a way that is developmentally appropriate can even become emotionally stronger than children who do not have to deal with the challenge of racism. In this chapter,

I offer specific suggestions for parents, teachers, and other caregivers to enable them to protect young children from becoming precociously affected by racism, thereby optimizing their chance to grow up believing they are as good as any other child.

Parents can do much to foster an environment that allows their children to become racially healthy, and teachers can lay the foundation for positive racial attitudes at preschool.

✷ SUGGESTIONS FOR PARENTS

Provide the basics. Children who are raised in a nurturing environment where they feel loved, supported, and valued have the best chance of developing a healthy self-image. However, experiences of neglect and abuse, whether physical or emotional, put children at risk for developing psychological and behavioral problems. How can children feel positive racial esteem when they do not even feel positive personal esteem?

Nurture self-worth. Parents should be careful about what values they convey to their children. How do they rate a person's worth? Do they employ a scale based on a person's physical appearance or race? Or do they assess character and achievements? It is difficult not to embrace society's values for specific physical characteristics, but an attempt should be made to foster values that place the physical self in its proper perspective. Parents play the most important role in their children's development of a positive self-image.

Human nature being what it is, physical appearance will always influence how people determine personal worth. But children should be encouraged to value others primarily for the kind of people they are and not for their physical appearance. Even when their children are very young, parents should listen carefully to how they criticize and compliment their children. What language do you use when you criticize or are angry at your children? Is skin color incorporated into your reprimands? Comments like "Get your black behind out of that chair and go pick up your things!" or "Nigger, don't you hear me calling you?" have no place in conversations between loved ones.

What are children usually complimented for? Are they usually praised for their physical features, like "good" hair or light complexion, or for their achievements, like singing a song or memorizing a nursery rhyme, and social skills, like helping a sibling or being kind to a playmate? How are skin color and other physical characteristics discussed? Comments such as "You're looking good. If only your nose weren't so wide" or "She's dark but pretty" are reminiscent of the comment familiar to many overweight females: "She's fat, but she has such a pretty face."

Helping your child view her skin color or race as an asset contributes to a strong self-concept. A dark-complexioned black mother once told me that one of her most cherished memories of childhood was her father's nickname for her, "BBG" ("Beautiful Black Girl"). She said that when she encountered the wider world, she did not feel inferior because for as long as she could remember, her color was regarded positively by her family and friends.

Keep the role of race in your child's life in its proper perspective. Some people have been brainwashed to believe that the most important thing about them is their race. But in reality, race tells as much about a person as shoe size. Children should not be brought up believing that their skin color or race is the most important thing about them. If they grow up in a home that places race in its proper perspective, children learn that it is only one of many aspects of themselves.

Although learning about one's racial identity and cultural heritage is important, learning about one's humanity is more important. Children who grow up in a loving home, preferably with both parents, have a better chance of seeing themselves as worthy and lovable.

Follow your child's lead. Unless a young child initiates discussion about skin color, be careful about bringing it up. Why impose limitations on children so young? Children do not usually think in terms of race and should be spared from having to do so until they can handle it. However, if the child initiates the discussion, by all means respond to her questions in a calm and supportive manner.

Empathize: try to see things from your child's perspective. Be careful about interpreting your child's words or actions from your own adult perspective. A preschooler might say "I want to be white," but her remark doesn't mean that she has the same concept of white as an adult, much less an enduring preference for switching colors and races. These types of whimsical expression are typical of the preschool phase. Don't make the mistake of shaming children because they express such desires. With love and support, they will become secure in themselves whatever their skin color or race.

Watch what you and others say about your child's color and other physical characteristics. Comparisons involving your child's physical appearance can damage his developing sense of self-worth. Thus it is important that you express your disapproval when tactless people make inappropriate comments about your child's appearance. If they accuse you of being too sensitive when you call them on their bigotry, don't be defensive. It is they who are not being sensitive enough.

A mother of a preschooler told me how she responds when visitors compare her daughters' physical appearance: "When people come to the house, they compare the children. They will say my oldest daughter has the 'best hair,' 'the prettiest complexion.' She will get the impression that she is better. I say to them, 'Don't do that because I'm trying to teach my daughters a different set of values.'"

Another mother threatened to stop seeing her best friend if she continued talking negatively to her daughter: "My girlfriend was hung up about her dark color. She said to my daughter when she was a baby, 'You don't like me because I'm dark' whenever the baby started crying. Then when my daughter got older [three years old], she said to her, 'You think you are cute because you are light.' Now she is twenty-nine years old and a schoolteacher. I was saying to this girlfriend, 'Look. if you don't stop, I will have to stop seeing you because I don't want my daughter raised with the same complexes and problems that you had.'"

Do not talk about people in terms of their skin color or race. Except in rare situations, like police matters, it is unnecessary to mention race or skin color. Parents who routinely describe people using skin-color and racial labels are sending a clear message about the importance of these labels.

Focus on developing your child's character and talents. Although physical appearance is important for children of all races, character and their own abilities are even more important—and more enduring. The child who learns to be thoughtful regarding others and develops her social and intellectual abilities has a better chance at having a happy childhood than one who focuses on her appearance.

Be careful not to pass on your own racial prejudice. Parents should be aware of the impact of their own biases on their child's developing ideas about race. Sweeping remarks about blacks, whites, Jews, Asians, or other groups reinforce racial stereotypes and are as harmful as feeding children poison.

A mother of a preschooler related how she made a deliberate effort to change the way she talked about whites to her children after a friend pointed out that whenever she mentioned whites, it was always for some wrong they did.

Be mindful of your own skin-color sensitivities. A mother disclosed to me her insecurities about her color: "I have always been self-conscious . . . about my coloring and her coloring. People would say, 'Is she your daughter?' Her father's a different coloring. I am chocolate and she is golden. People automatically think that she is beautiful because of her complexion. . . . I always thought that I was ugly because of my coloring." As this confession suggests, parents, especially those whose children are a different color, have to be careful not to transmit their own insecurities to their children.

Be brief. Keep your responses to your child's questions to the point. Preschoolers' questions are usually very specific. Elaborate answers can be confusing to a child who has a limited capacity to process information.

Be aware of your child's stage of race awareness. It is important to be aware of your child's stage of race awareness when responding to her questions and reacting to her statements about skin color (see the Appendix). Preschoolers think differently from older children and adults. They may use words that adults use for skin-color and racial matters, but they understand them in a completely different and usually innocent way.

Be careful what information about racism you share. Think carefully about sharing your experiences with racial bigotry with your young child. Ask yourself, "What purpose does it serve?" Preschoolers do not have the coping skills to handle the anxiety they may experience from learning distressing information.

Encourage your child to become acquainted with people of other races. Even if you live in a segregated community, you and your child can still have contact with other races via libraries, preschools, parks, and playgrounds. The younger your child is when he becomes accustomed to the reality that the world includes many different kinds of people, the more comfortable he will be in relating to people of other races. Remember that you are preparing your child for living in a global community in which racial isolation could be an obstacle to success.

Monitor your child's television viewing. Research has revealed that black children watch much more television than white children.[1] Parents, teachers, and others who care for black children must limit the amount of time the children spend in front of the television. Also pay attention to the programs your children watch to ensure that they are not exposed to a steady diet of racial stereotypes.

Avoid harmful stereotyping. Be careful about passing on stereotypes. Racism is just one of the many isms (including sexism, ageism, chauvinism, and lookism) that seeks to rob people of their inherent human dignity. Some people who become angry when they sense someone is being racist toward them do not hesitate to demean others for being handicapped, foreign, "fat," or "ugly." You can't teach your son that he is better than girls just because he is male and then expect him to be unbiased in other areas, such as matters of race. You cannot convey to your daughter that she is more valued than less attractive people of her race and then expect her to regard people of other races or with different physical attributes as her equals. Teaching children to appreciate their value as humans, as blacks, requires that they learn to respect the dignity of others who are not only a different color but may look, speak, and act differently from them.

Acquaint children with their own family history. For young children, something concrete, like a family tree made out of photographs, is an effective way to show them their connections to other family members and to older generations, like grandparents, great-grandparents, and others. However, I believe that it is just as important that children know about their immediate family. Some children are told much about their roots but know little about their birth father. The absent father is a big problem for many black children. Dealing with this absence can take a terrible toll on their developing self-concept. So if your child doesn't live with her father or see him regularly, before you go digging up old photographs of Grandma and Grandpa, it would be a good idea to pick up the phone and work on establishing or reestablishing that significant father-child connection.

Expose your child to a variety of books and dolls. Allow your child freedom of choice. Don't force your child to read only those books and to play only with those dolls or action figures marketed for blacks. Remember, childhood isn't about being politically correct.

Carefully select your child's preschool or day-care center. A child's preschool or day-care center plays a crucial role in his healthy psychosocial development. This environment must meet not only your needs for reliable, affordable custodial care but also your child's needs for cognitive and emotional growth. Too often, because of financial pressures, parents do not consider their child's cognitive and emotional needs sufficiently. Parents can be penny wise and pound foolish by placing their children in preschools or day-care centers that save money in the short run but do their children harm in the long run. For example, if parents are careful about the kind of language they use in front of their child at home (as I advise), but their child's teacher is not, their child may pick up negative racial information as well as other detrimental ideas. It is more important to shop around, spend a little more on child care, or go without something else than economize on your child's early experiences. Early learning is so deeply imprinted that it is better to do it right the first time than for the child to have to unlearn negative information that resulted from being placed in an environment where racial intolerance is fostered.

Some parents choose to place their children in a black preschool, while others choose a multicultural setting. There are advantages to each choice. On the one hand, a black setting offers some promise that the children will not experience racial prejudice. Some parents who make this choice want to provide their children with a safe cocoon, a place where they can be with "their own people" before they are thrust into a menacing world where they'll be judged by their race. On the other hand, a multicultural preschool enables the child to become accustomed to interacting with children of different races before ever learning about racial stereotypes. When deciding what kind of school environment they want their children to experience, parents have to weigh for themselves what is most important not only for their children's emotional well-being and future school success but also for their capacity to function in a multiethnic society.

Celebrate black heritage. Celebrating different "ethnic" festive days can contribute enormously to children's appreciation of their own racial heritage. Teach children about the story of the struggles and triumphs that help define "their" people. For example, Kwanzaa (Swahili for "first harvest"), a seven-day celebration that begins on December 26, is emerging as a unifying celebration for many blacks who have embraced it as an alternative to the traditional Christmas celebration. Kwanzaa, founded in 1966 by Maulana Karenga, a professor of black studies at a California university, allows blacks to "define and reaffirm themselves" by focusing each day of Kwanzaa on one of seven spiritual and communal principles: *Umoja,* or unity; *Kujichagulia,* self-determination; *Ujima,* collective work and responsibility; *Ujamaa,* cooperative economics; *Nia,* purpose; *Kuumba,* creativity; and *Imani,* faith.[2] For those who wish to escape the commercialism and racial alienation that they experience during the traditional Christmas season and instead celebrate the cultural traditions of their African heritage, Kwanzaa is a valuable energizing and life-affirming experience.

Some black parents feel that if they and their children celebrate Christmas, they are betraying their ethnic heritage. To be truly "African American," they think that they must only celebrate Kwanzaa. Why not celebrate both? One of the benefits of living in a multiethnic country is sharing at least the promise of a diverse society. In the final analysis, we share one culture. Thus it is important that a celebration like Kwanzaa (or Juneteenth, the celebration of the signing of the Emancipation Proclamation) not be used to foster a child's sense of separateness from her primary identity as an American but instead be used to promote an appreciation of her race's unique role in the mosaic of our American heritage.

✷ SUGGESTIONS FOR TEACHERS

Know your own color, racial, and social-class biases. You may be biased against certain children because of their race, color, or social class and not even be fully aware of it. If you favor some children over other children, they will be quick to sense it. It can have an adverse effect on a child to learn that whatever he does to win your approval, he cannot get you to like him. Developing a caring relationship with children is at the core of teaching them.

Teach children the Golden Rule. Help children to understand that they can make life better for themselves and others if they "Do unto others as they would like others to do unto them." You'd be surprised to learn how many children do not know this simple but important rule.

Teach information about race at the child's developmental level. Children may not be able to understand some information about race because they are not developmentally capable of doing so. Be careful of teaching them information about race that may prejudice or confuse them. It is best to allow preschoolers to use their own labels, provided they are benign, to describe people who are of different colors and races.

Don't overreact. If a child uses racial epithets or behaves rudely in other ways to other children because they are different in terms of color or race, respond to the situation as you would to any other form of disrespectful behavior. Don't make skin color or race an issue unless it becomes necessary to do so.

Have rules of conduct for your class. Enlist the children to help you generate rules about how the children should treat each other. Go over the rules repeatedly until you are sure that all the children understand them. Enforce the rules consistently and equitably. Regularly praise different children for keeping the rules.

Intervene swiftly with children who act out racial prejudices. Children who come from racially bigoted families can hurt other children by using racial epithets or refusing to play with them because of their skin color, the way they talk, the way they dress, and so on. Respond gently but firmly to prevent children who express racial prejudice from contaminating other children's perceptions. For example, when a child uses a racial epithet in anger, refer her to the rules generated by her classmates and say, "We agreed that we won't say any words that hurt each other in this class." If you are unable to manage the situation yourself, seek professional help.

Emphasize children's similarities rather than their differences. Teach children that their most important identity is not their racial identity but their human one.

Select books and videotapes that reflect racial and class diversity. Books and videotapes should show people of various races and social backgrounds. Remember that blacks, like whites, are a diverse people who live in different areas, work at a variety of jobs, and so on. Your selection of books and videos should reflect this diversity and not focus primarily on blacks from poor inner-city areas.

Choose dolls and toys that are representative of the different races. In their play, children tend to reenact their own experiences, their own fantasy world. Children who are provided with the opportunity to play with dolls and toys that represent people of different races are likely to come to see them as a normal part of the world, real or imaginary.

Select pictures of people for the classroom walls who are racially diverse. Whether you teach at a predominantly white school, a predominantly black school, or an integrated school, classroom pictures and murals should include characters and people of all races.

Don't make the mistake of the teacher at a predominantly black school who, in her zeal for promoting black children's self-esteem, created a mural of Mother Goose characters who were all black: there was a black Jack and Jill, a black Humpty Dumpty (are there black eggs?), a black Little Bo Peep, and so on. That mural was just as biased as one having nothing but white faces. The real world doesn't look like that, and the classroom's walls shouldn't either.

Find a buddy school. Teachers at a predominantly black or white preschool should establish ties with a buddy school with the opposite situation. At different times throughout the school year, the children and staffs can interact to mutual benefit. You can arrange art exhibitions of children's work, "Clean Up the Environment" days, museum trips, field days, and the like. Avoid activities or events that are competitive or that have ethnic themes. The idea is for children to get to know each other in collaborative and nonstigmatizing ways.

Facilitate interactions among children who are not playmates. Encourage children who do not ordinarily play together to do so. At this age, it is at least as important to help children develop their social skills as it is to teach them their ABCs.

Select different children for special roles. When you choose class helpers, think of rotating the children you ask to assist you. Avoid playing favorites as much as possible. Some teachers unthinkingly choose the most attractive white children in the class to play the leads in class productions. Sadly, too often these teachers don't even consider minority children for lead roles. All children deserve a chance to shine. You would be surprised at the talent some children have if you just give them a little encouragement.

Protect childhood. Preschoolers don't need to become familiar with man's inhumanity to man. There will be lots of time for them to learn about slavery, the Holocaust, and other horrific episodes in human history. Developmentally, preschoolers may find much of this information confusing, and emotionally, they may experience difficulty coping with it. Let them enjoy the innocence of childhood for as long as they can.

During the wondrous preschool years, caregivers exert an influence on children that they will carry with them for the rest of their lives. The culture of childhood in this country is strikingly similar across different social classes and ethnic groups. As I talk to and observe children from different backgrounds, I am amazed at how they generally have similar toys, recite many of the same nursery rhymes, enjoy many of the same books, look at the same cartoons, and view many of the same videos. Preschoolers, regardless of race, even learn their first cultural symbol, the Golden Arches of McDonald's restaurants, before they can recognize letters! They are more similar at this phase in their life than at any other time.

But race will exert different pulls as they grow older. Parents, teachers, and caregivers of all races can do much to preserve children's shared innocence of racial hatred and to ensure that they are not pulled away from each other by centuries-old misconceptions that divide the races. Much of the preschoolers' emerging attitudes toward skin color and race will reflect their caregivers' sensitivities and biases. Caregivers cannot pass on healthy racial attitudes unless they have them themselves.

In the next section, you will find a parents' quiz that allows you to assess how your own responses to racism and colorism may affect your preschooler. Your performance on the quiz will give you a sense of how well you are doing in raising a racially healthy child.

PARENTS' QUIZ: HOW ARE YOUR RACIAL ATTITUDES AFFECTING YOUR CHILD?

A. A black relative jokingly refers to your child as "that little nigger" in his presence. You . . .

1. Ignore it. Enjoy the joke. It's OK for blacks to use the *N*-word with each other.
2. Ask him to apologize to your child and not to use that word in your home.
3. Tell him, "That's not a nice word."
4. Angrily accuse him of demeaning your child.

B. A neighbor compares the hair textures of your two daughters in their presence, describing one of them as having "nice" hair and questioning why the other's hair is "so nappy." You . . .

1. Ignore it.
2. Calmly inform her that both of your children have lovely hair.
3. Tell her to mind her own business.
4. Angrily tell her off.

C. In conversation with you, your child's white teacher says that black children tend to have behavior problems. You . . .

1. Ignore it.
2. Ask him to explain his remark and how it relates to your child.
3. Tell the teacher that he is unfairly stereotyping black children.
4. Call him a racist.

D. You learn that most of the white preschoolers in your daughter's class have attended a birthday party for a white classmate but neither your daughter nor any of the other black children were invited. When your daughter asks you why she wasn't invited to her classmate's party, you . . .

1. Tell her that you don't know and suggest that she asks her classmate.
2. Empathize with her and offer a logical reason for her not being invited.
3. Discuss with her all the bad points about the birthday child and tell her she wouldn't really want to have gone.
4. Tell her that she wasn't invited because of her skin color.

E. Your child attends an interracial preschool. He tells you that an older white child said that he is "black." He asks you why this child called him "black" when he's really "brown"? You . . .

1. Tell him, "That's just a name."

2. Explain to him, in age-appropriate terms, the difference between skin color and race.
3. Ask him whether it bothers him to be called "black."
4. Tell him, "Of course you're black. Why are you making such a fuss?"

F. Your child tells you that she wants a white doll. You . . .
1. Ignore her request.
2. Give it to her as a birthday or Christmas gift.
3. Promise her that you will give her one, even though you don't really intend to because you hope she'll change her mind or forget.
4. Tell her that she can have only black dolls.

G. You're bothered that one of your child's favorite TV programs habitually uses racial stereotypes. You . . .
1. Ignore it. It won't affect him; he's just a child.
2. Don't allow him to watch the show.
3. Discuss the program with your child but allow him to continue viewing it.
4. Resign yourself to the fact that we live in a racist society; he might as well get used to it.

H. Your close friend often talks derogatorily about whites, calling them "honkies" or "white trash," when your children are around. You . . .
1. Dismiss it. It's just your friend's style. The children are too young to be negatively affected by these words.
2. Tell her to keep her prejudices to herself.
3. Mention to her that she should watch what she says in front of the children.
4. Resign yourself to the fact that we live in a racist society. Your children will hear this kind of talk everywhere.

I. Your child has said a couple of times that he wants to be white like his classmate. You . . .
1. Ignore his remark.

2. Talk to him about it but do not focus on the racial aspect of it.
3. Worry that he's developing a preference for whites. Tell him he shouldn't say such a thing.
4. Angrily tell him to shut his mouth and warn him never to say such a thing again.

J. A white clerk is rude to you while you are shopping with your children. You . . .
   1. Ignore him.
   2. Ask him to apologize for his rudeness. Maybe he's racially prejudiced, but maybe he's just having an off day. Depending on whether he apologizes, you either drop the matter or report it to his supervisor.
   3. Assume he is a racist and report his behavior.
   4. Angrily tell him off. Loudly call him a racist and a few other choice words as well.

K. Your sister blatantly favors her other-skinned nieces and nephews over your dark-complexioned daughter. You . . .
   1. Ignore it.
   2. Privately discuss your observations with your sister, allowing her an opportunity to explain her behavior. Tell her that if she continues her favoritism, you will not allow your daughter to visit her.
   3. Hint at your dissatisfaction with her behavior.
   4. Accuse your sister of being a bigot in the children's presence.

L. You overhear your son call his white playmate, who lives in the same neighborhood, a "honky" when they quarrel over a toy. You know he's imitating your husband. Within the half hour, the children are playing with each other again as if nothing happened. You . . .
   1. Ignore it. Your son doesn't really know what he's saying.
   2. Tell him that *honky* is not a nice word to say and that it hurts people's feelings. You also make a point of talking

with your husband about not using *honky* and similar words, especially around children.

3. Chuckle. Kids say the cutest things.
4. Discourage your son from playing with that child because all whites turn out to be trouble.

M. A black friend, complaining about her mistreatment by whites on her job, says in your children's presence that all white people are no good. You . . .

1. Ignore her. She's just having a bad day and needs to let off steam.
2. Mention that white people are no different from other people. Help her determine whether her problem is racism or something else. You make sure that your children hear your advice to her.
3. Commiserate with her. Share your own experiences of whites' mistreatment.
4. Advise her to sue her employer for racial discrimination. Also bring your children into the conversation and warn them to be on guard for whites who will take advantage of them too.

Scoring

If you scored mostly 1's: You have a tendency to dismiss situations that may be important to your child's development of healthy racial attitudes. You are inclined to invalidate your child's feelings and experiences as well as the negative effect you and others may be having on his emerging awareness of race. Work on listening more attentively to your child and becoming more aware of the effect of others' racial conversations and behaviors upon him.

If you scored mostly 2's: You validate your child's experiences but are careful not to interpret a situation as racist until you explore other explanations for it. When you determine that the situation is racially unfair, you respond constructively. Be careful, however, not to become complacent. Responding to words and behaviors that may or may not be racist is an ongoing challenge.

If you scored mostly 3's: You are inclined to underestimate the harmful effects certain words and behaviors may have on your child. You also reveal a tendency to interpret a situation as racial without first examining other possibilities. Work on considering alternative explanations to problems before presuming that they are racial.

If you scored mostly 4's: You have a disturbing tendency to impulsively interpret situations as racial without exploring other reasonable explanations for them. As a result, your words and behaviors contribute to the escalation of problems, thereby making positive resolutions more difficult. This tendency places your child at risk for developing a sense of racial inferiority and for overreacting to situations that may or may not be caused by racism. You need *immediate* help in developing a more balanced perspective in your racial attitudes in order to allow your child to develop healthy relations with people of other races.

PART TWO

The Waning of Racial Innocence

The Early School Years

CHAPTER FIVE

Shades of Brown and Black

How Early Grade-Schoolers See Color and Race

You've got to be taught to be afraid
Of people whose eyes are oddly made,
And people whose skin is a diff'rent shade,
You've got to be carefully taught.

You've got to be taught before it's too late,
Before you are six or seven or eight . . .
—R. RODGERS AND O. HAMMERSTEIN, *"You've Got To Be Carefully Taught"*

The world of school intrudes on the enchantment of childhood. This new world, ushered in by kindergarten, is more competitive and demanding than the home world. Even for children who have attended preschool, there is something different about going to kindergarten—the "real" school where "big kids" go. Most of the day is no longer devoted to carefree play but to learning the three R's. For many children, school can also be where they begin to learn their racial ABCs, including bigotry, intolerance, and prejudice.

Fortunately, given the developmental stage of children in the early school years, kindergarten to second grade, it doesn't happen right away. Unless they have been sensitized to race by their family or by others in their social circle, children only gradually gain an inkling of the meaning of skin color or race (see the Appendix).

The experience of Ruby Bridges, the black six-year-old who was chosen to integrate a white elementary school in Little Rock, Arkansas, in 1957, reveals how taking a developmental perspective is essential to appreciating children's understanding of race during the early school years. Ruby was the model for the little girl in that powerful Norman Rockwell painting, *The Problem We All Live With* (1964), who is shown being escorted by burly federal marshals past a menacing white mob that wanted to prevent her from entering the school building. In *The Story of Ruby Bridges* (later filmed for television as *The Ruby Bridges Story*), psychiatrist Robert Coles tells how this courageous little girl daily confronted the rage of whites but remained clueless about the nature of racism.[1] Despite the racial storm swirling around her, young Ruby could not understand the turmoil that enraged the older folks. She heard people in her family discuss racism, and she peered into its menacing face every day; yet as a black six-year-old growing up in the race-obsessed South, Ruby grasped little of what all the commotion was about.

Appearing in 1997 on *Oprah,* the popular television talk show, Bridges recalled that while playing, she would innocently repeat the catchy chant with which the angry white adults greeted her every morning outside her school: "Two, four, six, eight, we don't want to integrate!" Cognitively and emotionally, Ruby was too young to understand the meaning of these words, much less the racism that motivated them. Her innocence was a shield that protected her from the taunts and threats of harm that would have traumatized an older child. If Ruby, who confronted the angry face of racism every day, understood so little of what all the fuss was about, it should not be surprising that the average black child comprehends even less. Given her developmental stage of race awareness, a child of Ruby's age cannot fully assimilate information about race even if it is violently thrust into her consciousness.

SUDDENLY, DIFFERENCES MATTER

Developmental psychologist Jean Piaget referred to the stage of a child's life from age five to seven years as the preoperational, or "prerules," stage. During these years, children's race awareness reflects their cognitive development in that the youngsters do not comprehend the rules adults use to determine racial group membership. Thus they cannot understand that privileges are bestowed or denied based on race. But in the manner of the "little scientists" Piaget describes, children are busy accumulating bits and pieces of information that will eventually lead to a fuller understanding of the often subtle rules of racial relationships and functioning in society.

Around age five, children who have taken only the slightest interest in skin color or anything dealing with race suddenly seem to become acutely interested in both. They ask more and more questions, and they make observations, often at the least expected times. For example, five-year-old Autumn's mother vividly remembers this scene:

> The first time she even brought up race, we were sitting at the table and she just pointed to me, my mother, and her father. My mother's skin is dark, and Autumn just looked across the table. "Grandma, I'm white. How come you're brown?" . . . It was clear out of the blue sky as to why. Like everybody just stopped for a few minutes and thought about it. Why did she even ask us this question? So it must have been bothering her for her to just blurt it out. So my mother told her, "You're not white; you're just light." "No, I'm white!" I mean she was heavy on "I'm white. I'm not black." You know, it was like she didn't want to be black for some reason.

Differences in family members' appearances, especially their skin color and hair texture, will become an issue for children who look dissimilar to other family members. Like preschoolers, these children identify most strongly with their family. Unless the family makes skin-color differences a focus of attention—by making either negative or positive remarks about skin color—it is unlikely to become a major emotional issue for a child even if the child encounters racial problems in school. Autumn simply seems to be verbalizing her perceptions. At this stage of development, children are still very concrete—in Autumn's case, she perceives her skin color as closer to white than to brown or black, so she calls herself "white." The adults at the table misinterpret Autumn's statement by leaping to a conclusion about her racial preference. Such a distortion in the meaning of an innocent child's words can have a devastating effect on that child if it leads to teasing and ridicule by the adults in her life. Autumn, or other children in her situation, will learn that there is something bad about saying she is white, even though she has heard other people call people who have light skin "white."

"What Am I?"

When asked, "What are you?" five- and six-year-olds are most likely to reply "a boy" or "a girl" rather than mention color or race. When specifically asked, "What color are you?" children in the early school grades are likely to respond more accurately than preschoolers, describing themselves as "brown," "black," or "light-skinned." Some light-complexioned children describe themselves as "white," naming their skin color rather than their race. Children in this age group are less likely to use the idiosyncratic terms that preschoolers use, self-descriptives such as "vanilla," "chocolate," or "peach." Indeed, by age six, most children have adopted adultlike skin-color labels, but unlike adults, they do not attach any social meaning to these labels. Thus most children at this stage remain unaware of their *racial* identity, but some of them are learning that there's more to skin color than meets the eye.

Some parents believe that their children are aware of their race when they actually know only their color. Consider five-year-old Deanna:

INTERVIEWER: *What color are you?*
DEANNA: Brown.
Some people call someone who is brown "black." Can you be black and have brown skin?
No, I'm brown! You can't be black if you're brown.

Parents of light-complexioned children say that they have a particularly difficult task teaching their children the difference between their skin color and their race even when they devote considerable time to it. The mother of five-year-old Sherry said that her light-complexioned daughter once called herself "white" but now knew that she was "black":

> Sherry started saying she was white. I said, "No, sweetheart, you are not white." This went on, I would say, for three months, but I had to really get it across to Sherry that she is not white. It took a little time because Sherry is young, and she didn't really understand the different colors of brown. But [my husband] really helped her out a lot. He kept saying, "No, Sherry, you're black, or you're

> considered brown." He said, "Your race is black, but your color is brown." And . . . she kind of got the hang of it.

But only "kind of." When I asked Sherry to tell me the color of her skin, she described it accurately as "light brown." However, when I asked her to tell me her race, she did not seem to understand what I was talking about. When I specifically asked her if she was black, she denied it. What can caregivers learn from the case of Sherry and other young children confused about their race? Caregivers should be aware that children who are not developmentally ready to understand certain information will not change their thinking despite all the teaching and preaching in the world.

Like Sherry, five-year-old Gayle also correctly named her skin color. When I challenged her, her response was typical of children her age:

INTERVIEWER: *Suppose I say you're a black girl . . .*
GAYLE: I'm not a black girl! I'm light brown . . . light-skinned.
How do you know you're light-skinned?
'Cause when you get white and you'd turn this color. [Points to the inside of her palm.] When you get in the sun too long, when you're white, you turn this color. [Points to the outside of her palm.]

Learning the Color Spectrum

Skin-color differences are relative. Someone considered dark-complexioned in one family may be regarded as light-complexioned in another family. During the early school years, children begin to pick up on the finer distinctions among skin colors. Children will say that they are "dark brown" or "light brown" or even occasionally "middle brown." (Preschoolers rarely tell me they are "light-skinned" or "dark-skinned.")

By now, children are learning from their families and schoolmates that these finer distinctions matter. As journalist Brenda Payton observed in her essay "Black like Me," blacks in general are keenly aware of the variations in each other's skin colors, using words like ebony, bright, golden brown, "chocolate brown, cinnamon brown, paper-bag brown, high yellow, red bone, blue black, meringue, jet black, cafe au lait" to distinguish fine gradations in coloring.[2] Children eventually learn these fine color distinctions as well as the social status ascribed to them and their positions along the color continuum.

Generally, black children at the extremes of the brown color spectrum—either very light or very dark—are more likely to have negative feelings about their skin color, particularly if they are in contact with people with color biases. Children who are dark-complexioned bear the brunt of colorism. If they experience being less favored than lighter-complexioned children in their own family or at school, they will begin to devalue their own skin color and themselves. Unlike preschoolers, children at this stage of development are aware that there is a connection between their skin color and how they are treated by others.

However, having a dark complexion is a problem at this early age only if it is made into one. In *Nappy: Growing Up Black and Female in America,* Aliona Gibson, who grew up in northern California, recalled that she "can't remember ever being made to feel like I was less pretty because I was dark." She remembers "always being complimented on what a pretty little girl I was. Maybe that was [my parents'] way of overcompensating, to make sure that I didn't grow up hating being dark."[3]

Caregivers of dark-complexioned children should be mindful of encouraging them to think positively about their skin color. When talking about their skin, link positive words to "dark-skinned" like "beautiful bronze," "sweet chocolate," or "gorgeous ebony." These early positive associations will go a long way toward cushioning the negative messages that children are likely to encounter later in life.

At the other end of the spectrum, some light-complexioned children also begin to learn that there are positive associations with their skin color. They may sense that people consider them more attractive and treat them better than children who are darker. But the opposite situation also occurs. People in their family, neighborhood, or school may ridicule or exclude children whose only "sin" is having a lighter skin color. Eartha Kitt, the singer-actress (perhaps most widely known for her role as the Catwoman in the early *Batman* television series) disclosed in her autobiography the rejection she experienced from members of her extended family because of her "yella" complexion.[4]

I once counseled a dark-complexioned aunt who was raising a few of her nieces and nephews. With the exception of one light-complexioned six-year-old boy, the children all had coloring similar to their aunt's. When I first met this family, I recognized almost immediately that she disliked the light-complexioned boy. In her litany of complaints about him, she accused him of "thinking he's white" and "thinking he's better." I was meeting with this family because the boy had been referred to me for behavioral problems at home. But as is often the case, the problem was with the caregiver, not with the child. She acknowledged that she had failed miserably in trying to teach him that he was black.

If caregivers have unresolved conflicts about skin color, their children are likely to be affected, especially if any of these children are the "wrong" color. The aunt believed that light-complexioned blacks regarded themselves as superior to dark-complexioned blacks and had an easier life. Although there were other issues involved in this case, the aunt's dislike of her light-skinned nephew, a dislike based on her color prejudice, permeated every aspect of their life together.

And he knew that she disliked him and the reason why. When I met with him alone, he said that his aunt didn't like him because he was "white." So at an early age, this little boy was learning that there was something negative about his skin color from someone who was supposed to love him. Eventually, I recommended that this child be removed from his aunt's home because I suspected that he was being physically abused there. Unfortunately, my suspicions were later confirmed.

Learning Race by Hair

Some children, girls especially, begin to become aware of racial differences as a result of comparing the color and texture of their classmates' hair with their own. The mother of six-year-old Pam revealed that it was only after her daughter became fascinated by the straight, long hair of a white girl in her class that she began asking questions about racial differences:

> [Pam] has said, "I wish I had hair like . . ."—uh, I can't remember the little girl's name, but she picks at the little girl's hair in school. Because this is the one thing that the teacher called my attention to. She just loves to play with the little girl's hair. . . . The teacher said just lots of time she wants to get her attention or something, but she is busy playing with the little white girl's hair. She thinks that the white girl's hair is so pretty. If it wasn't for the hair, I don't think she would notice color difference.

I had a similar fascination as a child. When I was in the second grade, a girl with waist-length, straight, black hair sat in the seat in front of me at school. I thought that she had the prettiest hair in the world. Although I was often complimented on my hair, I felt ambivalent about it because it took such a big effort for my mother, and occasionally my aunts, to wash and style it. I did not look forward to having my hair done. It was a revelation to me that my classmate's hair was "naturally" straight and that she didn't have to go through all that I had to go through to make my hair straight. Hair was one of the first things that I learned that differentiated whites and blacks.

Hair plays a central role in a black girl's unfolding knowledge of her racial and feminine identities. Not only is she learning that certain types of hair are associated with certain skin colors, but she is also learning more about her own attractiveness. Five-year-old Toni's mother told me that she was bothered by her daughter's comparison of her own hair to that of her classmates:

> She's on an ego trip about her hair. . . . [The relatives of] her father, they're mixed. . . . Their hair is straighter. And on my side, it's majority black, so our hair is more nappy. . . . In her school, [among] the other little black kids, she notices that their hair is really coarse and that she's got a little softer grade. So if I let it out, she goes through one of those ego trips, you know, flipping the hair . . . like "I'm gorgeous" or something. So I try not to let her hair out much, you know; I keep it braided.

Children, especially those who attend predominantly white or integrated schools, may learn that there is something different or even odd about their hair. Whites and children of other races who are not familiar with blacks' hair are often curious about their hair textures and styles. They may ask questions or make observations about blacks' hair that may seem rude or offensive to a black child, like "Why is your hair sticking out?" or "Why does your hair look like *that* after you go swimming?" However, early grade-schoolers' questions and comments seldom reflect the malice that may be characteristic of older children's remarks.

According to black children I have talked with, the most common word that white children use to describe blacks' hair is *puffy* or *poofy*. When they are older, around age eight, black children with "puffy" hair may be subjected to teasing about their hair. For example, after overhearing comments at school about a classmate's "puffy" hair, Beverly, a six-year-old, told me that her sister also had puffy hair. She described her own hair as "good" hair because it didn't "puff up" when it was washed, whereas her sister's hair was "bad" because it did. Beverly's mother was irritated that her daughter had "learned" at school that her hair was "better" than her sister's hair.

Even at predominantly black schools, black children can be subjected to judgments about their hair. They face comparisons about who has "good" hair and whose hair is longest. A seven-year-old girl told me that she didn't know that she had "nappy" hair until she went to school with other black children.

Some white girls actually envy black girls' hair because black girls can wear their hair in so many interesting styles. I met a six-year-old white girl who could not understand why her hair couldn't be styled in luxuriant braids like the hair of her best friend, a black classmate. The white girl thought that her friend looked cute wearing her hair in different styles of braids with color-coordinated barrettes and was frustrated because her mother couldn't style her hair like her friend's. The white girl's mother tried to style her daughter's hair in braids, but despite her best efforts to secure them, they would inevitably loosen or unravel. When the subject of hair differences came up in class, the girls' wise white teacher explained how different people had different types of hair and showed how each type had its own special qualities. Each girl left school that day appreciating the uniqueness of her own hair.

Color Choices in Self-Portraits

Black children in the early grades seem to be more aware of their skin color than children of other races. Some black children, especially those who are lighter or darker than family members or who attend color-conscious schools, begin to be aware of the emotional and social benefits and liabilities of their color. This growing awareness of skin color and hair texture is reflected in their self-portraits. Early grade-schoolers are more likely than preschoolers to use the appropriate color to represent their skin and hair.

A kindergartner's mother and her friend noticed the difference in skin-color awareness between black children and children of other races in her daughter's class at a parents' open-house event. The children's self-portraits were displayed on the classroom walls with information on how each of them had charted their skin, hair, and eye color. Snapshots of the children were posted next to the self-portraits.

> There was one little boy. . . . He's very dark. . . . We had to look at his [photo] 'cause he had charted "My eyes are black, my hair is black, and my skin is black." . . . He used a black crayon . . . and colored it in. So we said, well, let's find him, let's see what he really looks like—and he really was actually black. I mean really dark. Then there was a little Chinese boy that had written down that . . . his eyes were blue, his hair was brown, but his skin was green. I said, "Why does he think that his skin is green?" . . . We're laughing at the picture. It was me and my girlfriend—we were laughing about it. . . . And we kept going down the chart. . . . We found a lot of the little white kids and the Chinese kids were coloring their skin green, blue, yellow—any old color, whereas the black kids used black and brown.

When whites and children of other races depict themselves in colors other than their own tones, people don't accuse them of wanting to be another color. If black children do the same thing, however, they are said to hate their color. Surely something is out of kilter here.

"I'll Be This Color Forever"

By age six, most children are *beginning* to understand that skin color is a permanent part of the body. Unlike preschoolers, early grade-schoolers think that their skin color cannot be easily changed by magical means (for example, wishing or repainting).

They are aware that the sun, to which they attribute amazing powers, can change a person's skin color. However, many early grade-schoolers' understanding that skin color is a permanent part of a person's identity is still shaky. If they are pressed, their initially sound responses change. Consider my conversation with six-year-old Shirley:

INTERVIEWER: *Can a person change her color and become another color?*
SHIRLEY: No.
Why not?
God have to do it.
Why does God have to do it?
Because you can't do it by yourself.
Could I get God to make me another color now?
No. He might be asleep.

Like preschoolers, some early grade-schoolers have noticed that they were a different color when they were babies. But unlike preschoolers, who have a magical explanation for their skin-color change, grade-schoolers, like five-year-old Melanie, attribute the change to a natural phenomenon:

INTERVIEWER: *What color were you when you were a baby?*
MELANIE: Black, I mean white.
You were white when you were a baby?
Yeah.
How do you know you were white?
God made me that color. . . .
Are you still white? [Melanie shakes her head.] How come you became black [as she had previously described her skin color]?
I growed, and I growed, and I growed.
How did you become black?
I keeped getting in the sun.

For many children, the sun is the major player in causing skin-color changes. Most children seem to understand the connection between level of exposure to the sun and the darkening of the skin. For example, six-year-old Shirley told me that when she was a baby, she was "tan," but now she is "brown." When I asked her why her color had changed, she said, "I stayed in the sun too much." But Shirley seems to have an unrealistic fear of the sun's power to change her skin color:

INTERVIEWER: *Did you ever want to be another color than you are?*
SHIRLEY: Yes.

Can you remember when it was?
I think it is now. [Giggles.]
Why do you want to be another color?
Because I won't look as dark.
Well, why don't you want to look as dark?
'Cause I might burn up.
You might burn up? Why might you burn up if you're dark?
If I get blacker and keep on getting blacker, I might burn.
You might burn? Did you ever see that happen to anybody?
No, but I saw it on a cartoon one time, and the little girl was getting a tan.
And what happened when she was getting a tan?
She said ouch!

Early grade-schoolers' developing understanding about skin-color permanence is reflected in how they approach this topic in real life. A friend told me that she was certain that her six-year-old twin daughters understood that their skin color was permanent until she took them to see Santa Claus. They saw a black Santa at one mall one week and a white Santa at another mall the next week. One of the twins said to the second Santa, "How come you were black at the other mall?" The Santa was rendered speechless, and the little girls were puzzled when their mother burst out laughing. She realized that both her daughters thought that Santa had changed color as he moved from one mall to another. Their reasoning was illogical to the mother but made perfect sense to her children, given their stage of development. If there is only one Santa, how else can one explain his skin-color change?

"My Color Makes Me Me"

Most early grade-schoolers I've interviewed tell me that they do not want to change their color, contradicting the conventional wisdom that black children would prefer to be white. Most children, like five-year-old Kenya, seem very attached to their parents and family and fear abandonment if their skin color were to change:

INTERVIEWER: *Did you ever want to be another color?*
KENYA: **No.**
Why not?
Because I want to be the same color as my mother is. If I'm not the same color as my mother is, I can't be my mother's child no more.
What's the matter with that?
Then you'll have nobody to feed you or anything.

Since children at this stage of race awareness generally have some idea that their skin color is permanent, a grade-schooler who says that she wants to be white means something quite different from a preschooler who says the same thing. Usually, the preschooler is caught up in a fantasy world and wants to change color because of a momentary whim. The grade-schooler, by contrast, may be signaling that she is becoming aware of the privileges accorded to whites or that she is feeling some distress that she attributes to being brown or black.

When a child says, "I don't want to be black" or "I want to be white," one has to be very careful in deciphering the meaning. It is tempting to interpret the child's words from an adult's perspective, but a child at this age does not think like an adult. The question to ask when a grade-schooler *repeatedly* expresses a desire to be white is, "What is happening in the child's life to make him feel that he would be better off being another color?"

I've met only a few black children at this stage of development who have expressed a desire to be white. One was a first-grader, who attended a predominantly white school:

INTERVIEWER: *Have you ever, for even a little while, wanted to be another color?*
CLAIRE: **Yes.**
Which color did you want to be?
White. Only for a little while.
When was this?
That was a long time ago.
And why did you want to be white?

Because I thought it was better-looking, but now I want to be black; I want to be brown.
Why did you think white was better-looking a long time ago?
Well, I was littler then.
And why did you think white was better-looking?
Because I didn't know better then. That was when I was in kindergarten.
But what happened in kindergarten . . . that made you think that white was better-looking?
I just thought it was better, but then my mom heard on the news that whites were getting killed down in Africa, so I wanted to be black, I mean brown.

Another child told me that she didn't want to be brown anymore because there was no one in her predominantly white neighborhood to play with. Indeed, experiencing social problems is the major reason children give for wanting to change their color. Consider the case of a six-year-old dark-complexioned black girl who upon her arrival home from school one day asked her mother to "take this color off and get me another color." The mother was stunned by her daughter's words. As she said to me, "It was like she was asking me to take her color off like you'd remove a wrapper from a crayon and put another one on. Isn't it strange to think that way?" No, not for a first-grader: *that's exactly how they think!*

Fortunately, the mother responded to her daughter's distress compassionately. When she discussed the situation with her daughter, she learned that her daughter's previous complaints about keeping friends were more serious than she had realized. Her daughter believed that "none" of her classmates liked her because she was black. Although her daughter's classmates were mostly white, the mother concluded it was not her daughter's race but her personality—she was shy and sensitive—that was the cause of her social problems. As it turned out, the mother was right. The mother addressed the true root of her daughter's problem by teaching her daughter skills to enable her to relate better to her classmates. By the time her daughter left elementary school, she was a member of a close group of friends of different races. Attending a predominantly white school did not lower her self-esteem, impair her social skills, or diminish her ability to relate to other blacks.

Of course, there are situations where children are ostracized by other children not because of their limited social skills but because of their skin color and other physical differences. During the early school years, however, this situation is unusual unless children are in an environment where racism is tolerated.

Fear of Being White

Amid all the talk about black children wanting to be white, little attention is paid to the opposite situation, their fear of being white. I was surprised to learn from my conversations with children that for some of them, this is a major concern. For example, while interviewing six-year-old Sharon, I noticed her mother, who was listening to our conversation in an adjacent corner of the living room, throwing me a worried glance. Her daughter, who was light-complexioned, had just revealed that whenever she got into fights with her sisters and cousins, they teased her and "make me feel bad" about being "white." Sharon said that although she frequently "told on them" for teasing her whenever she got into fights with them, they would tease her all over again about being white. In Sharon's family, being white was regarded as a negative thing. Sharon explained to me that white people were "mean because they use guns and kill people."

As I sat on the floor talking with this little girl and feeling her anxiety rise as she talked about whites, it occurred to me that she was talking about white people the way some young children talk about the strangers whom their parents warn them against. Strangers, they have learned, are bad people, "other" people, different from us. When I asked Sharon whether she knew any white people, she said that a family member had pointed some out to her on the bus. At a tender age, Sharon had already absorbed a negative stereotype of whites, even though (or perhaps because) she had hardly any contact with them. It is no wonder that Sharon wanted to change to a darker complexion to look more like her siblings and cousins.

WHAT DOES COLOR HAVE TO DO WITH FAMILY?

During the early school years, children develop a greater awareness of the connection between their own skin color and the skin tones of other family members. However, it would be a stretch to say that they fully understand the role that heredity plays in their skin color. In fact, they have at best only a shaky grasp of the relation between the physical characteristics of parents and children. Many parents and teachers are surprised that children can be exposed to all types of information, for example, through books, television programs, and classroom instruction, about procreation but still don't quite fully understand it. Early grade-schoolers often initially appear to be quite knowledgeable about this topic, but after you talk with them for a while, it becomes obvious—usually hilariously so—that their information is jumbled. Reflecting their early stage of cognitive development, they often intermingle snatches of facts about procreation with their own creative ideas. Unlike preschoolers, they have an inkling of the biological connection between mothers and their children. But they do not understand the genetic basis of skin color. Although most children seem to know that their mother had something to do with their skin color, they are not quite sure what. My conversation with six-year-old Jessi, who is light-complexioned, was typical of children who have only a limited understanding of the relationship between biology and their skin color:

INTERVIEWER: *How did you come to be that color?*
JESSI: **I don't know . . . 'Cause I didn't go in the sun much.**
But how did you come to be that color?
My mother.
How did your mother make you that color?
I don't know.
But what did she do to make you that color?
I think she ate starch.

Early grade-schoolers believe the father's color should match the mother's, but many of them, including children from two-parent families, do not recognize the role fathers play in determining their skin color, as this following dialogue indicates:

INTERVIEWER: *How did you come to be that color?*
CHELSEA: **Because God made me that color.**
Why did God make you that color?

> **Because that's the color my mother was.**
> *Why did God make you the color your mother was?*
> **Because if you're not the color your mother was, you might not be your mother's child.**
> *Why not?*
> **Because they don't look like alike.**
> *How does it matter if they don't look alike?*
> **Because my mother is black; and if I'm not black, my mother can't be black. I can't be my mother's child.**

When I show early grade-schoolers an assortment of photos of children of various races and ask them to select the children who belong with parents of different races (white, black, Asian, and biracial), most children will group family members primarily according to skin color, not necessarily by race. Although they put Asians and whites in the same family, they are unlikely, as preschoolers do, to place light-skinned blacks in with them.

Early grade-schoolers tend to expect family members to match, even if they themselves are from families with skin-color variations. Children's notions that family members should have matching skin colors can cause problems in real life. Five-year-old Kelly's mother told me about her daughter's surprise when her baby sister was born with a skin color noticeably different from that of the other members of the family: "Kelly asked why [the baby] was so dark. She took more after my side of the family—she's a little browner. She's lightening up now, but she was really brown when she was first born, and Kelly couldn't understand why she wasn't the same color as her. As a matter of fact, my mother couldn't even understand why she wasn't the same color. Hey, there's two sides to the family!

Children who find it confusing to understand that members of their family can have both "brown" and "white" skin will have a tough time learning about race. In Rebecca Carroll's *Sugar in the Raw,* a remarkable collection of reminiscences by adolescent black girls who describe what it is like to grow up black, one teen recalls the difficulty she had grasping this concept as a young child:

> My mom is very light-skinned, which sort of threw a wrench in my process of figuring out stuff. . . . My grandmother on my mother's

> side was very dark, and I remember asking my mom, "How can a white baby come out of a brown mommy?" Of course, everyone laughed at me, but it was something that I was honestly wrestling with. My mom kept telling me she was black, but I didn't believe her for the longest time, not until later on, when I understood the way society deals with race and culture. Then I just took her word for it.[5]

Occasionally, children this age realize that it is possible to have people of different colors in the same family. In the midst of explaining that family members have to have matching colors, six-year-old Alana suddenly changed her response. Alana, who described her own color as "brown," had initially said that the light-complexioned girl could not be the child of dark-complexioned parents:

INTERVIEWER: *Why couldn't she be their daughter?*
ALANA: **Because she doesn't have the same skin color.**
Why should she have the same skin color as the mother and father?
I forgot! She don't have to 'cause my daddy is light.

Although children at this stage of race awareness are observant of skin-color differences, these differences do not carry the meanings, either negative or positive, that some adults give them. So it is not surprising that children do not see the incongruity between their insistence that families have matching skin colors and their own reality, where some members of their families have pronounced skin-color variations.

One out of two marriages in this country ends in divorce.[6] Because of the high rate of remarriage and the prevalence of informal living arrangements, many children will spend some portion of their lives in stepfamilies or blended families, where members may share little physical resemblance. For young children, physical differences, like skin color and hair, are not important unless people close to them make them so. As children grow older, however, depending on how people react to skin color and other physical variations within their families, these differences can become a major cause of conflict between family members.

I sometimes conduct an exercise that involves showing gradeschoolers a picture of an interracial couple (black and white) and pictures of children of various skin colors and then asking them to select pictures of the couple's children. Since most children in this age group believe that the members of a family should have matching skin colors, it is not surprising that most of them refuse to see the interracial couple as parents of the same children. For example, when I showed six-year-old Claudia the photos of an interracial couple and asked her to select the children who belonged with them, she demurred:

CLAUDIA: **No, I don't want white with black.**
INTERVIEWER: *Why not?*
'Cause it don't match.
Can't this mommy go with this daddy?
No.
Why not?
'Cause they just can't!
But how do you know they can't?
'Cause I never seen a white lady with a black man.

Five-year-old Cher's response in the following dialogue is revealing in that she assumes that an interracial couple would not be together because there would be conflict in the relationship:

CHER: **A white mommy? A white mommy and a black daddy?**
INTERVIEWER: *What's wrong with that?*
Look at her.
Can't they be a mommy and daddy?
[Shakes her head.] . . . 'Cause.
'Cause why not?
The mommy won't like the daddy.
Why won't she like the daddy?
'Cause.
'Cause why?
The daddy won't treat her right.
What will he do?
Kick her out the bed.
Why won't that daddy like that mommy?
'Cause she white and he black.
So what's wrong . . . ?

The children won't like the mommy and daddy.
Why not?
'Cause the mommy's white.

Black children's resistance to assembling an interracial family reflects not only their reality (very few of them are acquainted with racially mixed families) but limitations in their cognition. Their tendency to assemble families of similar skin color indicates their need to replicate the world they know. For them, whatever they are used to is how things should be.

The few early grade-schoolers whom I have witnessed assembling mixed families cite reasons other than biology for doing so. Usually, they had experienced their own parents' separation, divorce, or remarriage. For example, when six-year-old Desiree, whose parents had recently separated, assembled a mixed-race family in which the children resembled only the white mother, I asked why none of the children looked like the black father:

DESIREE: **That is because . . . they . . . she got divorced and married another man.**
INTERVIEWER: *She got divorced and married another man?*
Yeah.
Why did they get divorced?
Because they were having a hard time together.
What kind of hard time?
Like fighting, like arguing, like Dad and Mama.

Learning "Groups": Sex Comes Before Race

Most children in the early school grades are not developmentally inclined to look at people in terms of groups, much less groups solely defined by skin color or race. So if you ask them to describe another child or adult, they are unlikely to mention skin color as a defining feature.

When I give five- and six-year-olds a pile of photographs of children of various races (black, white, and Asian) and ask them to put children together who belong together, they, like preschoolers, are most likely to categorize people initially by gender. Thus girls, regardless of their race, are grouped with girls and boys with boys. Only when I specifically ask them to sort people into "black," "white," and "Chinese" groups do they try to do so. Although, like preschoolers, they do not always use these labels accurately, unlike preschoolers, they seem to rely on more than skin color alone to determine who belongs in the different groups.

Most of them are beginning to understand that the word *black* means something more than just skin color, and so, unlike preschoolers, they include *both* dark- and medium-brown-complexioned people in their "black" group. For example, Meisha had initially described the medium-complexioned blacks as "brown." However, when I asked her to put all the "black people" in one group, she included the medium- and the dark-complexioned people in the black group. Her reason for calling them black is typical of that of other early grade-schoolers:

Interviewer: *Why do you call them black?*
Meisha: I can't figure out that one either.
So how do you know they're black?
'Cause they're brown.
But if they're brown, why do you call them black?
I don't know.
Who did you hear call them black?
My aunt, my mother, and my father.

Unlike preschoolers, most early grade-schoolers do not categorize light-complexioned blacks with whites; instead, they put them in a separate group, variously called "light-skinned," "light brown," or, as one child described them, "tan black." Although most children are not yet able to articulate it, they are beginning to realize that something other than skin color is used to determine a person's "group." Most children at this age, particularly those who have been carefully taught to distinguish light-complexioned blacks and whites, seem to know that light-complexioned blacks are not white, but they don't see them as black either.

Early grade-schoolers' "white" group usually consists of Asians as well as whites. Consider six-year-old April's explanation for using the word *white:*

INTERVIEWER: *Why do you call them white [referring to the children whom she identified as "white"]?*

APRIL: ***White* is a better word than *peach*.**

Why?

I think cause blacks like it better than *peach*, 'cause they would be calling them the "peach people."

Although some children seem aware that there are physical characteristics other than skin color, such as hair color and texture, that are associated with people of different colors, only a few children can describe what these differences are. Five-year-old Joy was an exception, as the following dialogue indicates:

JOY: **White people have different hair from black people.**

INTERVIEWER: *Why is that?*

God gave the hair to them, and they cannot take it off.

But why did God give them that kind of hair?

'Cause they white people. . . . 'Cause God did not like the black people hair on the white people.

Well, why not?

'Cause . . . 'cause God think everybody be laughing at white people got black people's hairs on.

Most children do not spontaneously categorize Asian people in a separate group but rather assign them to the "white" group. When pressed to do so, most of them can identify Chinese people, yet only some of the children can give a reason for calling people Chinese. Apparently children acquire the concept "Chinese" before they can articulate it. I have met children who are familiar with the word *Chinese* but who were unable to identify Chinese people. They associate the word with a type of food or a restaurant rather than with a group of people.

Early grade-schoolers are much more likely than preschoolers to be aware of other racial and ethnic labels, although they do not always use them accurately. Depending on the region of the country in which they live, children spontaneously use terms like *Puerto Rican, Mexican,* and *Japanese* to describe some of the people whose photographs I show them. When children talk about these groups, they do so more in terms of their different language and less in terms of their different physical appearance (for example, a five-year-old said, "Mexican people speak Spanish"). On rare occasions, I've also heard children call people "spics" and "honkies."

Occasionally, I've met early grade-schoolers who sort the photographs of children of various races on a basis other than gender, skin color, or race. For example, six-year-old Shannon made only two piles of the photographs of children of various races. She called one pile "Americans" (all the blacks, of varying skin color, and all the whites) and the other pile "Japanese" (Asians). Her family's extensive travel seemed to have influenced the way that she viewed people—in her case, from a national rather than from a skin-color or racial perspective. For Shannon, Asians were foreigners; she did not comprehend that some people who looked Asian could also speak English and be Americans. It is difficult for children at her developmental stage to understand this concept.

ARE PEOPLE OF DIFFERENT COLORS DIFFERENT?

As children are learning to distinguish people on the basis of skin color and other physical characteristics, they are also sensing less obvious differences between people of different colors. This is one of the key differences between how preschoolers and early grade-schoolers think. When I ask preschoolers whether there are differences between brown or black and white people, most of them don't seem to have a clue about what I'm talking about. They don't see any differences, other than skin color. However, by age five or six, children begin to sense that there are more differences between people of different colors than meet the eye. Some children may not be able to identify these differences, but they know that something about the black and brown people makes them different from the white people.

Prior to the civil rights era, the social differences between whites and blacks were much more obvious, especially in the South, where blacks were prohibited from using the same public facilities (for example, water fountains, restrooms, theater sections) as whites. The biographies of people who grew up in that era reveal that as young children, they sensed differences between blacks and whites (for example, in what they were or were not allowed to do), but cognitively they could not grasp these differences. Gladys Knight, the famous singer, poignantly remembers how at age six, as a child growing up in the segregated South of the 1940s, she was oblivious to the differences between blacks and whites. When she encountered a segregationist sign, she didn't know what it meant: "My mom tells me when I was six, I stood pondering the signs over two water fountains that said WHITE and COLORED and then I asked her, 'Momma, what color is water?' I never got an answer."[7]

Some children tried to figure out just what those differences were, and no one has described the effort more poignantly than Anne Moody. In her superb autobiography, *Coming of Age in Mississippi,* she movingly writes about growing up in the 1940s in the segregated South. As a young child, Moody tried to figure out the difference between whites and blacks that adults insisted existed but that children were unable to see. Until about age six, she was unaware of any difference between her and her white playmates. Then one day, her mother forcefully separated Anne from her white playmates in the white section of their local movie theater, where Anne had followed them while her mother was talking to one of the white children's mothers. All the children, both whites and blacks, cried inconsolably at being forced by their parents to separate. None of the children could understand the adults' explanations for why they had to sit in different sections of the theater: "All the way back to our house, Mama kept telling us that we couldn't sit downstairs [in the theater], we couldn't do this or that with white children. Up until then I never thought about it. After all, we were playing together. I knew that we were going to separate schools and all, but I never knew why."

Anne became obsessed with finding out the difference between whites and coloreds that allowed whites to have privileges denied to coloreds: "'There is a secret to it besides being white,' I thought. . . . Then my mind got all wrapped up in trying to uncover that secret." In the fashion typical of a preoperational child, Anne set out to learn this secret. "One day when we [Anne, her siblings, and their white playmates] were all playing in our playhouse . . . I got a crazy idea. I thought the secret was in their 'privates.' I had seen everything they had but their privates and it wasn't very different from mine. So I made up a game I called 'The

Doctor.'. . . I examined each of them about three times, but I didn't see any differences. I still hadn't found that secret."[8]

A white colleague of mine also grew up in the South, in the 1950s. Like Anne, around age six, she also started wondering about the differences between colored people and white people; all the colored people she knew seemed to be very poor compared to the whites she knew. One cold day, as she drove with her mother through a run-down black neighborhood, she became worried about whether their dilapidated homes were warm. So she asked her mother why the colored people didn't live in better homes. It was the first time that she remembered her mother, who was one of the only whites in their community to befriend blacks, being at a loss for words. When her mother finally answered, she responded in an uncharacteristically disingenuous tone of voice: "They don't like to work." My colleague said that she never again asked about the differences between coloreds and whites because she learned then and there that the question made adults uncomfortable.

Although *obvious* discrimination is no longer sanctioned, some black children I've interviewed sense that there are differences between the black or brown and white people, but they aren't quite sure what those differences are. Consider my conversation with Dee:

INTERVIEWER: *Are black people and white people different?*
DEE: **My friend Lydia, she said white people have . . . black blood, and black people have red blood.**
Do you believe her?
No, I believe they both only have red blood.
Why don't you believe her?
Because white people can't have different kind of blood.
Why not?
Unless God made them have it.

Based on the information that she learned from a movie, six-year-old Desiree also saw differences between blacks and whites:

INTERVIEWER: *Are black people different from white people?*
DESIREE: **Yeah.**

How are they different?

Because they didn't . . . the blacks didn't make slaves out of the whites; the whites made slaves out of the blacks.

Children who see differences between the races are in the minority. Most of the early grade-schoolers I have met do not believe that there are differences between people of different colors, except for skin color and, in the case of some Asians and Latinos, language. Interestingly, most grade-schoolers, even those who live in poor communities, do not see whites as being economically advantaged. At this age, black children generally do not yet have the stereotype that whites have more money or better things than they do. Many young children's idea of "rich" is having lots of toys and candy.

Different Meanings for Black and White

Some black parents are concerned that their young children's developing ideas about racial and ethnic groups will be adversely affected by the culture's insidious messages about black and white people. They point to the associations that are made with the colors white and black. White is seen as being associated with things that are honorable and good, while black is associated with things that the opposite.

For example, the villain in westerns wears a black hat, the hero a white one; the color of christening and wedding gowns is white, the color of mourning clothes is black. Phrases like "the black sheep of the family" connote that black is shameful. But people rarely allude to other, opposite associations with these colors: black is the color of elegance, sophistication, and wealth (for example, in the expressions "black gold," "black opal," and "black label"), whereas white is also the color of cowardice, sickliness, and death.

Some Africans I've met have associations with the colors black and white that differ radically from American views. This difference was brought home to me by a white American priest who spent several years in Kenya and became an elder of the tribe he served. He learned that the Kikuyu tribe with whom he worked associated black with life and white with death and suffering. During his initial period in Kenya, young children used to come up to him and pinch him to see if he were still alive. They could not understand how someone without color, seemingly bloodless, could be alive. When a child was born into the tribe, the child was kept inside his home until his melanin had come in and his skin had darkened: parents did not consider their child presentable until he had a darker postbirth color.

Various cultures have different associations with the colors black, brown, and white (for example, in China, white symbolizes death and brown life). As children mature, they should learn that associations with these color words are all relative. So to use these colors to make such absolute distinctions is ludicrous.

Teaching Skin Color and Race: Some Activities

One way to minimize your child's color consciousness is to teach her that skin color is just a covering and that people of different colors are far more similar than different. It is best to wait until your child asks about racial differences before addressing the topic. Make your conversation fun. Since children at this stage of development are very concrete, it is helpful when you talk to them about the concepts of racial differences and similarities to draw analogies to things that they can actually see, touch, or taste. Here are some examples:

- One mother I've read about used M&M candies to teach her five-year-old child the concept that people are different outside but on the inside they are essentially the same: although the M&M candies are different colors on the outside, inside they are all dark chocolate.
- You may be interested in Patty Green's ginger cookies, which are geared specifically to teaching children about racial similarities and differences.[9] The cookies, dark and white chocolate on the outside, are the same color and have the same taste on the inside. She also has a line of cookies from different countries, including China and Mexico, that includes fun facts (numbers from 1 to 10, common phrases, the country's flag).
- I've often told my children that different kinds of people are like flowers in a huge, beautiful garden. The garden is so much more interesting with its many different kinds of flowers than if it only had one kind. And even the flowers that seem

alike, like roses, have many different kinds. People are like flowers. We are many and different, but we are all part of a magnificent garden. Young children seem to resonate to this image, one that comes especially alive for them if your conversation takes place in a garden or park or even while placing some flowers in a vase.

Teachers can also find many helpful suggestions for fostering healthy racial attitudes in young children in works by L. Derman-Sparks[10] and the staff of Teaching Tolerance,[11] a project of the Southern Poverty Law Center.

Do White Children See Race Differently?

Johnny Lee, a white man who was a former imperial wizard and a founder and recruiter for the Ku Klux Klan Youth Corps, vividly remembers his experience when he was five and saw a black man for the first time. Johnny said to his father, "Look, Daddy, there's a chocolate-covered man." Daddy replied, "No, son, that's a nigger." Lee said that it was at that moment that "the seeds of hatred" were planted that resulted in his life in the Klan, a life he later repudiated.[12]

Unlike young Johnny, white children who have not been sensitized to race ascribe little importance to skin color.

Relatively few studies have been done on how children of other races, including whites, become aware of racial differences. Those available suggest that skin color is not as salient an issue for white children at the early grade-school stage of development as it for blacks.[13] It is understandable that young white children do not tend to regard skin color as important, since racial prejudice is generally not a factor in their lives.

I am impressed by how little race seems to matter to many of the white young grade-schoolers I encounter. Most of them, from families of friends and acquaintances, attend integrated schools or live in mixed-race communities. Their answers to my questions about race are similar to Ian's, a six-year-old white youngster. Ian described the colors of the white and black people as, respectively, "whitish" and "brownish"; he can identify the "Chinese" people and says that he has friends who speak Spanish, although he doesn't have a special name for them. Like black children who do not come from racially obsessed families, Ian did not spontaneously describe or categorize people by skin color or race. Despite my repeated promptings, Ian could not think of a single way, other than skin color, in which blacks and whites differed. Although his level of understanding about how people get their color and his awareness of the existence of different racial groups was similar to that of black children, skin color did not seem as emotional an issue for him as it was for some blacks.

I have heard of Latino and Asian children for whom "race" became an emotional issue when they were subjected to teasing and other mean behavior because of their accents, their limited fluency in English, their different types of dress or the lunches they bring to school. Fortunately, however, most early grade-schoolers, regardless of race, do not seem to have stereotypes of themselves or of people who are different colors. Like preschoolers, they are inclined to see people as individuals rather than as members of a group—color, racial, or otherwise. Because of this developmental advantage, these early years are an optimum time for children of different races to get to know each other, before they become aware of the stereotypes that in time will rob them of their racial innocence.

I suspect that children in other countries with a history of racial discrimination develop race awareness in ways similar to American children. Several years ago, I met a lovely white six-year-old at the home of friends of friends while visiting Australia. From the start, she seemed very comfortable with me, unlike a few of the adults, all gracious people, who it seemed to me were trying a little too hard to appear at ease with a black person. Circumstances led to my spending much of the afternoon talking and playing games with her. It wasn't until much time had passed and we rejoined the adults' conversation that she began to ask me about myself.

First, she asked questions about my skin color (like "How did your skin color become brown?" and "Will it change back?"). Next, she asked me about my full lips. Her parents understandably were discomfited by her questions and took turns trying to dissuade her from asking me anything else. Actually, it was all quite amusing. The parents were growing increasingly tense trying not to offend me, while their daughter, oblivious to their discomfort, became increasingly more persistent in her questioning. To make matters worse, their guest was not being very cooperative with the parents' efforts to restrain their daughter.

In spite of my assurances that I didn't mind answering the questions, the parents continued to try various strategies to silence their daughter, all the while doing their utmost not to appear anxious. Eventually, they found some pretext to escort her from the room. She had never seen, much less talked to, a black person before, and her curiosity was perfectly normal. I knew that to her, skin color and lip shape were just physical attributes, not the hot potatoes they were to her parents. When we said good-bye later that day, I felt a tinge of sadness; I wondered if I visited her again several years in the future whether she would see my color more than she would see me.

Even at this stage of development, children who have not been exposed to the racial prejudices of their family and society retain the remarkable gift of obliviousness to the social baggage attached to race. Dr. Laura Schlessinger, author and nationally syndicated talk show host, once told a marvelous story on her show about a childhood incident that illustrates this point. When she was a girl, she had a piano teacher named Charlie. Whenever he came to her home to give her piano lessons, he greeted her younger sister by hoisting her on his shoulders. One day, about a year after Laura had been taking lessons, Charlie did not hoist her sister on his shoulders. Instead, he bent down and gave her a candy. Her sister said, "Charlie, your hands are black!" This was the first time her sister had noticed Charlie's skin color despite all the time they had known each other. Although she had been oblivious to his different skin color when she was younger, as she grew older, she was developmentally able to see the difference. Dr. Schlessinger concluded: "Racism is not congenital; it has to be learned."[14]

~

Although early grade-schoolers are more advanced in their understanding of skin-color differences than preschoolers are, they generally have not yet acquired the color consciousness of the society in which they are growing up. If children are not developmentally predisposed to think negatively about their skin color or race, why do some black children have such low self-esteem? In the next chapter, I suggest that in the minority of cases where self-esteem is a problem, there are more likely culprits than race.

CHAPTER SIX

Black Children's Self-Esteem

The Real Deal

It is the conventional wisdom that poor self-esteem is rampant among young black children because they are ashamed of their skin color. Some studies support this view; most do not. My own experiences, observations, and research have convinced me that black children, like children of other races, are likely to grow up feeling good about themselves if they are raised in nurturing families and communities. Conversely, the factors that cause a white child, or a child of any other race, to have self-esteem problems can lead to similar problems in black children. In cases of low self-esteem, it is important to ask, "What is going on in the child's life to make him dislike himself?" Some people don't ask this question because they are afraid of what they'll find.

For young children, the world consists almost exclusively of their own family and its immediate environment. The larger social context, beyond family and school, is not yet on the radar screen. According to psychologist Erik Erikson, children's primary psychosocial task at this time of life, around ages five and six, is to develop "industry," that is, self-confidence, self-discipline, and competence. They are supposed to learn the formal skills of life, how to play by the rules, and be a team member. If they do not learn these life skills, they become subject to feelings of inadequacy and inferiority.[1] Parents and other primary caregivers play a critical role in their children's developing ability to deal with the challenges that arise at this time of their life. Over the years, I've observed three crucial ways in which parents' behavior and attitudes affect their children's developing sense of self-worth. In this chapter we will look at these three influences: parents' disciplinary style, children's relationship with their parents, and attitudinal impoverishment or enrichment.

PARENTS' DISCIPLINARY STYLE

It is relatively easy to spot young children with poor self-esteem. They may exhibit behavior problems at home or school. They may be painfully shy and withdrawn or, conversely, aggressive; they may have difficulty getting along with their peers; they may even have problems learning.

A few years ago, I was consulted on the case of a dear little black kindergartner, DeAndre, who had several problematic school behaviors: hitting and kicking other children, disrupting the class, and being generally oppositional to the teacher. DeAndre's mother told me that the way she "controlled" him was by "whipping" him. She said that he wouldn't dare do the things at home that she heard he was doing at school. She obviously loved her son, but she mistakenly believed that "bringing him up right" involved whipping him "when he needed it." Her physical punishment did not meet the legal definition of abuse because it left no marks on DeAndre's body, but it certainly left indelible marks on his psyche.

His mother couldn't understand why, even though she "whipped" him, he continued to act out in school while remaining an "angel" at home. When I met him, he seemed to be a child with a broken spirit: he showed little emotion. In truth, DeAndre was a very angry little guy who loved his mother but was afraid of her.

His white teacher reported that she had had similar problems with some of her other black students, especially boys. She was as sensitive and caring a teacher as one would find anywhere, but she seemed to have the impression that being black caused children to have behavior problems. But race has little to do with the behavior problems of these children: the true culprit is physical punishment.

In August 1997, the American Medical Association published the results of an extensive study that found that the more children are spanked, the worse they will behave over time.[2] However, a million such studies will not change the minds of parents who are convinced that physical punishment is necessary to raising well-behaved children.

DeAndre's mother could not see that there was a link between how she disciplined her son and his aggressive behavior toward other children and defiance toward the teacher. Only once did I see a flicker of understanding; this occurred when his mother recognized the words he reportedly used while he was hitting another child as the ones she yelled at him while whipping him. But according to her, DeAndre was having problems at school because his white teacher just didn't know how to manage black children. She is not alone in thinking that way.

The Belief That Hitting Works

Many parents in the black community hold a similarly strong belief in the value of corporal punishment. They believe that more severe methods are needed to discipline their children. If black caregivers hold the view that their own children need more severe discipline than the children of other races, what's the rest of the world to think?

A grandmother, Mrs. Lawson, to whom I was providing parenting guidance, called the alternatives to physical punishment that I offered "the white people's way." According to her, these alternatives would not work for blacks: "White children, when you tell them to do something, they go do it. You have to pop black children before they'll listen to you."

Any white person who uttered these or similar words would be tagged a racist. I knew that Mrs. Lawson was devoted to her grandchildren, but I also knew that she fervently believed that she would be doing them a disservice if she didn't "pop" them when they misbehave to teach them right from wrong. She was following a style of discipline she had learned from her own mother. She admitted to me, however, that she had modified her mother's approach: her own beatings are not as severe as her mother's, to avoid leaving marks that would cause "the system" to remove the children from her care.

I was disheartened to listen to Mrs. Lawson's accounts of how she was brutalized—there is no other word for it—as a child. I had been told similar stories by many older blacks (as well as by whites and Latinos) who grew up in the first half of this century, but I was nonetheless appalled to hear once again about the kinds of physically punitive things that were done—and continue to be done—to children in the name of discipline and love.

Our many conversations did not convince Mrs. Lawson of the potential harm that she was doing to her grandchildren. Although she disliked being beaten as a child and acknowledges that her mother, by today's standards, would have been considered abusive, she defends her mother's need to use harsh discipline. Mrs. Lawson says that as an adult, she understands that the way that her mother disciplined her was "all for my own good; it made me the person that I am today." As I reflect on the difficulties she has shared with me about her life, her history of emotional problems, and the descent of some of her adult children into the drug world, I wonder whether she has really thought through the relation between the "discipline" she received as a child and the person she became. Can she come to see the effect it seems to have had on her children and may yet have on her grandchildren?

Of course, the mode of discipline they chose to use is only one aspect of parenting, but from what I've observed, it has a critical influence on children's self-concept. I am convinced that children who are regularly subjected to physical discipline, as well as emotional maltreatment, are more likely to have emotional, behavioral, and other problems not only in childhood but also later in life. Most of the children in the early grades who have been referred to me because of their behavioral problems have been subjected to regular physical punishment that has caused them harm.

"Spanking," "whipping," "paddling," "popping," "beating," or whatever name corporal punishment goes by, is an unnecessarily harsh way to deal with children's behavior problems. It teaches children that the use of physical violence—for that is how children experience it—is justifiable when people "mess up." When they are routinely subjected to physical punishment, children learn more about fear and aggression than about internal control and self-regulation. Moreover, physical punishment can create a lingering animosity between caregivers and their children that can be very harmful to their relationship.

Hitting to "Toughen" a Child

I've been told by many black parents that they rely on physical punishment not only because it is what they learned from their own parents but also because the world is tougher for black children. From their standpoint, strict physical punishment is an effective way to toughen their children to deal with a hostile world.

A mother and I had an ongoing discussion for several months about the value of physical discipline. She believed it was the most effective way to keep her children "in line" and therefore threatened it daily and employed it at least weekly. One day, when I thought she had finally run out of arguments for relying on whippings and seemed to be seriously considering switching to the nonpunitive methods we had been discussing, she sprang a new argument on me. In a moment of frustration for her—and of revelation for me—she said, "Well, if I don't beat them, 'the man' [that is, the white man] will. If they don't learn at home, then the white man will throw them in jail or kill them when they don't do what they're supposed to."

Fear of the white man's punitive reach seems to be one of the major underlying reasons why many black parents and other caregivers use harsh discipline with their children. This fear certainly has its roots in the early history of white oppression of blacks, particularly through slavery, in this society. Unfortunately, few experts have addressed this issue. Black children, particularly those of poor and working-class backgrounds, are generally required to grow up faster than white children, to take on more responsibilities at a younger age, and to endure harsher consequences for not fulfilling their caregivers' expectations.

Blacks and whites, regardless of their social class, have similar priorities in their parenting, one of the most important being raising a well-behaved, "God-fearing" child who has good manners and respect for others. Many black parents regard physical discipline as an important tool to help them accomplish this goal. Black parents often quote the biblical injunction "Spare the rod, spoil the child." Indeed, the black church plays a major role in promoting the reliance on physical discipline. When I was a child, I heard numerous sermons on the value of beatings. I can still recall the uneasiness I felt at hearing the adults' loud "Amens" as the preacher exhorted them to beat their children when they misbehaved in order to keep them on the right path.

A few years ago, I finally got up the courage to challenge this advice when I heard it given yet again in a passionate Sunday sermon by a black minister at a church I occasionally visit. I was reluctant to approach this minister; his leadership has had a very positive influence on the community. But I felt compelled to discuss with him his parenting advice to the congregation.

In his sermon, he gave an example of the regular beatings he endured as a young boy whenever he disobeyed his parents. One day, when his parents discovered that he had neglected some chore, they told him that his father would "whip" him later that day. However, as was their custom, they did not tell him precisely when the whipping would take place. The minister said that the long wait was even more dreadful than the actual whipping, and he noted that at the time, he "hated" his parents for torturing him.

Then, it seemed to me, he skipped over a large part of the story and began talking about how much, as an adult, he appreciated that his parents loved him enough to give him those whippings. Wait a minute, I said to myself. What happened to all that hate you were mentioning a moment ago? And I thought, What were the psychological consequences to that little boy you used to be, a little boy who was trying his best to be a "good" child but who inevitably, like all children do, messed up and then was subjected to painful blows from loving hands that hurt for a long time?

After the sermon, I asked the minister whether he had ever considered suggesting alternative disciplinary strategies for misbehaving children. A man generally renowned for his loquaciousness suddenly became tongue-tied. He acknowledged that he hadn't given much thought to other methods of discipline because he'd been taught that responsible parents used physical punishment. But he seemed open to considering other methods; indeed, by the end of our conversation, he invited me to "educate" him about alternate methods of discipline.

The idea that blacks deserve a "whipping" when they mess up is deeply ingrained in the American psyche. In that sense, whipping is seen by prejudiced whites as an appropriate means for disciplining blacks who refuse to do whites' bidding. For example, Congressman Gerald Solomon, a white man, caused a national furor when he said in a speech before the House of Representatives that UN Secretary-General Kofi Annan, a black African from Ghana, "ought to be horse-whipped" for his negotiations with Iraqi president Saddam Hussein. Congressman Donald Payne, a black man, called Solomon's words a "racist insult" that reminded him of "the painful image of a black person being whipped into submission by a white master." Solomon apologized; he could not understand how his words could be interpreted as racist.[3] But the white colleague who brought this story to my attention doubts that Solomon would have used the same words to chastise a white man. Whipping is not a humane way to deal with the perceived transgressions of adults—or children.

Spanking Is "Cultural"

The conventional wisdom, held by many blacks and whites, is that physical punishment is part of blacks' cultural heritage. I have often heard blacks justify spanking their children because "that's the way blacks do it." Similarly, I have heard social workers and other professionals, both black and white, say "it's a cultural thing" that blacks use physical punishment for their children. But the use of physical punishment is not unique to black culture: it is a standard practice in many, if not most, cultures worldwide.

Studies show that many white Americans rely on corporal punishment as much as black Americans do. However, research suggests that they tend to rely on it for different reasons. Blacks tend to employ physical discipline to teach, whereas whites tend to resort to it in anger. The class status of parents is also relevant. Middle-class parents, especially those who have benefited from parenting classes and books, tend to employ nonphysical methods of discipline, especially for older children, while lower-class parents tend to employ corporal punishment.

Given the prevalence of physical punishment among so many different cultures, including white American culture, spanking is not a "black thing." But many blacks believe that it is. This mistaken belief is making life worse for black children and harming, not helping, their development. If this idea is "cultural" for blacks, it is not so because it is rooted in African-American culture, or in the African culture that preceded it, but instead because it was adapted from the brutal attitudes of the slave masters from the white European cultures of past centuries.

The Legacy of Slavery and Black Parenting

The legacy of slavery seems to be the major influence on the disciplinary methods of blacks. Harsh physical punishment was one of the main ways slave owners controlled their slaves. Vicious beatings were administered even for minor infractions.[4] Frequently beaten themselves by their masters, black adult slaves in turn beat their children. Through the years, this legacy of corporal punishment has been passed down from one generation to another as a means of disciplining children.

James Comer and Alvin Poussaint, black psychiatrists and authors of *Raising Black Children,* note: "Under the harsh social conditions of the past many black parents had to force their children to obey so that they would not violate any of the racial rules and bring harm to themselves or their families. This led some parents to establish hard-and-fast rules with severe punishment for even minor disobedience."[5] Unfortunately, although many oppressive practices associated first with the slavery era and subsequently with the segregationist era have been eliminated as blacks have gained equal status in this society, unhealthy parenting practices that are rooted in those times have endured in too many black families.

Black Skin Shouldn't Get Whipped!

I hold few absolutes in regard to parenting, but one is that *children should not be hit, spanked, beaten, "popped," "whipped,"* or whatever name this dehumanizing practice goes by.

Harsh physical punishment is particularly harmful to black children. Corporal punishment is harmful for any children, but for black children it carries a particularly high risk because of the stigma that their skin bears in this society.

We live in a society in which many whites still regard dark-skinned people as inferior: less worthy, less intelligent, and less attractive. When black children are spanked, for whatever reason, they learn *at the hands of their own caregivers* that they are not worthy to be treated in a more humane way. This is the same message that white society in the United States has traditionally sent to blacks. The stick, the whip, the belt, the shoe, the hands—whatever implement is used to deliver the blows to a child's dark skin signals that that child deserves to be hurt. Is this the kind of message we want to send our children?

Are Black Kids Disciplined More Harshly?

Talk show host Oprah Winfrey recalls, "I wanted to be a white kid because they didn't get whippings. . . . They got talked to."[6] As a child, she saw how the white parents on television shows like *Leave It to Beaver* dealt with their children's misbehavior, and she quite logically concluded that all white children were disciplined that way. (It wasn't until she was an adult that she realized that many white parents—unlike their fictional counterparts on TV—also use corporal punishment.) Oprah was beaten so badly as a child that she bled from the wounds that resulted. Just as the positive aspects of the way she was parented no doubt contributed to her success, the negative aspects, particularly the way she was disciplined, contributed to personal problems that she has revealed to her audience.

As a child, I, too, believed that white children were not beaten. Moreover, because we black children got beaten when we misbehaved but the white children with whom I was acquainted weren't beaten, I thought that people believed that black children were not as important as white children. Do you know the story behind the phrase "whipping boy"? Supposedly, when a royal child misbehaved and was deemed deserving of punishment, a stand-in was designated to receive the blows in his stead. The royal offspring was regarded as too precious to be whipped, so a child from the servant class received his punishment for him. It makes sense that some black children wonder whether they are as valued by their parents as white children are by their parents, given the harsh treatment they receive at the hands of the very people who are supposed to love them.

The impression that white people don't use physical punishment is commonly held by many blacks I've met. In a parenting workshop I recently gave, a black mother said that white people don't spank their children and then pointedly noted: "You see how they're turning out." She then described a scene in a supermarket where a white mother repeatedly told her young child not to do something and he persisted in doing it. She said that a black parent would have "gone upside his head." A few audience members voiced their agreement with her. This anecdote illustrates the widely held perception in the black community that whites are too permissive with their children. White parents are perceived as allowing their children to get away with things that black parents would never allow.

Good Reasons Not to Spank

The bottom line is that physical punishment is a major risk factor for later emotional and learning problems. Parents who use physical punishment are playing Russian roulette with their ability to control their own use of force and the ability of their children to tolerate it. Some children, for whatever reasons (for example, genetic predisposition, temperament), are more likely to be psychologically harmed by harsh physical punishment than others, and there is no way to predict which child is most vulnerable.

Recent research has shown the harm that physical and emotional maltreatment (like frequent yelling) does to the brain. Abuse affects learning, frustration tolerance, impulse control, and much more.[7] From what I have seen, an awful lot of blacks experience problems as adults that stem, at least in part, from the severity of their discipline as children.

Those of us who follow children for several years as they develop witness the following scenario all too often. The infant starts out as an emotionally healthy child. Things are fine at age one, but by age three, the caregiver is describing what a handful the child is and how he doesn't listen. By age five or six, the teacher is reporting that the child has behavior problems. By age seven or eight, people are talking about a child who is "out of control." The tragedy is that most of these caregivers are devoted parents, doing the best that they know how to raise their children. But they find it hard to escape parenting practices that have been passed down to them from the time of slavery. The reach of the lash is long.

I am convinced that gentler discipline is more effective in fostering children's emotional health, including their self-esteem, because I've observed the positive impact on children's self-concept when their parents switch from corporal punishment to other methods of discipline. I've seen wonderful examples of positive developments in children's lives when their caregivers learn more effective ways to discipline.

The parents of six school-age children come immediately to mind. The mother's idea of good parenting was to keep an immaculate home and to make sure that her children were well fed, clean, and well behaved. She and her husband believed in the efficacy of physical punishment; that's the way that they had been raised, and it had worked for them. They saw corporal punishment as the most reliable way to get their children to obey them and stay out of trouble.

This couple came to me when their daughter was having behavior problems in the second grade. By any measure, their daughter was a child with a poor self-concept, but race had very little to do with it. She was a very anxious child, described to me by her parents as "sneaky" and "moody." When she thought that her classmates were picking on her, she struck back by calling them names or fighting, behaviors that increased the conflict and further alienated her from the other children.

When I advised her parents, among other things, to avoid physical punishment and use alternative disciplinary methods, they were very skeptical. "That psychology stuff is for white people," they told me. Only out of a sense of desperation, prompted by an increase in their daughter's behavior problems, did they decide to try the alternative nonpunitive strategies that I had suggested. Gradually, they observed an improvement in their daughter's behavior. They came to understand that the true object of discipline is to *teach,* not to punish. No other professional experience gratifies me as much as guiding caregivers in their transition from harsh physical discipline to gentle discipline and to observe, over a period of time, the positive effects this change has on their children's behavior and the caregivers' own satisfaction with their parenting.

The biggest obstacle many parents face in giving up physical discipline is their belief that no other method will be as effective in managing their children's misbehaviors. As an exasperated black father of a five-year-old once said to me, "If I give up beating my son, what else will I have to control him?" He could not see that beating his son was ineffective. Although physical punishment, combined with abusive words, would temporarily stop the boy from misbehaving as long as his parents were watching him, he resumed misbehaving when their backs were turned. As parents, we need to find a way to free ourselves from the slave mentality of needing to control our children and move on to learning how to discipline them in ways that foster their self-discipline. I helped this father see that there are more effective ways to give his son discipline than beating him.

Parents who use harsh methods to discipline their children are likely to have suffered harsh discipline themselves as children. They don't want their children to experience the pain they endured. What they do want is for their children to "grow up right." Most of these parents are very receptive to learning effective alternative ways of disciplining their children if counselors approach them as guides to becoming the best parents they want to be rather than condemning them for being "bad" parents.

I must emphasize that *emotional and verbal maltreatment is just as harmful to a child's development and self-concept as physical punishment.* Abusive, belittling, and demeaning words directed toward the child can be as emotionally hurtful as whippings or spankings are physically painful. Just the other day, I overheard a father warning his son, "I'll knock your teeth down your throat" if the boy did not stop his misbehavior. The father's words scared me; imagine the effect on his young son!

No physically or emotionally abusive punishment fosters healthy development. When we use humane methods to *discipline* our children, we send a powerful message of their worth and do much toward nurturing healthy self-concepts.

✱ WHAT TO DO INSTEAD OF SPANKING

Reinforce positive behaviors. Success is the best teacher. Acknowledge the child when she is behaving well, and she is more likely to continue behaving well. Some parents are critical of their children when they misbehave but are less likely to praise them for behaving well. Get in the habit of acknowledging your child's positive behaviors. *The ratio of praise to criticism should be at least 3 to 1:* three compliments, smiles, or pats on the back to one reproach or reprimand. Keep criticism to the absolute minimum, and try not to cite more than one major negative a day. Remember to hug and kiss your child daily and tell her that you love her. If you cultivate a good relationship with your child, she is more likely to work hard to please you.

Ignore. If the misbehavior is not a big deal—if it is not dangerous to life or limb and does not violate an important family rule—let it go. Sometimes a stern stare is enough to let the child know you disapprove of his behavior. Save "no" for important misbehaviors. Remember that children are not supposed to be perfect.

Redirect. Especially with younger children, it is often helpful to guide them to redirect their energy to a more appropriate activity. For example, if your child is pulling the cat's tail, gently guide her to her toy cart so that she can pull that instead.

Use timeouts. Set aside a place in your home—a special chair or spot—where your child can go to calm down after a reprimand. This strategy is particularly useful for young children (ages three to seven). Timeouts should be used sparingly and should be limited to one to five minutes, depending on the age of the child. After a timeout, ask your child, "Tell me what you are learning." Helping your child reflect on his misbehavior provides an opportunity for him to gradually learn to avoid it.

Apply natural consequences. Whenever possible, require that your child undo any damage done. For example, if your child spills juice on the kitchen floor, require that she clean it up. If she damages the property of another family member, require that she replace it or pay for it, even if payment installments last several months.

Withdraw privileges. When children violate family rules, take away privileges such as television viewing, playing video games, spending time with friends, and going on family outings.

Assign chores. All family members should have regular chores. Chores for misbehavior are in addition to children's routine chores.

Impose fines. Children who are able to understand the consequences of their actions can be fined for specific misbehaviors, such as hitting another family member. Limit fines to only a few specific misbehaviors. (This punishment assumes that the child receives an allowance.)

Assign exercises. Some parents of older children in good physical condition find that exercise can be a useful disciplinary strategy. Have the child do a specific number of repetitions—twenty pushups, say, or ten laps around the yard—when he engages in certain misbehaviors. This strategy can be effective if used judiciously, but one must be careful that children do not come to associate exercise with punishment.

Be respectful. How you talk to your child is also important. Talk to your children respectfully even when they misbehave. Talk to them the way you expect them to talk to you. *Label the behavior, not the child.* It is the *behavior* that is bad or wrong, not the child. Belittling or demeaning children when they misbehave lowers their sense of self-worth, induces resentment, and does nothing to teach them how to improve their behavior. Dealing with misbehavior rationally and respectfully and focusing on ways children can work to improve their behavior encourages children to develop self-discipline.

CHILDREN'S RELATIONSHIP WITH THEIR PARENTS

Children who have a close relationship with their parents are more likely to develop a positive self-concept. Research shows that children who have two parents who are involved in their lives do better in school and are less likely to get into trouble than children who come from single-parent homes. Unfortunately, black children are more likely than children of any other race to grow up in single-parent, female-headed families.[8]

Over the years, debate has raged in political and academic circles about the impact of the absent father on the black family. Scholars, politicians, and others have tried to explain this trend toward single parenthood, which seems to have accelerated since the 1960s, when the civil rights movement led to dramatic changes in black life in the United States. Part of the explanation lies in how the welfare system (in particular, Aid to Families with Dependent Children) was structured so as to create a situation in which poor fathers had no incentive to live with their children. In some cases, several generations of female-headed families have lived "on welfare," and few of the children in these families have developed relationships with their fathers.

Fathers Who Abandon Their Children

Fathers who, for whatever reason, have little or no involvement in their children's lives are harming those children. Many black children's self-esteem problems can be traced, at least in part, to their fathers' lack of involvement in their lives. Experts point to financial factors as the explanation for black fathers' absence from their children's lives. In my opinion—an opinion based on both personal and professional experience—poverty is *not* the main reason many of these men essentially abandon their children. Some men prefer a carefree lifestyle that does not involve the encumbrance of raising children. Many white children also face hardship as a result of absent fathers, but given the obstacles society places in black children's path, black fathers have a particular responsibility to provide their children with consistent love and support in their formative years.

By age five, children who are not in regular contact with their father are likely to begin to ask questions about him. Some of them will develop an aching "father hunger" that is painful to witness. They'll call practically any man with whom they have a nodding acquaintance "Daddy." I recall the case of a five-year-old boy whose mother consulted me after his kindergarten teacher threatened to suspend him because of his behavioral problems. Although there were other causes for this boy's behavioral problems, his primal need to have a relationship with his father explained much of what was troubling him. He had begun to call different men whom he met "Dad." His mother admitted that she shooed him away when he tried to ask questions about his father, from whom she separated when the child was an infant.

Adults often underestimate children's need to have both parents involved in their lives. I've heard some mothers claim that they can be "both a mother and father" to their children. This is a next-to-impossible task. Many a mother has managed, usually with the extraordinary support of family and friends, to raise emotionally healthy children. But such mothers are the exceptions; most single mothers whom I've met do not have an extensive support system.

More often than not, their children pay a heavy price when they do not experience the companionship and support of a father or father surrogate. As children grow older, many of them begin to blame themselves for their father's absence in their lives. They think it was something lacking in them that caused their father to abandon them.

Judith Wallerstein and Julia Lewis studied children of divorced families over a period of twenty-five years. They found not only that white, middle-class children of divorced families experienced serious emotional problems in their childhood but also that the impact of their parents' divorce spilled over into adulthood and led to difficulties in forming close relationships.[9] Black children who have parents who have never even tied the knot may experience additional emotional problems due to the more complete absence of many of their fathers from their lives.

Some parents believe that an absent father has a greater negative effect on a boy's self-esteem than on a girl's. I have observed that some boys in the early grades who lack a close male role model are more likely to begin a steady slide into major problems as they grow older. A supportive father is in a better position to teach a boy how to be a man. A woman, no matter how remarkable she is, is likely to experience considerable difficulty fulfilling the role of a caring father.

In fact, the effect of an absent father is just as damaging to girls. I've worked with many girls in the early school grades who desperately craved a father figure. Occasionally, mothers and other caregivers have expressed concerns to me about their young fatherless daughters' inappropriate attention-seeking behavior with men. Girls who do not have fathers are less likely to learn about the variety of fulfilling relationships they can have with men. Nicky Marone, the author of *How to Father a Successful Daughter,* suggests that fathers are essential to girls' development of self-esteem.[10] The negative effect of the absence of a father on a girl's developing self-concept intensifies as she matures.

I know black men who have the financial resources to raise their children but who have had little or no involvement in their children's lives. For example, a black professional I once knew, a "big shot" in the local civil rights movement, quickly ended a relationship when his girlfriend became pregnant with his child. He made it clear that he would have no part in raising the child. This man had a clear vision of his role as a champion for civil rights but had a blind spot regarding his obligation to provide his own child with the basic human right of having a relationship with her father.

Black fathers in previous generations generally made great efforts to raise their children in spite of greater racial discrimination and hardships than black men face today. Even during slave times, when black males were denied legal status as husbands and fathers, black slaves endured much to live on or near the same plantation as their children. The female-headed household is a relatively new phenomenon for black families. For example, in the Harlem neighborhood of New York City, as late as the mid-1960s, the majority of black children lived with both parents; today most of them spend at least some of their lives in single-parent families.[11]

Little is written about the millions of black men, some with limited financial resources, who are wonderful fathers. Throughout the years, I've met many of these men, some of whom have made enormous sacrifices to raise their children. Some who no longer have a relationship with the mothers of their children continue to honor their obligations as fathers. Nevertheless, I'm amazed when I read about some famous black men—in politics, sports, and entertainment—who can afford to help raise their children but have little, if any, regular involvement in their children's lives beyond monetary support payments. *Some black men regard these celebrities as role models.* If they, with all their resources, are *not* involved in their children's lives, why *shouldn't* ordinary men who are less privileged feel justified in abandoning their own children?

Fathers who abandon their children, financially or emotionally, should be held accountable by their family, friends, and community to fulfill their responsibilities to their children. I have a relative whose college-educated son fathered a child out of wedlock. Not long after the child's birth, this young man ended the relationship with his girlfriend. When his mother learned that he was not supporting his child, she told him that she would have nothing to do with him unless he fulfilled his obligations to his child. He now supports and regularly sees his daughter. I know this man well enough to say that he would have done neither without his mother's ultimatum.

There are encouraging developments in our society. More black males seem to be becoming committed to fulfilling their responsibilities as fathers. Movements like the Million Man March and Promise Keepers are bringing attention to the critical need for fathers to remain involved in raising their children.

A New Trend: Missing Mothers

Like their peers of other racial and ethnic groups, black mothers are the mainstays of their families. In many years of working with families, I have learned that I can almost always count on a mother or a grandmother to be there for a child who is experiencing problems growing up. I've known many black mothers who have made enormous sacrifices to bring their children up right, with or without the support of their children's fathers.

Although today most mothers continue to be central to their children's lives, some are shirking their responsibilities. In the past decade, some mothers, like too many fathers, have succumbed to pressures and temptations and consequently absented themselves from their children's lives. The crack cocaine epidemic—a modern form of slavery—that began in the mid-1980s is mainly responsible for this devastating phenomenon. As a result of this scourge, some black children have little or no contact with their mothers.

Some of these children have been placed in the foster care system. Sometimes they are placed with a relative, usually an overwhelmed grandmother with limited financial resources and declining health. Here's a disturbing thought to ponder: what happens when today's missing mothers become tomorrow's irresponsible grandmothers?

Traditionally, blacks have relied on their extensive kinship networks in raising children. But under such an arrangement, the children's biological parents, especially their mothers, usually continued to play a central role in their children's lives. Mothers didn't simply abandon their children to lead lives of self-indulgence. Instead, their separation from their children was usually undertaken to improve the financial conditions of the family.

My work with children in kinship care and foster care makes me particularly aware of the life-altering impact the absence of birth mothers can have on the lives of their children. Although some of these children are fortunate to find loving homes with relatives or foster or adoptive families, too many of them are allowed to languish in the system, pining to be reunited with mothers who seldom, if ever, contact them. Many absentee mothers have turned to drugs or alcohol to cope with their troubled lives. Most love their children but are unable to free themselves from the grip of their addictions despite numerous attempts at recovery. Mothers who cannot get themselves in shape to care for their children can doom those children to miserable lives.

Another serious problem is that although some of these addicted mothers can't or won't get their lives in order so that their children can be returned to them, they refuse to agree to the termination of their parental rights. Thus children who are not fortunate enough to have fathers (often the father is unknown) or relatives who are interested in raising them end up being shifted from foster home to foster home until they reach adulthood. Many of these children move out of the foster care system straight into the juvenile justice system; that is, they pass from dependency to delinquency. In 1997, a federal law was passed that reduces the time allowed parents who have had their children taken away from them by state agencies to meet the conditions to have their children returned. Only time will tell whether this law enables many more abandoned children to grow up in stable homes.

Little has threatened the survival of the black community more than the disturbing incidence of drug abuse among black mothers. Mothers are indispensable to the preservation of a people's culture. Fortunately, there seems to be a new energy sweeping black communities across the country. The Million Woman March of 1997, like its predecessor the Million Man March, showed, among other things, women's interest in improving the lives of their children.

ATTITUDINAL IMPOVERISHMENT OR ENRICHMENT

Another crucial influence on children's sense of self-worth is their parents' attitude toward their race and their life. Some social scientists blame racism and poverty for the self-esteem problems they perceive in many young black children. For example, Kardiner and Ovesey say blacks, in reaction to the pervasive racism they have historically experienced, have become a people of "self-hatred" who pass this hatred of their race to their children.[12] Most of us who grew up in families and communities with confident, optimistic, and productive blacks realize that self-hatred does not characterize most blacks.

As a clinical psychologist, I recognize that what some people untrained in mental health see as "self-loathing" is more likely to be depression. Among the hallmarks of depression are poor self-esteem and low energy. In my work with black children who are experiencing emotional and school problems, I've met parents who appear to be depressed, though they have not received a diagnosis or sought help. Some of these parents have apparently grown weary of dealing with the multiple problems (many I suspect ultimately stemming from racism) in their daily lives. They seem to have given up the struggle. That does not mean that they dislike themselves or their race; rather, it means that they dislike and resent the obstacles society places in their path. The problem for children is that parents who don't put much effort into improving their own lives pass on certain negative attitudes and behaviors to their children, which can in turn have a negative impact on their developing sense of self-worth.

Poverty and how parents deal with it can also adversely affect their children's self-esteem. The gains of the civil rights era have produced a thriving black middle class, but there is also a black underclass, one that, according to Cynthia Tucker, editorial writer for the *Atlanta Constitution,* may be worse off now than thirty years ago.[13] Children growing up in very poor families often have difficulty obtaining the basic necessities, including adequate health care, child care, and education, that are essential for healthy development.

The odds against blacks in this society challenge them to have positive attitudes about life's prospects. I am disheartened when I see the evidence of continuing racial discrimination in housing, employment, education, banking, and elsewhere and when I realize how few whites truly comprehend this reality. But blacks cannot allow themselves to become defeated by these obstacles. Because of people like Rosa Parks, who refused to be relegated to "her place" at the back of the bus, conditions for most blacks have improved since the era of Jim Crow laws. It is up to this generation to continue the struggle.

Considerably more help is needed from both the public and private sectors to lift black families who have been left behind out of the quagmire of poverty. Advocates of the current welfare reform movement seem to have the right philosophy: help people gain financial independence rather than remain dependent on welfare handouts. But much more needs to be done to provide adequate educational opportunities and job training so that parents can qualify for jobs that will enable them to support their families.

Though government policies are important, children's welfare generally depends as well on the attitude their parents take toward dealing with the challenge of being black in this society. Do they choose to see the glass as half empty or as half full? Unfortunately, parents who choose to see the glass as half empty pass along negative attitudes to their children about their prospects in a race-conscious society. Some of them may "talk the talk" that their children will do better than they did and grow up to be "somebody," but they don't "walk the talk." They do not make the efforts necessary for improving their own or their children's lives. Thus, early on, their children are set up to fail.

Black Americans, especially those from economically disadvantaged backgrounds, have limited alternatives compared to most white Americans. But they still have choices about how they lead their lives and the kinds of values they will pass on to their children.

People who have the attitude that they are exempted from being responsible parents because they are poor or black just don't cut it. Just as it is important that parents have adequate financial resources to support their families, it is also crucial that some of them work to combat negative attitudes that limit their vision about the possibilities for their own lives and those of their children.

Children, up to at least age six, have a marvelous ignorance of their economic circumstances, including poverty. As long as they have someone who loves them, sufficient food, a decent place to live, and a few toys, young children, even in deprived circumstances, are capable of having relatively happy childhoods. Many people who grew up in what some would describe as an impoverished environment do not remember it as such. Whoopi Goldberg, the actress and comedian, grew up in poverty but didn't realize it until she became an adult. Because of her mother's imagination, resourcefulness, and devotion to her children, Whoopi was able to lead a basically contented childhood.[14]

Many children I've worked with are growing up in families whose problems are only partly explained by their limited economic circumstances. Negative attitudes and behaviors also contribute to how people fare in life. For example, parents are their children's first and most important teachers. Children will look to them for guidance in their approach to life's opportunities and obstacles.

Parents can teach their children an important lesson just by believing and passing on to their children the idea that they do have a chance to "make it" in this society. But some parents teach, by their words and actions, that not much is expected of their children because of their race. They tell their children, "This is a white man's world," and they can't expect to go far in it. Such negative messages are likely to have a tremendous impact on their children's lives as they grow older.

Poet Langston Hughes wrote that life for blacks is not a "crystal stair"; it is a never-ending struggle.[15] Life may be challenging, but parents should teach their children early on that they *do* have choices about the path they take in life, and must show their children, by how they lead their own lives, how to develop healthy life habits that allow them to pursue their dream. Parents who teach their children positive values do much more to enrich their children's lives than parents who simply resign themselves to leading limited lives because they find it too hard to do battle with racial bigotry. Admittedly, the negative experiences many blacks have faced make it challenging to remain optimistic about the prospects of success for blacks in this society even when they do all the right things. But it pays to remember that two-thirds of black Americans do *not* live in poverty. Moreover, most poor black families do not fit the stereotype of the dysfunctional family. Jonathan Coleman, author of *Long Way to Go,* said that when he set out to study the lives of inner-city blacks, he expected to find rampant dysfunction among them. Although he found some, he also met many families who, despite myriad obstacles not faced by the average white family, led rich and rewarding lives.[16]

Blacks have historically been a proud, resourceful, and hardworking people. Society needs to do a much better job in guarding against discrimination and providing adequate education, job training, and opportunities for decent jobs so that parents of the children of the black underclass can support themselves and their children.

But all that will not be enough unless parents also do their part. Caring and supportive parents are crucial for raising psychologically healthy children. Black parents have a special responsibility to their children, who, because of their skin color, are likely to face challenges that many other children cannot even imagine. With love and nurturance from their families and support from society, black children have as good a chance to grow up feeling positive about themselves and their prospects as any other children. *If parents do not honor their responsibilities, why should society care more than they do?*

~

Black children who have poor self-esteem usually experience problems that can be directly traced to the caregiving they receive. Racism can play a direct role in shaping children's self-esteem only after they have developed to the stage where they can comprehend race and racial distinctions. For younger children, the effects of racism remain largely indirect, impinging on their lives through economic and social influences that can be tempered by positive familial influences. But families cannot protect their children from the effects of racism by themselves. As I shall discuss in the next chapter, schools and communities also play a crucial role in shaping children's ideas about skin color and race.

CHAPTER SEVEN

How School Influences Children's Awareness of Color and Race

Children who are fortunate enough to come from families that do not teach them skin-color or racial prejudices will confront the existence of these realities once they start school.

My younger son, then five years old, came home from school one day very upset. It was Black History Month, and he and his class had been learning about Martin Luther King Jr. He cuddled up next to me on the couch and spluttered out what he had learned that day in school: "Mom, my teacher said that some white people . . . no, some black people . . . brown people. Why do they say brown is black? I think she said it was the white people who shot him. He was bleeding and there was blood everywhere. Why did they shoot him?"

The more he talked, the more obvious it became that he was more focused on the gory details of King's death than anything that the teacher must have told him about King's achievements. It is not surprising for a young child to be upset about the frightening details of such an event, for it is difficult for a young child to process them. My son also seemed confused about the skin color of the assassins. As yet, he did not talk about people in terms of their skin color, and I was saddened that one of the first bits of information that he learned about "whites" is that they are "bad" people who killed Dr. King.

Young children are not developmentally prepared to process certain information the way adults do. Presenting a child with sensitive information when the child is not yet able to understand it can do more harm than good. For a few days following his lesson on Martin Luther King, my son repeated the gory aspects of King's assassination as if he were working through a situation he was having difficulty coping with. Occasionally, he asked me to explain, for example, by asking "Why do they call brown 'black'?" and later, "Why are white people mean?"—for by then he had learned that it was "some white people" who killed King.

I was dismayed that my son had to deal with this kind of information at such a young age. I still can't determine what purpose it served. The central message about King should not be his violent death but his heroic life, and all whites should not be blamed for his death.

Not every teacher is capable of teaching about the struggle for racial equality. It is not like teaching the three R's. Not only is adequate knowledge needed, but special skills like sensitivity, objectivity, and empathy are essential. Otherwise the teacher can botch the job and do more harm than good to children's developing awareness of race.

If children are to learn important lessons about race, it is best that they learn them the right way the first time. What they are taught should be adjusted to their developmental stage. Having to unlearn misunderstood lessons takes much more effort and can be emotionally harmful.

BRINGING COLOR TO THE CLASSROOM

My younger daughter, six years old at the time, came home a few months into the school year and described an assignment her teacher had given the class that day. The teacher was instructing children on how to graph their physical characteristics to determine how many children in the class fell into different categories. She asked them to stand up whenever the statement she made described them. These are the statements that my daughter remembered: "Stand up if you are white." "Stand if you have blond hair." "Stand if you have brown eyes." "Stand if you are black." "Stand if you have blue eyes." Apparently, some children, including my daughter, were confused about when to stand since only a limited number of skin colors was mentioned. (She was waiting for "brown" to be mentioned, but it was not called.) A conflict erupted when one child told another child to sit down when she stood up with the "white" group because she should have stood up with the "black" group. So a class exercise that was intended to teach children how to graph turned into one teaching them about race.

At recess the same day, my daughter and about five of her friends, a racially mixed group, reenacted the teacher's assignment. When a white classmate said, "Stand up if you have white skin," a couple of girls stood up. Then the white girl told one of them to sit down because her color looked "a little different" from the color of the other white girls. Then another child told the white girl herself to sit down also because her skin was "kinda brown." The argument about who was what color escalated until one of the girls said that she wasn't interested in playing anymore.

As many caregivers know, children will argue about practically anything, but in this case it is unlikely that they would have argued about skin-color differences if the teacher hadn't initiated the topic in a way that confused them. She had used a racial categorization of color, and she had wrongly assumed that all the children had picked up the lexicon that translates what is literally brown into what is socially black.

In our conversation after school that day, my daughter asked me why the teacher did not ask the brown and peach people to stand up and why people were called colors that were different from the ones they actually were. Her question led to our first discussion about race. As I expected, when I tried to answer her questions, she did not fully comprehend. Developmentally, she was still at the stage of racial innocence, a period I wished that I could prolong.

I don't think that it's the school's role to teach children about skin color and race. Making skin color or membership in a racial group an issue in the classroom can be divisive. It is especially important during the early grade-school years that children learn more about their similarities than their differences. My child's teacher should have chosen something other than skin-color differences to show children how to graph. Hopefully, this book will also teach teachers that young children think of their color as *color,* not as a sign of race.

Years ago, when racial discrimination was officially sanctioned in this country, it was traumatic for some children to learn that they were "colored" or "Negro," especially in so public a place as the classroom. James Weldon Johnson, in *The Autobiography of an Ex-Colored Man,* poignantly describes the emotional ordeal of an elementary school–aged, light-complexioned boy of mixed-race (black and white) parentage who learned his racial identity in an integrated school in the South during the pre–civil rights era:

> One day . . . the principal came into our [class] room and, after talking to the teacher said, "I wish all the white scholars to stand for a moment." I rose with the others. The teacher looked at me and calling my name, said: "You sit down for the present, and rise with the others." I did not quite understand her, and questioned: "Ma'm?" She repeated with a softer tone in her voice: "You sit down now, and rise with the others." I sat down dazed. I saw nothing and heard nothing. When the others were asked to rise I did not know it. When school was dismissed I went out in a kind of stupor. A few of the white boys jeered me, saying: "Oh, you're a nigger too." I heard some black children say: "We knew he was colored."
>
> Perhaps it had to be done, but I have never forgiven the woman who did it so cruelly. It may be that she never knew that she gave me a sword-thrust that day in school which was years in healing.[1]

Negative Lessons from Schoolmates

Even today, when racial discrimination is illegal, some black children, depending on the type of school they attend, may face difficulties because of their skin color or race. Although during the early school years most children are not inclined to focus on other children's complexions, it only takes one or two children who have been sensitized to skin-color differences outside of school to cause problems for other children whom they regard as different.

Aaron, a handsome second-grader with an ebony complexion, was referred to me because he was having behavioral problems in school. He frequently got into fights with other boys in his class, which resulted in repeated visits to the principal's office. Aaron said that some of the boys teased him about being "black." He couldn't understand the reason that they teased him: "It's just skin." Interestingly, Aaron's color became an issue only when conflicts erupted with a small group of boys over his aggressive style of play. Angered by something they believed Aaron did to them, the boys retaliated by making fun of the obvious thing that made him different from them: his darker skin color. The fact that they all attended a predominantly black elementary school didn't seem to matter much.

This kind of situation, where skin color is used as a weapon, is typical for children in the early school years who have been sensitized to racism. Aaron felt that his teacher ignored his complaints about the other boys' teasing, so he handled the situation the best way that he knew how: by fighting.

Children may learn from their schoolmates that their skin color is more valued than other skin colors. One of my friends was puzzled by her five-year-old son's sudden interest in skin-color differences, which became apparent soon after he entered an integrated kindergarten class with an Asian teacher. According to his mother, "He started having lots of questions about why he was different from the rest of us. I explained the reason lots of times, but he still didn't get it." His parents became quite concerned when he began saying things that indicated that he thought that his lighter complexion was better than their dark complexions. They blamed other children at his school for fostering their son's negative attitudes.

Other Types of Prejudice

Other children also learn their value at school. For example, Latino, Asian, or other nonblack minority children who attend a predominantly white or integrated school are more likely to be the object of curiosity and even ridicule when a conflict arises with a schoolmate who has been sensitized to skin-color differences prior to entering school. The mother of one of my children's classmates told me how upset she became when her then seven-year-old daughter complained that a classmate had called her a "fat Chinese." When the daughter told her mother of the taunt, her mother responded: "I hope you were proud." The daughter remarked that she didn't feel that the classmate who called her fat said it in a "nice way." It was only then that the mother realized that whereas she was concerned that her daughter had been teased about being Chinese, her daughter, who was svelte, was more bothered about being called "fat." The negative tone of her classmate's voice had troubled the daughter, but since race was not something the child was aware of, being called Chinese did not upset her; being called "fat" did. But by being linked with the perceived insult "fat," "Chinese" took on a negative connotation. The daughter did not complain to the teacher because she feared that the classmate would taunt her even more.

This child's situation reminds us that race is not the only target of prejudice. The young classmate had already absorbed and adopted society's prejudice against fat people. The mother's focus on racial prejudice typifies the tendency of people of all races to ignore the pain of prejudice that others (in this case, overweight people) feel throughout their lives.

More generally, little girls and little boys learn early on that some among them are more attractive, popular, better at sports, and so on, than others. Schools should try to minimize the effects of the different types of prejudices and treat each child as an equally valued human being. In reality, parents have to settle for a bit less on all fronts, including race.

A SCHOOL'S RACIAL COMPOSITION MATTERS

Although school plays a critical role in the child's emerging consciousness of skin color and race, the impact varies with the school's racial composition and the degree of sensitivity and skills of the staff in dealing with these issues. There are costs and benefits to attending different types of schools. Black children who attend predominantly white schools are likely to have different experiences from those who attend predominantly black or racially integrated schools.

Because school plays such a significant role in shaping a child's racial consciousness, it is very important that parents select the school for their child carefully. Unfortunately, many parents, because of financial circumstances, have only limited choices about where they send their child to school. For many parents, such considerations as the school's location, safety record, and academic quality are more important than its ability to promote positive racial attitudes. Parents and teachers have to become personally involved in ensuring that the racial atmosphere is conducive to their school's success.

Black parents who can afford to be selective about their child's school often face a difficult choice: quality or diversity? Unfortunately, many high-quality private schools are predominantly white. They have the resources to maintain high academic standards and to ensure the safety of their students, but they lack the diversity and commitment that are crucial to developing healthy racial attitudes. Public schools are more likely to have a diverse student body but too often lack the resources that promote academic success. Middle-class black parents who do not reside in "good" school districts must decide whether it is better to send their children to a school where they will receive a good education but as black students will stand out as different, or to a school where they will receive a mediocre education but will be part of a racially diverse student body.

However, parents who remember their own schooling, and those who already have older children in school, will realize that most children do not attend schools that are ideal in every way. Children can do well in school in spite of some negative experiences with racial prejudice or other problems. The best approach is to choose a school that is capable of doing a superior job academically and socially and to become involved in the school that you choose for your child to make sure that it delivers on its promises.

Whatever choices parents face, it is important for them to be aware of the benefits and limitations of schools with different types of racial mixes.

Attending a Predominantly White School

Several older black students whom I have asked to reflect on their experience at predominantly white elementary schools describe their experiences as mostly positive. Unless adults made it an issue, race was not a problem for them during the elementary school years. Although some of their classmates made occasional comments about their darker skin and curlier hair, only a few of the black students I spoke with remember these comments as being pejorative. Many of these children developed close friendships with classmates of other races. In contrast to interracial friendships in adolescence, those in the early school years have an excellent chance of thriving because children do not generally judge a child's racial allegiance by whom he hangs out with.

Unfortunately, some black children who attend predominantly white schools have terrible experiences. Some don't recognize that race was the reason they were mistreated until years later. A colleague, now in her thirties, is still distressed when she remembers her ordeal as the only black in a predominantly white kindergarten class located in a wealthy suburb in northern California. Even when the teacher isolated her from her white classmates (by placing her desk away from those of the other children), ignored her during classroom discussions, and barred her from using the classroom bathroom, it never occurred to the kindergartner that it had anything to do with her skin color. Like most children her age, she thought that it was her fault that the teacher didn't like her.

The kindergartner's parents did not learn of their daughter's predicament until she made an innocent remark about something the other children were allowed to do that she wasn't allowed to do. As she remembers it, when her parents learned of her mistreatment, "all hell broke loose." Her parents talked with the offending teacher and then with the school principal. When talk produced no positive results, her parents led a neighborhood march to the school that resulted not only in changes in their daughter's treatment but in the school's agreeing to conduct staff training on cultural sensitivity. In spite of the community uproar about the racial discrimination to which she was subjected, it was years before the youngster understood that she was maltreated because of the color of her skin. This is not surprising, given her early stage of race awareness.

Early Experiences with Classroom Prejudice

Although one hopes that such blatant discrimination would not be tolerated today, subtle forms of racism still exist in some classrooms. Children may not *recognize* racism as such in their classroom, but their parents report that they can tell by the things that their children complain about that they *feel* it. They feel it when their teacher seldom chooses them to answer questions, spends less individual time with them, overreacts when they misbehave, and always selects white children for the lead roles in school productions.

Research supports children's feelings. An extensive study, based on videotapes of teacher-student classroom interactions, showed that teachers, even those who consider themselves sensitive to gender and racial issues, are astonished to learn that their classroom interactions revealed gender and racial biases.[2] That is, teachers are more likely to call on and to give the most positive reinforcement to white boys and the least attention to black girls. Of course, a black child doesn't have to attend a predominantly white school to experience discrimination. Teachers who have a bias against something, whether it's skin color, race, class, weight, attractiveness, or something else, are present in all types of schools. But at a predominantly white school, the black child may feel more alienated: not only does she look different, but she may also be treated differently. So her difference is magnified and is likely to adversely affect her developing self-concept.

Some children also experience maltreatment by their classmates. They are made to feel less welcome or are even excluded from their classmates' play groups. Usually, their exclusion is instigated by a bully who is imitating his family's racial prejudices.

Black children are not alone in feeling alienated by white teachers and classmates' racial biases. Children of other persecuted minority groups also have similar experiences. One of the saddest cases I know concerns a Chinese girl who attended a predominantly white kindergarten in the 1960s. As the adopted daughter of white parents who lived in the Midwest, she felt rejected by her white classmates. In a story in *People* magazine, she recalled still painful memories of her experience in kindergarten: "The other children wouldn't touch me. . . . I damned God for making me Chinese."[3]

This was clearly a case of child abuse. The teacher was at least partly responsible for the ostracism this kindergartner experienced. There are many things she could have done to facilitate interactions between this child and her classmates.

Facilitating Interracial Friendships

One of the advantages of the early school years is that friendship groups are rather fluid. Exclusive cliques and clubs tend not to develop until later. Thus children who may initially not be inclined to play together are more likely to get to know each other if they are encouraged to do so. Teachers have the ability to intervene in children's play to structure interactions that will provide children with opportunities to get to know each other.

One place to start is with choosing teams. Instead of asking children to pick their own teams for classroom activities or sports, teachers should choose team members using a random method, such as a lottery or a numbering scheme (for example, line the students up and then choose every third or every fifth child to be on a given team). Students on a teacher-selected team are more likely to spend time with children they would not ordinarily choose to work or play with. This approach is useful for fostering a sense of belonging not only for children who are of different races but also for children who, for one reason or another, tend to be among the last chosen for classroom group activities and for sports teams. I've heard many parents complain that because of shyness or poor sports ability, their child is among the last chosen for various school groups and teams. By encouraging interaction among different children, the teacher sends a very important message that school is a place where everyone is supposed to make an effort to get along and work together. Most young children are very malleable; they simply do not have the attention span or the emotional commitment to hold on to skin-color or other biases for long unless these are constantly reinforced by older children and adults. If teachers do not tolerate racial bullying, whether in the form of teasing or pressuring classmates not to play with certain children, such bullying can be effectively curtailed.

The Pain of Looking Different

One of the most difficult things for black children who attend predominantly white schools is the scarcity of other children and adults (for example, teachers and administrators) who look like them. This can lead to feelings of isolation and alienation. Clarence Page, black Pulitzer Prize winner and syndicated columnist, reported that his son didn't want to go to school because he said the other children didn't look like him.[4] Some children who have difficulty fitting in may begin to express a desire to be white, however fleeting it might be. Other children deal with these feelings in other ways.

Thus it is important that predominantly white schools enroll more than a few token students to decrease their black students' sense of differentness. Schools have an obligation not only to support their students' academic development but to nurture social and ethical development too.

Some black parents fear that their children will lose their racial identity if they associate with white children. They worry that their children will come to identify more with white children than with black ones. I've heard people characterize some black children who attend predominantly white schools as "acting white," that is, identifying more with white children than with blacks in their speech, behavior, dress, and values. In an op-ed article in the *San Francisco Chronicle*, a black mother recounted a disturbing incident that illustrates the problem. Her daughter, Kelly, and a white classmate, first-graders at a predominantly white school, were walking home together when they encountered a group of black teenagers. "The classmate suggested that they cross the street to avoid the 'black boys.' Kelly crossed the street—she was as worried about her safety as her white friend. I was alarmed that she'd absorbed the notion that members of her own race were a threat to her. I couldn't have my child afraid of black teenagers. She would eventually be a black teenager."[5]

The incident motivated the mother to consider transferring her child out of the predominantly white school. If this incident was her only reason, the mother may have overreacted. Black children need to know that some people who look like them will try to harm them. Black-on-black crime is a major problem in the black community. Just like any other race, blacks have good and bad people.

Finding Good Role Models

Black children at predominantly white schools have to deal with not seeing people who look like them on the staff. They may see black people in subservient positions, like janitors and cafeteria workers, but no black teachers or school administrators. Young children may not consciously register the absence of black authority figures, but this absence sends a subtle message to them, and to white children, that all the important people are white. At a predominantly white school in my liberal community, students rarely see a black person in a position of authority except at their seasonal basketball games, where some of the referees are black. Although that is better than nothing, it feeds into the stereotype that blacks are good only at certain activities, like sports.

One has to be careful about making assumptions about a person's attitudes because of race. Over several years of consulting to schools, I've met white teachers, though fortunately few, who seem to be racially prejudiced. Others I've met went to extraordinary lengths to support their black students, sometimes even taking on the role of surrogate parent. I've also met black teachers who fulfill every black parent's dream for the way they inspire and support young children. Unfortunately, I've also met a few black teachers whose treatment of black children was no better than that of racist whites.

Parents can do something to address the problem of the scarcity of minority role models at their children's schools. They can start by lobbying school officials to recruit minority principals, teachers, and other support staff. They need to spread the message that having minority teachers is not just beneficial to black children's education (in the full sense of the word) but also to the education of white and other children.

There are several other ways to bring black role models into the school. Black guest speakers can be invited to speak to classes on a variety of subjects. Black high school students can help out with tutoring, coaching, and various other extracurricular activities. And most important, black parents themselves can volunteer to spend time at their children's schools. Parents who volunteer—as classroom parent, library helper, reader, or in some other capacity—do an enormous service to their children because, in the final analysis, parents are their children's most important role models.

Questions to Ask When Considering Sending Your Child to a Predominantly White School

Are the school administration, faculty, and other staff welcoming to black students and their families, not just in terms of what they say, but also by what they do?

How many other black students are in your child's class? In the school?

Does the staff have similar expectations for black and white children's academic performance and school behavior?

Is the staff sensitive to the issues of black students?

Does the school have a reputation for producing successful black students?

Do you feel comfortable talking with your child's teacher and principal about your concerns relating to your child's education and school experiences?

Does your child have opportunities (for example, scouts, sports, clubs) to interact with black children and adults?

What's your child's personality? For example, is your child outgoing and confident enough to handle the pressures of being different?

What is the racial composition of the faculty and staff?

Does the curriculum include black history, preferably integrated into American history?

Are blacks adequately represented in books, other media, and the pictures that are prominently displayed in the school?

Does the school invite meaningful parent involvement in school policies and curriculum?

Is there an active black parents' group at the school?

Attending an Afrocentric School

For some black parents who have become disenchanted with the public educational system that seems to be failing black children, an Afrocentric school is seen as salvation. Statistics on many black children's school performance are disturbing; on most measures of school achievement (including grades and standardized tests), when compared to other racial groups, black children are at often the bottom of the heap.[6] Some experts and parents believe that black children will do better in schools that are administered and staffed by blacks. Some blacks view African-American cultural immersion schools (similar to Chinese, Japanese, or Spanish immersion schools) as the best way to educate, motivate, and promote the self-esteem of their children, as well as to teach them about their African-American heritage. Anecdotal evidence suggests that some children benefit enormously from attending these schools. For example, San Francisco has adopted a districtwide education model called the I Rise Project, which some parents say has improved their children's school performance, increased their knowledge of African history, and bolstered their ethnic pride.

However, other parents have expressed concerns that an Afrocentric curriculum deprives their children of a well-rounded education. For example, Enola Williams, executive director of the Portola housing project, said, "I want our kids to be taught what every other kid is taught. . . . What do we know about American history? What do we know about the Constitution? What do we know about the Bill of Rights? Those are the things our children need to learn."[7]

Afrocentric schools may be the best choice for some children. But the academic success that some of these schools promise may come at an exorbitantly high social price if, in promoting ethnic pride, they teach children that whites are the enemy and blacks are superior to people of other races. An Afrocentric curriculum must be designed so as not to alienate black children from their *American* heritage or to foster the very racial prejudices that they were founded to counteract.

The risk of promoting racial prejudice in these schools is considerably greater than in schools where racial diversity and harmony are goals. A school that has a political agenda that promotes racial separatism may teach historical distortions mirroring the distortions typical in Eurocentric curricula.

Such a school can do serious emotional and cognitive harm to young children because, unlike older children and adults, most early grade-schoolers are not developmentally capable of distinguishing fact from propaganda. For example, if a second-grader is repeatedly told by his teacher that whites are "bad people" who "always stole blacks' stuff away," as a second-grader once told me, he is more likely to believe it than a teenager, who has a deeper knowledge of history and more experience with whites. Since early learning is difficult to unlearn, children who are taught distorted facts when they are young are more likely to experience difficulties believing the truth when they are taught it later on in their lives.

Another issue for children who attend Afrocentric schools in their elementary school years is that they become accustomed to being around only blacks. Thus they may become as uncomfortable in a mixed-race setting as are many whites from racially exclusive backgrounds. This may place them at a disadvantage when they later pursue school and job opportunities in the multiracial America of the twenty-first century.

The mother of a five-year-old told me that when she moved homes, she transferred her daughter from an integrated to an all-black school. Her daughter's first comment after she returned home from her first day at her new school was, "How come all the kids at school were black and brown?" Her earliest concept of what a school looked like included people of various colors. As Daniel Goleman pointed out in his best-selling book, *Emotional Intelligence*, educational and professional success are highly dependent on a person's social skills. Children who learn early in their life how to get along with people of diverse backgrounds have a distinct advantage over children who do not have this experience.[8]

Things to Consider When Planning to Send Children to an Afrocentric School

Does your child have opportunities to interact with children and adults of other races?

Does the school provide a balanced view of the races?

Does the school provide a well-rounded education?

Does the school have books and other media that feature pictures of people of various races?

How do the benefits compare to the costs of sending young children to single-race schools?

Does the staff express skin-color or racial biases?

Attending an Integrated School

The ideal school environment is a racially integrated one that *actively* promotes racial harmony. The earlier children attend such a school, the better off they are, since their earliest ideas of how the world is organized will include the important notion that people are different. This world will be the one with which they will be most familiar and the one they in which they are most likely to feel comfortable. Unfortunately, integrated schools are increasingly difficult to find. A national study, headed by Harvard University professor Gary Orfield, indicated that "since 1980, white flight from cities to suburbs and lax federal enforcement of school desegregation plans had produced increasing racial segregation in the nation's public schools."[9]

Although in some regions of the country mandatory busing, whose aim was to integrate the schools, has succeeded in improving the educational opportunities of black students, often, due to the resistance of some whites, it has failed to work. Some blacks who had strongly supported mandatory busing have since become disenchanted with its unfulfilled promises and are now turning their attention to improving their own local schools. But that is a formidable goal. The age-old question about whether separate schools can be really equal still lingers, decades after the landmark 1954 Supreme Court decision that said they cannot. From what I've seen, it's difficult to have equality without integration.

The Tinsley Plan is a voluntary busing program in the Palo Alto Unified School District in California. Some educators say that it should be a model for school integration plans for the rest of the country. The plan's advocates say, "Kids are not born prejudiced, they learn it." This approach is sensitive to the developmental need of children to learn about each other while they are still young. To achieve its goal of early integration, the district restricts first-time enrollment to students in kindergarten, first, and second grade, so students of various racial and ethnic backgrounds can get to know each other early on. Thus the program "seeks to ease minority children into white classrooms at an age before children learn to distrust those who look different."[10] (I'd also like to see white children eased into black classrooms in high-quality schools.)

It makes sense to bring children from different cultural backgrounds together while they are young so that they can get to know each other before their ideas of different people are affected by racial stereotypes. During my early school years, I attended school with many Latino children. Although there is a strong negative stereotype of Latinos in this society, I have not been influenced by it because my earliest memories of Spanish-speaking children were of bright and friendly classmates.

There are other promising avenues to achieving school integration. Charter schools, independent public schools that were introduced in the 1980s and have shown "explosive growth" in the 1990s, are emerging not only as a response to the poor academic performance of blacks and other disaffected groups but also as a way to achieve racial integration. The New Village School in Berkeley, California, is one of the nation's only charter schools "to explicitly state antibias teaching as its mission."[11]

Over the years, I've met many children, of various races, who have extolled the benefits of attending an integrated elementary school. Black adults have reported that it has made them feel more comfortable with people of other races, and they believe it has given them an advantage in the work world. Whites have said that it has made them less tolerant of racial stereotypes concerning blacks and other minorities. Most interesting, some whites who have attended integrated schools become ill at ease when in later grades they are transferred to predominantly white middle schools and high schools.

However, integration does not automatically produce racial harmony unless such harmony is *actively* pursued. Not only is the involvement of parents important, but the commitment and sensitivity of the principal and teachers are essential if children are to learn how to get along with one another.

In addition to racial understanding, schools must actively promote academic achievement. Parents play a crucial role in supporting their children's academic success. Alan Krueger, an economist and an expert on education at Princeton University, maintains that "one of the most firmly established findings in social science is that children's success is positively related to their parents' income and education."[12]

Teachers also play a major role in students' school success or failure. As Professor Richard Elmore of Harvard University has observed, with the appropriate training, teachers can learn to recognize and encourage children's potential rather than bemoan their deficits.[13]

I agree with Elmore. Over the years, I've met many black children who attribute much of their school success to teachers, including white teachers, who expected them to do well and made extraordinary efforts to support them in their schoolwork.

Things to Consider When Planning to Send Your Child to an Integrated School

Is the school truly integrated?

Does the school offer the same educational opportunities to all its students?

Does the curriculum include black history and literature?

Is the staff integrated?

Does the school display pictures of blacks and other minorities?

Are teachers sensitive to the issues of black students?

TEACHERS ARE THE KEY

Regardless of the racial balance of the school your child attends, teachers have a crucial influence on early elementary children's developing ideas about race. By what they say and what they do, teachers model for their students, who are at a very impressionable age, how they should treat other people, especially those who are different. Over the years, I've met many dedicated teachers who are very sensitive to their roles as models for their students, but I've also met a few, of various racial backgrounds, who display prejudiced racial attitudes and behavior; these latter threaten to poison their young students' developing self-concepts and ideas about race. Following are suggestions for ways teachers can foster healthy racial attitudes.

✱ TEACHING THE RACIALLY HEALTHY CHILD

Be fair, respectful, and kind. Practically everything comes down to your students' and their parents' perceptions of how you and the school treat them. Often today, too much emphasis is placed on cultural sensitivity; human sensitivity is infinitely more important. If you try to be caring and understanding, children and their parents will feel it and, more often than not, respond in kind.

Be aware of your own prejudices. Some well-meaning teachers fail to realize that by the things they say and do, they are sending signals about values. Do you have a pattern of showing favoritism to some children? Who are the children you tend to call on in class, choose to do classroom errands, or to be the leads in class productions, and so on? At this age, children are very sensitive to other children receiving preferential treatment. "It's not fair!" is a common exclamation they use when they feel unjustly slighted. Children, including black children, who start learning too young that they can't expect fairness begin to internalize a sense of inferiority.

Post classroom rules of behavior. With the participation of the children, generate classroom rules of behavior based on the Golden Rule. Encourage children to treat each other as they would like to be treated. These rules should be few in number (not more than ten).

Avoid talking about people in terms of skin color and race. Unless they have been sensitized to racial differences, most young children are not inclined to think about people in terms of racial categories, so why foster this way of thinking about people in your classroom? Early grade-schoolers will quickly pick up on the words that you use to describe others.

Emphasize children's similarities rather than their differences. It is important that children at this age learn to appreciate what makes them similar because they'll have an awful lot of time later in life to learn what makes them different. Children at this age respond well to concrete examples; for example, you could use different-colored M&M candies to show how people are different on the outside but the same on the inside. Teach them about their shared heritage as human beings and Americans. You can do exercises where they generate their own lists of ways they are similar. After they have a good grounding in the ways they are similar, discuss how they are different. Talk with them about how their uniqueness contributes to the grandeur of the whole, as in a mosaic or a garden.

Adjust your teaching of historical information to the child's developmental stage. Choose carefully what you teach early grade-schoolers when you present lessons dealing with race relations. At this age, children do not need to dwell on slavery, assassinations of great leaders, or racial riots. If you decide to tackle these potentially divisive issues, remember that you cannot expect five- and six-year-olds to process such information the same way that teenagers do. Younger children are cognitively very concrete and are likely to interpret the information literally or to fail to keep past events in clear perspective. (For example, a six-year-old told me that Martin Luther King Jr. had freed the slaves.) One of the first historical facts many black children learn about whites is that they enslaved blacks. It is detrimental for children to learn this information at such a young age. They could begin to fear that whites could enslave them or end up believing that all whites are bad people. Ask yourself, "What is the purpose of children learning this information?" If you have doubts about its value to their development, don't teach it. Children will have ample time to learn it later in life.

Don't overreact to children's words that appear to be racial. Even if a child hurls racial epithets at a classmate, be careful not to interpret her words as you would those of an adult. Although the child may realize that her words are hurtful, she does not have the same racist attitude as an adult. Responding in a calm manner, with a phrase such as "We don't use those kinds of words in this class," perhaps backed up with an appropriately stern expression, should tell her that you mean business. Complain to parents or the principal only when your efforts are not effective.

Encourage children to play with classmates who are different. Most early grade-schoolers are eager to please their teacher, so if you suggest that they should play with other children, they are more likely to do so. Some children, whatever their race, because of their personality, physical appearance, or poor social skills, have a hard time making friends. Since at this age most children are not yet cliquish, you'll have more of an opportunity to introduce new faces into their fluid groups. Arrange class activities so that children get to work in different groups.

Find something special about each child. Find something special about each child, write it down, and let the child know it. Keep a small notebook on each child and from time to time tell the child that you are recording your special memories of him to treasure when he is no longer in your class. Each month, invite the child to choose a sticker from the ones that you offer, and then ask him to tell you something special about himself that he wants you to write in the book (if he is able to write a special word, encourage him to do so). You'll be surprised how far such a small effort will go in making children feel special.

Cultivate a positive relationship with parents. Early in the school year, get to know each of your students' parents so that when concerns arise, you already have a foundation on which to build. Teachers and parents are busy people, so it is understandable that you won't have large amounts of time to spend on tête-à-têtes. An occasional phone call or postcard (if you need to, recruit a volunteer to help) saying something nice about the child's schoolwork or behavior or mentioning that you really enjoy having the child in your class can make a welcome difference to parents who usually hear from teachers only when there is a problem.

Use books, videos, wall pictures, and other items that represent people of various races. If you've read this far, you may appreciate by now the importance of reading material, wall pictures, and videos that include blacks and other racial minorities. Don't make the mistake of thinking that if you "bring out the colors" during Black History Month or on Martin Luther King Day, you've done your part. Fostering positive racial attitudes is a year-round activity.

Provide as much support as possible in helping children do well academically. Many black parents are understandably anxious about their children's school performance. Some of them see bright, curious children enter school only to lose their excitement and interest in school by the third or fourth grade. Encourage children who do well in school to continue doing so. Children who begin to show learning problems should receive assistance as soon as possible. Any delay is very costly to black children, who aren't given as many opportunities to succeed as children of other races.

✷ QUESTIONS FOR TEACHERS TO CONSIDER WHEN SELECTING BOOKS, POEMS, SONGS, AND VIDEOS

Teachers commonly ask me how they can choose books (and other works) to avoid promoting racial biases in their classroom. A few years ago, at a conference on cultural sensitivity, I met a white elementary school teacher busily rummaging though a bunch of books and booklets trying to find information to guide her in choosing books and other classroom materials that would foster healthy racial attitudes. She left frustrated. Many people complain that teachers are insensitive to the effect of biased materials on black children, but precious little information is available to provide specific guidance on how to select age-appropriate books and other materials. Here are several questions to ask.

Is it developmentally appropriate? For example, a story that is about black slaves and white masters may be more harmful than enlightening to young children's developing concept of race. Early grade-schoolers may have difficulty processing the information in the story; they may have trouble separating what has happened in the past from what can happen in the present. They may think that whites will enslave blacks again. They may assume whites to be bad people. Children may also act out these roles on the playground, perhaps causing unnecessary pain to black classmates who are coerced into playing the roles of slaves. Why introduce conflict between children of different races when it is not necessary?

Is there a message that children can understand? A little boy listened to his teacher read a story about the Underground Railroad that carried the slaves to freedom. He missed the point of the story because he thought that it was about a real railroad. Children's thinking is very concrete during the early years. It is important to remember this when you select books and other materials.

Does it refer to races or ethnic groups by the names children at this age would use to describe them? As I've tried to show in this book, often young children do not use the words adults use to describe people of different races. In fact, unless they come from racially sensitive families, they are unlikely to see skin color as a distinguishing feature. A child may call a person "brown" when a book refers to him as "black." I do not think it is the school's role to teach children the appropriate racial names of groups. Yes, in time they will learn these names, but in my opinion, children should be allowed a little while longer to see others through their own eyes. (Wouldn't it be wonderful if children never had to learn racial names?) I think that if you are interested in teaching them a name, teaching them to call themselves "American" is a good start. They should learn that lots of different types of people are called by this name.

Are the characters stereotyped? Many older works present blacks mostly as poor inner-city residents, Mexicans as immigrants, Native Americans as living on reservations, and so on. Increasingly, there are new works that reflect the diversity that exists in different racial and ethnic groups, so it is important to update the works you share with children.

Does it affirm the racial group that is mentioned? For example, two teachers, one from a traditional school and one from a school with a more progressive attitude, differed on whether the song "Ten Little Indian Boys" posed a problem. The traditional teacher thought it was just a fun song and accused the other teacher of reading too much into it. The other teacher, a conciliatory type, asked the traditional teacher to substitute "little Jewish boys" for "little Indian boys" and see if it still didn't matter to her what group was mentioned in the song. The traditional teacher immediately understood why some people would consider the song offensive. It may be all right to use a song if you substitute neutral words for words that may be offensive.

Is it relevant to the children in your classroom? Black children who read mostly about white children are being taught to view themselves as irrelevant or marginal. Although some schools will have an occasional book on blacks, they may not routinely incorporate these books, and other related materials, into their lesson plans unless it's Black History Month or Martin Luther King's birthday. Unlike years ago, there are many books about black children available to teachers and others, so there is no excuse for not having a variety of books about blacks and other minorities.

Does it refer to an ethnic or racial group by the name that its members call themselves? The point here is not whether "black" or "African American" is more appropriate; these are both considered positive references and are often used interchangeably. Pay attention to other names, such as "Oriental," which may be used to make a point in the story, poem, or song but may have negative connotations for group members. Young children are quick to pick up names that can be used to tease other children.

What is the purpose of using stories, songs, or videos that are heavily laden with racial or ethnic references? Young children's natural inclination is not to view people in terms of skin color, much less race, so if your purpose can be accomplished with the substitution of another work that does not use racial and ethnic references, consider making the substitution. Why promote this limiting way of thinking when it is not necessary? Of course, if your intention is to present different races in a positive manner, sharing an affirming work can be helpful.

Are any of the "ethnic" characters allowed to transcend their racial or ethnic membership to provide important information or entertainment value to students? For example, a classic book like *Huckleberry Finn* is more than the depiction of its characters. Some hypersensitive adults focus on its racial stereotypes, but children are more likely to be interested in the personality and the various adventures of the characters rather than their race. *Huckleberry Finn* was one of the books that motivated me to learn to read when I was a child. Because children do not view things the way adults do, they may not see the bigotry that some adults see in this ageless story. Teachers who are concerned about the portrayal of blacks in certain works (for example, the way they speak, behave, and dress) may balance their selection of stories by offering others that depict blacks of different backgrounds.

Does it ridicule or demean something very important to a racial or ethnic group? A story I heard on the radio told of the anguish of an Asian boy who dreaded going to school on the morning following a particular episode of *The Simpsons* in which Bart made fun of the god of the Asian boy's religion. As the boy anticipated, some of his classmates teased him by calling him the unusual name of the god that they had heard on the show. Young children are very impressionable and quick to imitate characters that they find appealing. Thus it is important to avoid stories or other works that present these temptations until children are more mature.

What type of speech do the characters use? Blacks, like whites and other groups, use a variety of dialects and accents. Though it may be important for authenticity to choose some stories with black characters who speak nonstandard English, it is essential that most of the books and other works use standard English.

What do the children gain from it? Too often, our politically correct era robs children of the sheer joys of stories, songs, and pictures that some people deem offensive. Stories and other works can be enjoyed not only for the enlightenment they provide but also for the sheer pleasure they give.

The early grade-school years should be a time of wonder and excitement for children. Most black preschoolers I've met look forward to going to school, but something strange seems to happen along the way to too many of them, something that dashes their early promise of doing well in school. For too many black children, by the time they reach the third or fourth grade, eagerness to learn is gradually replaced by a growing disinterest in school because they have picked up the message that school is not too interested in them, so why try?

As we have seen in Part Two, it is important that black children receive caring parenting and inspiring schooling if they are to become invested in a society that sends them ambivalent messages about their worth. As we shall see in Part Three, once children enter the later years of elementary school, they face expanding horizons or looming failure, depending on the nurturing they received in their early years. As their racial innocence wanes, they may find themselves in a world of narrowing prospects or one of wonderful possibilities. The path they will follow depends on how they've come to see themselves and their race.

PART THREE

Reality Bites

Race Awareness in Middle Childhood and Adolescence

CHAPTER EIGHT

Fading to Black and White

How Children in the Middle Years See Race

I have a dream that my four little children will one day live in a nation where they will not be judged by the color of their skin but by the content of their character.
—Martin Luther King Jr.

Children can be cruel. Around age seven, traditionally known as the age of reason, children begin to adopt the illogic of adult's color and racial biases. Some of them use this knowledge to tease and exclude children. During the middle childhood years, extending from ages eight to twelve, children's growing awareness of skin-color differences becomes transformed into an understanding of race.[1] After the warm and fuzzy years of early childhood, when children were more malleable and open to learning about different people, they reach an age when they are increasingly influenced by society's racial stereotypes.

Charmaine, a ten-year-old, was referred to me for school behavior problems. When I phoned her fifth-grade teacher (at a predominantly black inner-city school) to obtain her perspective on this child's problems, the teacher asked whether I had met Charmaine. I had. The teacher responded, "Then you know what her main problem is: she's dark-skinned. The other kids tease and bother her a lot about it. Her self-esteem is very low." For the first few months of the school year at what was for her a new school, Charmaine's classmates did not call her by her real name but by the nickname "Blackie." The teacher's voice wavered: "You know, I'm a child of the sixties. We thought we'd solve this race thing back then. It grieves me to hear these kids teasing each other about skin color and hair, even eye color. It's seems nothing has changed. It's like the sixties never happened."

Charmaine was growing up in a multiproblem family. She lacked the emotional resources to deal with the taunts of her classmates. Her poor grades and increasing behavior problems reflected the emotional turmoil she was experiencing as the result of her classmates' rejection as well as the dysfunction of her own family. Fortunately, she had a teacher who understood her difficulties and a counselor who wanted to help her; with their guidance, Charmaine had a chance to develop skills to deal with her situation.

KNOWING AND EXPERIENCING THEIR COLOR AND RACE

When asked, "What are you?" children aged eight to twelve are more likely to say they are a girl or a boy than to identify themselves by race. However, when the question is repeated, they are more likely than younger children to mention their race. Consider my conversation with eight-year-old Tatiana:

INTERVIEWER: *What are you?*
TATIANA: What do you mean?
What are you?
I am a girl.
What else are you?
I am black.
What color are you?
I am brown.
Well, why do you call yourself black?
That's the name people call people with brown skin.

Interestingly, although the term *African American* is gaining favor among some segments of the black community, very few of the children I interviewed in this age group describe themselves as "African American." Children say that it's just not a term other children use. One boy said that one of the only times he heard any of his schoolmates use the term *African American* was in response to a black schoolmate who called him a "nigger." The schoolmate responded that he wasn't a "nigger," he was a "black African American." A fifth-grade teacher said she rarely hears her students use the term, perhaps because "the word sounds too academic" to children.

Predictably, children whose skin color is at the extremes of blacks' color spectrum, either very light or very dark, have the most difficult time coming to terms with their racial identity if they are not supported by family and friends. Light-skinned children receive mixed messages: some blacks call them "white" as a put-down, while other blacks grudgingly regard them as "better" because of their lighter complexion. Children, particularly girls, learn that people assume that they think they are better-looking because of their lighter color. I've met several light-complexioned girls who were hurt when some darker-complexioned girls, who didn't even know them, automatically assumed that they considered themselves "better." An eleven-year-old black girl, whose class attended a function with another school, told me that a dark-skinned black girl from the other school, whom she had never met, picked on her continually throughout the time their classes met. The light-complexioned girl was sad to learn that the other girl had assumed she considered herself better because of her lighter complexion. By the middle childhood years, if light-complexioned children are around sufficient numbers of these prejudiced children, they learn that the assumption of this "attitude" is inextricably linked to their lighter complexion. Unfortunately, too many of them spend the rest of their lives defending themselves, trying to convince other blacks that they are one of them.

Dark-complexioned black children also have a tough problem. Unlike light-skinned black children, they are unquestioningly accepted as black but are often demeaned for their dark color and described as "ugly."

As children learn to identify themselves as "black," they are also learning the various negative connotations of the word. An elementary school teacher told me that she often reminded her fifth-grade students that "black is not an insult; it's a description." She noticed that when some children were upset at each other, they linked three words: "You ugly, black [expletive]." Children also hear other disparaging words about their race. Some children said that friends refer to each other as "nigger," not as a put-down, but in ordinary conversation.

At this age, black children, and to a lesser extent children of other oppressed racial minorities, are also becoming aware of their low social status relative to other racial groups. However, children's natural inclination to feel positive about themselves continues to cushion them against the negative impact of racism on their self-concept. Children's self-image in middle childhood is still influenced mostly by the treatment they receive in their families, schools, and communities. However, if children feel that they do not fit in with their peer group because of their skin color or race, that can negatively affect how they feel about themselves.

A black man disclosed on a popular television talk show that his childhood experiences continued to influence his self-image well into middle age. Because of his light complexion, he didn't feel that he fit in with the other black boys in his neighborhood, who called him "red" and "dirty red." He longed to be as dark as they were, and so he tried various things to darken his skin. But to his dismay, nothing worked. In adolescence, during the heyday of the civil rights movement, he adopted a militant "attitude" like that of his darker-skinned buddies, but he still felt like an outsider because the "attitude didn't go with light skin." It took him years to recover from this childhood pain.[2]

Black children who live in or who attend schools in predominantly white communities are particularly susceptible to feeling like they don't "fit in" if they are not accepted there. But feelings of alienation are not unique to blacks. Children of other historically persecuted minorities—racial, religious, or cultural—also wrestle with identity problems when they are faced with being different from their peer group. For example, film director Steven Spielberg, as a young Jewish boy growing up in a non-Jewish neighborhood, tried various ways to fit in with his buddies. He even used a clothespin on his nose in an attempt to make it look like the noses of his friends. Whenever his grandfather called him by his Jewish name when he was playing with his friends, he was embarrassed.[3] Wanting to fit in—not to stand out in appearance, name, dress, or any other way—is natural for children in this age group, who crave acceptance by their peers.

The developing identity of children, especially girls, is affected by the extent to which they measure up to the prevailing standard of beauty not only as it pertains to skin color but also to hair, facial features, and body type. Like Spielberg, Oprah Winfrey, the talk show host, admitted that in her childhood, she wore a clothespin on her nose in bed at night in an attempt to make it narrow. She wasn't trying to look white; rather, she believed that other people thought a narrow nose was more attractive.[4]

Black Children in White Families

Black children of white adoptive or foster families face unique issues in defining their racial identity. Generally, children use their parents or primary caregivers as a reference point in learning who they are, not just racially, but also in terms of what values they hold, spiritually, socially, and so on. By the middle childhood years, children tend to be embarrassed by their parents even if they are of the same race; children whose parents are of a different race may feel even more uncomfortable if they are teased about their parents' racial differences. Their racial heritage is more likely to be a major problem if the family lives in a race-conscious community or the children attend a school where they are exposed to negative messages about racially mixed relationships or minorities.

One of the biggest problems for parents and children in adoptive and foster families who are of different races is dealing with the questions that inevitably arise when they are together in public. If the adults learn how to handle these questions graciously rather than reacting defensively, their children will learn that it is OK to be who they are. I know a white mother who used to dread appearing with her black adoptive daughters in public, but not because she was ashamed of her children. She was upset about the effect that stares and invasive questions were having on her daughters. Strangers' questions had not bothered her so much when her daughters were younger, but she became increasingly concerned about their effect on her girls as they entered middle childhood and began to understand why the strangers were asking questions.

I advised the mother that her daughters would take their cue from her: if she interpreted the strangers' questions as racist and expressed her views to her daughters, the impact was more likely to be negative. However, if she handled strangers' stares and questions positively—if she treated the strangers as curious people inquiring about an interesting family—she would be more likely to pass on positive messages to her daughters. Of course, some of the inquisitive people *are* racists, but that is not the point: the point is how she and her daughter *choose* to react to them.

This mother, adopting the more positive approach, came up with standard answers to questions she was routinely asked. Soon people's stares and questions bothered her less and she was able to appreciate her daughters' company more. Studies show that if they have supportive schools and communities, black children who are raised in white families have as good a chance of growing up feeling positive about themselves as black children raised in black families.

Biracial Children

Children of mixed racial ancestry (usually black and white) confront challenging issues as they come to terms with their racial identity in the middle childhood years. The biracial children I have talked to are likely to identify their race as "mixed" or "black and white." However, I have met a few children who say they are "black." They came from families who expected them to choose sides.

"Choosing sides" can be a wrenching decision for any child who is emotionally attached to both parents (even if one of the parents is absent). It is analogous to a divorce where a child who loves both parents is pressured to choose to live with only one of them. Even if a biracial child physically appears to be of one race, the burden of allying only with that one race can be emotionally costly. Some biracial children also learn, almost by osmosis, since people rarely actually come out and say it, that it is important to conceal the side of their racial identity that is deemed unacceptable by the people around them.

The daughter of a black mother and a white father who had separated early in the child's life grew up in a black community. By the fourth grade, the girl had become acutely aware of her friends' and their families' negative attitudes toward whites. She lived in fear that one day her school friends would discover that she was part white and that they would ridicule or, worse, reject her because of her "tainted" heritage. Children of mixed heritage whose physical appearance is white and who are growing up around racially prejudiced whites confront a similar situation.

Insecure biracial children may overcompensate for not being fully one race by "acting" more "black" or "white," depending on which group's acceptance they are seeking.

I knew a fair-haired nine-year-old girl who I never would have guessed was biracial when I first saw her. The child lived in a black community and had come to strongly identify as black to gain acceptance from the other children in her neighborhood. As someone observed, she became "blacker than black" in order to prove her identity. She lived with more pressure than any child should have to deal with.

Biracial children should not be pressured to identify with only one side of their racial heritage. Having to renounce part of who they are can be psychologically costly to them. If these children are confronting such pressures from people in their environment (whether family members or schoolmates), caregivers should try to minimize this pressure. Biracial children who grow up around people who accept them are likely to have a strong sense of self-worth. Several of the biracial children I know who identify themselves as "mixed" come from families and schools where race is not a dominant issue.

Biracial children who are secure in their dual heritage are at an advantage when they enter adolescence, where the pressure to choose sides in this undeclared racial war is likely to increase. Although at this stage, children tend to be quite cliquish, they rely less on race than on other things (for example, shared interests, personality, physical appearance) to decide who belongs in their groups.

"Hey, It Doesn't Wash Off!"

By age eight, most children understand that their skin color is a permanent part of their body. Unlike early grade-schoolers, older children can not be easily swayed from this belief even if they are challenged. Consider my conversation with eight-year-old Jelani:

INTERVIEWER: *Can a person change her skin color?*
JELANI: **No.**
Why not?
That's what you were born with.

Suppose you wanted to be another color. Can you change?
No, no . . . not unless you had an operation.
An operation?
Like Michael Jackson.
Michael Jackson had an operation?
Yeah, it turned him white.
Why did he do that?
He thought white was better.

Children in this age group understand that race is a permanent part of their identity. (For the record, Michael Jackson has attributed his skin-color change to a skin disease, not to cosmetic surgery.) If children at this stage express an interest in being a different color or race, this desire has deeper implications than for a younger child. Children who attend predominantly white schools are more likely to admit that at some time they wanted to be white. A fourth-grader named Vicky, a child from a middle-class family, told me that she didn't like being different; she hesitantly confessed that she once felt "weird" about being one of only two black children in her class. However, Vicky said that recently she has come to appreciate the value of being different and to realize that it "would be boring" if she looked like everyone else.

Several black children, almost all girls who attend predominantly black schools, have admitted to me that at least sometimes they desired to be white because they wanted the longer and easier-to-manage hair that they associate with whites.

Generally, however, children in the middle childhood years express contentment with their racial identity. They see race as *part* of who they are but not yet as the *central* factor in how they define themselves that it can become in adolescence. Some studies show that black children's self-concept during the preadolescent years is comparable to that of white children.[5] Children derive their sense of self-worth from various things, including their relationships with family and friends, their physical appearance, their interests, and their abilities. Interestingly, at this age, earning good grades is one of the prominent factors in black girls' sense of self-worth but not in black boys' sense of self-worth; for the latter, athletic ability begins to gain more prominence.

Realizing That Race Is Genetic

By age eight, most children are more or less aware of the origin of babies, but they are often embarrassed to talk about it unless repeatedly prodded. They understand that heredity plays an important role in determining racial identity. Unlike younger children, most older children are aware that both fathers and mothers are involved in determining their skin color. Children in this age group are clearer on the logic of heredity, often mentioning terms like *eggs, sperms,* and *genes* in conversations on this topic. Consider my conversation with ten-year-old Latifa:

INTERVIEWER: *How did you come to be the color that you are?*

LATIFA: **Because . . . um . . . Jehovah God created us, and, like, our genes tell us—say what we are going to be—what color we're going to grow up, and, like, our genes tell us what color we're going to be and stuff.**

How did you know that your genes told you what color you're going to be?

On TV.

How did your genes know to say that you would be that color?

Because sometimes they know lots of things 'cause they're not inside our body but our genes are.

Yes, but where did the genes get the information from? Can you figure that one out?

No.

How come you, your sister, and your mother are the same color?

Because she raised us?

Uh-huh.

And she married . . . the man who gave her the babies was half brown.

Yes?

And . . . he was this color. [She points to the tan color card.]

He was tan?

So tan is half brown and that way they made us brown.

When asked to choose the children who belong to parents of various races, children in this age group are more likely to assemble families according to race, rather than by skin color. Unlike younger children, they do not mix different racial groups (for example, Asians and whites) in the same family. Older children are less likely to insist that family members' skin colors should match; they are more likely to include members of various hues in the black families.

Children in this age group accept the interracial (white and black) couple as parents of the same children. Unlike younger children, they do not hesitate in identifying the children that belong to this couple, as illustrated by ten-year-old Dion's explanation for choosing the photos of light-complexioned children as belonging to the interracial couple:

INTERVIEWER: *You choose those children for those parents?*
DION: **Because you have to be half dark and half white.**
Why is that?
If their two colors [Points to the photos of the couple] are blended together, they come out like that. [Points to the photos of the children.]
Really? Where did you learn that?
Guessed.
Do you know anybody who has kids like that?
Yeah. [Mentions a schoolmate's name.] . . . One of her parents is still black but very light. Then she came out like this. [Points to the photo of the light-complexioned girl.]

LEARNING RACIAL STEREOTYPES

By age eight, most children can accurately classify people by race. When asked to sort photos of boys and girls of various races into groups, older children are more likely than younger children to categorize by race than by gender.

At this stage of their development, children also begin to show a most troubling aspect of what they are learning about the different races: racial stereotypes. Their tendency to see people stereotypically is consistent with their stage of cognitive development. Psychologist Jean Piaget characterized the stage of children's cognitive development from ages seven to twelve as "concrete operations." According to Piaget, children at this age tend to think of things literally, in black and white—no pun intended.[6] Children in this age group are developmentally inclined to view people categorically. Growing up in a race-conscious society that stereotypes certain races negatively and others positively makes it all the more difficult for them to appreciate people objectively. Cognitively, it is advantageous to be able to handle lots of information about different groups of people quickly, but in the process, the information often becomes distorted. For example, if children are taught to view whites as "bad" people, whenever they see a white person, they'll see him as bad, even though he may not fit this stereotype.

When I asked children of this age whether whites were different from blacks, several responded that whites "think they are better than blacks." Others noted that whites made blacks slaves. It seems that one of the earliest messages black children learn about people called "white" is that they are exploiters.

Children in this age group also say that blacks differ in other ways from whites (and from other racial and ethnic groups—Puerto Ricans were often mentioned on the East Coast, Chinese and Mexicans on the West Coast), for example, in their speech, walk, dress, food, and music preferences.

If we focus on children's perceptions of how blacks differ from whites, we see the emergence of several stereotypes. For example, children say blacks and whites differ in speech (blacks "use more slang"; whites "try to talk perfect"), dress (blacks are more fashionable dressers), walk (children demonstrate the type of bobbing stride popular among some black males), and music preferences (blacks enjoy more dynamic music). Blacks are described as more social than whites; their neighborhoods are seen as livelier, with people mingling outside on their porches and streets, while whites' neighborhoods are described as quieter.

More alarming are some of the negative stereotypes black children are picking up about their own race, especially stereotypes dealing with intelligence and behavior. It isn't until the late primary school years that children begin to mention that whites are smarter (reasons include "they get better grades" in school; more tutors and teachers are white) and blacks are "badder" than white (reasons cited include "on television they kill more people").

The emerging tendency of children in this age group to embrace the stereotypes of the different races predisposes them to experience difficulties dealing with people who do not conform to these stereotypes. Black children from different socioeconomic backgrounds may have trouble relating to one another if their perceptions of what a black person should be differ. For example, black children from middle-class backgrounds who speak "proper" English are often accused by children from low-income backgrounds of "sounding white" or "speaking funny"—of being "Oreos," black on the outside, white on the inside. Black adults who hold racial stereotypes also expect black children to speak, act, dress, and in other ways conform to the black stereotype; when they don't, these children are accused of "acting white" or "trying to be white." As they enter adolescence, it can become very difficult for black children who do not conform to the stereotype to be accepted by their black peers.

How Stereotypes Develop: Looking at the Media

Once children are at the stage when they are able to recognize different races, they gradually acquire stereotypes about them from a variety of sources. Although their family, friends, and school (see Chapter Two) continue to influence their perceptions, other sources like television, films, and music become increasingly influential.

Much has been written about the role of the media in perpetuating negative stereotypes of blacks. Films and particularly television are powerful influences on children's perceptions. Although more blacks are seen in more diverse roles in movies and television today than ever before, they continue to be disproportionately portrayed as disreputable characters, including criminals, prostitutes, drug addicts, and destitute people. Children who have a steady diet of these stereotypes may become confused or form negative impressions of blacks even though most of the blacks they know bear little resemblance to these celluloid images.

Children are bombarded with images of blacks as deviant. In one newspaper story, a black girl complained that she was offended that most of the films about black youth focus on drugs and gangs. A friend's sixth-grader said that when her school announces it will show films about blacks, she can predict that they will deal with people who have racial problems or are involved with crimes. She has seen many films about "normal" white people, but she cannot recall ever viewing a film in school about "normal" blacks.

The present generation of black children is faring much better than those of earlier times in terms of the images of blacks they see on the screen. They see blacks in positions of authority and influence unimaginable years ago. But Hollywood still has a long way to go before demonstrating that it recognizes most blacks to be "normal," just like most whites.

Film director Spike Lee has strongly protested the negative stereotyping of blacks in films. "I've never said that every African American image in film has to be angelic. . . . Just that there has to be a balance. The African American community can learn a lot from the Jewish community. If somebody says something derogatory about Israel or the Jewish people, there'll be letters, telegrams, demonstrations. African Americans have to do the same thing, because that stuff works."[7]

Learning from Television

Children tell me that they learn many of the negative stereotypes about their own race, and positive stereotypes about whites, from television.

When I was a graduate student at Harvard University, a physics graduate student from India, who resided in the same dorm as I, asked me if he could talk to me about something that had been bothering him. Over several months of friendship we had discussed a variety of subjects, none dealing with race. I was taken aback when he asked me whether blacks were as loud and rowdy as they were portrayed on television. He and his dormmates (students from various countries) were struck both by the difference in the portrayals of blacks and whites and by the differences between the blacks on television and those they encountered in real life.

Welcome to America! If a sophisticated man has difficulty reconciling the projected and the real images of blacks, think of how confusing it is for children, especially those of other races who have only limited contact with blacks. Children are more vulnerable to negative stereotypes than adults who have more experience and judgment to process the information.

A 1998 landmark study by Children Now, a national children's advocacy organization, found that compared to other minority groups, blacks are overrepresented on television. However, they are usually depicted as negative stereotypes. The study revealed that children of all races say that on television shows, whites are portrayed as "smarter, richer authority figures, while minorities—usually African Americans—are shown as poor, lazy, silly and criminal."[8]

Of all the programs on television, news programs, particularly local news shows, are among those most likely to perpetuate negative stereotypes of blacks. They routinely portray blacks as troublemakers and seldom show them as exemplary citizens. These real images have a powerful effect on the child's developing awareness of racial stereotypes. A friend told me how upset her ten-year-old daughter became when she learned that a local rapist, who had eluded the police for several weeks, was identified as a black man. "See," she said to her alarmed mother, "that's why people are afraid of blacks." Until that moment, her mother hadn't realized that her daughter had internalized this negative stereotype.

In fact, the stereotype of blacks as criminals is so ingrained in the American psyche that some whites have the notion that they will be believed if they blame blacks for crimes they themselves commit. (Two notorious examples in recent years were a mother who drove her car into a lake, drowning her two young sons, and a man who shot his pregnant wife to death. Both initially told the police the culprit was "a black man" to deflect the investigation from themselves.)

Years ago, I found myself habitually cringing at the local television news whenever the criminal of the day, frequently a black man, was discussed. I decided not to allow my children to watch television news programs until they were old enough to develop critical skills for processing the information they heard. Several months ago, I was quite pleased when my teenage daughter caught the racial biases of a local news story in which a white college student falsely claimed to have been abducted and raped by a black man whose composite was repeatedly shown on television and plastered all over the region. As my daughter pointed out, although the accusation was proved to be false within a day, the white student's recantation was not as widely publicized as the composite drawing of the black man.

Although there are significantly more black professionals and government officials today than ever before, one would not realize it by watching most news programs, whose anchors and reporters continue to be predominantly white. Leaders and experts shown on television are usually white. (A study a few years ago of the experts who appeared on the influential news show *Nightline* found that most of them were white males.)[9] So children who watch news programs also acquire the notion that all the truly knowledgeable and influential people are white.

I was reminded how accustomed I had become to the image of white experts when I was viewing the story of Bobbi McCaughey, the Iowa mother who gave birth to septuplets in 1997. When the news anchor announced that she would be interviewing the obstetricians who delivered the babies, I was all prepared to see white male doctors when two black females appeared on the screen instead. I called my children to see the interview because there are so few times when news programs show blacks as articulate and knowledgeable as these doctors on any issue other than race, poverty, entertainment, or sports. Parents should use those rare moments on television when blacks are shown in nonstereotypical ways to let their children see blacks who are as "normal" as the people they are accustomed to seeing in their own lives.

As mentioned earlier, because blacks have such a high rate of television viewing, TV exerts a disproportionate influence on black children's development. Parents should closely monitor their children's television viewing and discourage them from seeing programs that routinely stereotype blacks. It is important to teach children to think critically about the images they see. Complaining to television stations that regularly broadcast negative stories on blacks can also be helpful.

Racial Lessons in Music

Music has always played a defining role in the way blacks view themselves, whether it be as the children of a God who would one day release them from their earthly bondage that the slaves envisioned in their hymns or as the romantics of the Motown beat. Gospel remains a mainstay in the lives of many blacks, but the romanticism of the popular music of just a couple of decades ago has given way to a harsher sound that some say reflects the cruel reality of today's black underclass. Nowhere has the impact of this music been greater than among preadolescents, who are developing an understanding of race and the impact it will have on their lives.

It is hard not to be shocked by some of the words that come out of children's mouths as they sing along with songs espousing violence, hatred, and sexual exploitation. Many black children are strongly influenced by the hip-hop music of this generation, particularly "gangsta rap." Several years ago, a father sought my advice about what he should do about the music that his eleven-year-old daughter was listening to for several hours a day. He didn't want to alienate her by banning her music in their home, but he felt that many of the rap songs she sang along with were downright "evil." He was especially bothered by the violent and misogynist lyrics that referred to women as "bitches" and "ho's." Try as he might, he could not find a single redeeming thing about this music. My inclination was to pass his objections off as an intergenerational conflict and to counsel compromise, since previous generations of parents, including those of my baby-boom era, have always found something to criticize about their children's music. However, his absolute condemnation of the music persuaded me that I needed to listen to some of the songs in question before offering advice.

The lyrics of a couple of the rap songs he complained about were so offensive that I found it difficult getting past the first few seconds of them. Like the father, I found the gratuitous violence and the scathing descriptions of women deeply disturbing. Suddenly something a male teacher had complained about just a few weeks earlier made sense. He was hearing more allusions to "bitches" and "ho's" and violence in his current students' playground conversations than he had heard in all his previous years of teaching, which were many.

There is also positive rap, but it is not as big a moneymaker for the record industry as negative or gangsta rap. Positive rap holds out the promise of a much needed revival of the grand poetic tradition. But it is gangsta rap that holds sway among the youth culture, for children of other races as well as blacks, despite its toxic messages.

Will Smith, the actor and popular rap artist, puts it well when he distinguishes gangsta rappers from positive rappers like himself: "It is easy to grab your dick and curse and just spew out misogynist rhetoric. . . . Doing what we were doing—speaking proper English on a rap record rhyming about being punched in the eye and taking it, not pulling out some giant gun—that's the hard part."[10]

Much has been written about the negative effect of gangsta rap on young blacks. In his insightful essay on the genre in *What's Going On,* Nathan McCall defines the principal message of gangsta rappers: "They say it's admirable to be hard, unfeeling towards the world. Underlying all the tough talk is a deep depression, an angry, suicidal pessimism about life and an eerie preoccupation with death and dying."[11] Not surprisingly, some gangsta rappers claim that it's "just language," so what they sing about doesn't matter. But as McCall points out, language matters greatly: it is what rules the world; it has started wars and cemented peace. Children who regularly hear that violence is the answer to even minor slights, that police deserve to be shot, that females are to be used and discarded, cannot escape being negatively influenced by these words. Parents are noticing that this message is reaching their impressionable children, who are learning that they have to become "hard" to be "cool." Gangsta rap does not elevate the human spirit, as historically most black music has done; rather, it reduces humans to no more than their basest instincts. Much needs to be done to improve the bleak lives of the children and families of the underclass, but gangsta rap is not the answer; it just makes their situation worse.

What's most ironic is that many of these rappers seem to believe that they are "socking it" to white society with their hateful messages when it is white music moguls who profit most and white youth who are among the most ardent fans of rap. Meanwhile, countless black children are being exploited; they aren't even aware of the harm done to their minds, lives, and self-image as black youth.

For example, consider how negatively females are often depicted in these songs. When I was growing up, elegant male groups like the Temptations, the Four Tops, and others sang that black girls were to be cherished, looked up to, and loved in songs like "My Girl" and "I Can't Help Myself (Sugar Pie Honey Bunch)." I seldom heard anyone, much less a young girl, called a "bitch." That sort of flagrant insult simply wasn't tolerated. A girl I know was recently infuriated when a black boy in her fifth-grade class, intending to indicate his interest in her to another classmate, referred to her as "my bitch." But she knew if she complained she would invite further abuse. Why didn't the teacher reprimand this abusive student?

Some teachers say such language is now commonplace. A black elementary school teacher lamented that girls "just aren't protected anymore" as girls were in her generation. It depresses her to hear the abusive language her young girl students have to tolerate, and it angers her to realize that there is little she can do about it. Of course, abusive language directed at young girls is not totally caused by gangsta rap, but rap has played a large role in vulgarizing the language children use with each other.

The bottom line is that the lyrics of many rap songs give children detrimental messages about their race and, for girls, their gender. Parents and teachers will need to help children sort out these messages. Although rap is a great artistic form, the only real popular poetry in our common culture, when it is misused to spread messages of violence, hatred, and misogyny, it should not be allowed to pollute children's minds. Adults need to be firm in their resolve to promote positive messages in their homes and classrooms, especially for young children who have not yet developed the cognitive skills to judge what is healthy for them.

It's revealing that some parents have such difficulty deciding whether to permit their children to listen to gangsta rap. Most of these parents would have no difficulty deciding what constitutes a healthy diet for their children: they would not feed their children only candy and potato chips every day. A healthy mental diet is just as important if a child is to develop properly. No way around it, gangsta rap is junk food.

Some black women's groups have called for the censoring of gangsta rap. But one has to be very careful about advocating censorship in a free society. A boycott would be better. Gangsta rap is basically a commercial venture. A refusal to pay hard-earned money for it may be the best way to curb its appeal.

THE IMPORTANCE OF STRONG COMMUNITIES

Children who spend most of their formative years in segregated communities will have different experiences from those who live in integrated or predominantly white communities. They may attend a school with children of different races, but unless they go to a school that actively promotes racial harmony, these students will feel more comfortable among "their own." But growing up in a segregated community does not necessarily lead to negative racial attitudes or give children the idea that their future is limited—unless they receive negative messages from that community.

Many have claimed that during the era of segregation, black communities in general were stronger than during the present era of integration. In the postslavery, pre–civil rights era, strong communities allowed blacks to survive, and even prosper, despite Jim Crow laws and various other forms of oppression. The memoirs of people as diverse as Harvard professor Henry Louis Gates, attorney Johnnie Cochran, and singer Gladys Knight all have a common thread: the pivotal role their segregated communities played in supporting them.[12] These communities offered a safe haven from the racism that blacks inevitably encountered when they ventured into the wider world. Unfortunately, the high crime rate and drug infestation in some of today's low-income segregated communities make them more of a threat than a refuge for young children.

Much has been written about the disintegration of black communities across the country when the black middle class bolted for greener suburban pastures. The arrival of equal opportunity allowed them to live in predominantly white communities previously closed to them. Although there are thriving segregated middle-class black communities all across the country, suffice it to say that there are many more poor segregated black communities that have been devastated by the multiple blows they have sustained since the glory days of the civil rights movement, particularly from the crack cocaine epidemic.

Through my work in some of these communities, I see how race begins to shape young children's view of the world. Black children from low-income neighborhoods notice the differences between the affluence of the white communities that they drive through and the poverty of the communities that they live in; the opulence of the malls they visit and the shabbiness of the local business area; and the quality of schools they can only glimpse from afar and the squalor of the actual schools they attend. Unlike younger children, older children in the late primary school years are cognitively capable of using their observations to reach conclusions about the connection between race and privilege. In so doing, they begin to see the world not as "we" but as "them" (whites) and "us" (blacks).

The messages children receive from the older members of their community, as well as from the greater society, are crucial to how they interpret these observations. Are they encouraged to see themselves as shapers of their own destiny or as victims of an uncaring and racist society, trapped in their community with no hope of improving their lives?

One of the earliest messages some black children get from society is that they are not provided with the safety that most white children expect as their right. When I was around age twelve, I witnessed a residential burglary in progress. I was alone at home in Brooklyn, New York, when I saw a man on my next-door neighbor's roof, breaking and climbing through a window. I was initially hesitant to call the police, for I imagined the burglar might spot me and figure out that I reported him and come after me. But the positive image I had of the police, mostly from television, emboldened me to report the crime. When I phoned the police, I urged them to come quickly as the burglary was still in progress. Hours later, after I had given up hope, two white policemen finally turned up. The adults in my family were not surprised that the police had taken their time to respond to my call. I learned a disillusioning lesson that day: blacks in certain neighborhoods are not a priority for the police.

Many of the children I work with who live in low-income communities have a negative image of the police's ability to protect them. As an adult, I find it even more painful now to observe that some black communities are not even a priority to their own residents. I've visited homes where the adults treat it as "normal" to prepare for a night of drive-by shootings as the result of drug activity that plagues their neighborhoods. Communities that relinquish their responsibility to provide basic safety and to keep their homes and streets in good repair do inestimable harm to their young children. Children get the message that their lives are not important. Of course, it is best if communities have the support of the authorities to ensure their children's safety and improve other conditions that imperil them.

Consider the predominantly black housing projects of Lockwood and Coliseum Gardens in Oakland, California. Prior to the assignment of a black police officer, Jerry Williams, to the neighborhood as part of a new venture in community policing, even the police avoided the neighborhood as much as possible due to its heavy drug traffic and high crime rate. According to Williams, "The people in this community were being held hostage in their own homes." When he initially patrolled the area, he was greeted with open hostility by the residents, including the youth, who had little respect for the police. Eventually, thanks to training in "health realization," a model pioneered by Dr. Roger Mills, Williams learned to look for the good in the community residents rather than regard them as the enemy, as he had been trained to do. As a result of his attitude change, Williams was able to form a partnership with the residents that resulted in profound improvements in the life of the community: the previously high murder rate has remained at zero for several years, drug traffic has ceased, and children play outdoors again. Williams started a foundation, Healing Our Future, for inner-city junior high school students to teach them that they can influence their lives.[13]

The story of the revitalization of this community shows the advantages of a partnership between government officials and community residents. There are other communities across this country that do not have the luxury of such partnerships but that by their determination and ingenuity are able to reduce crime and improve other conditions anyway. The bottom line is that adults need to attempt to improve neighborhoods that negatively affect their children's lives.

~

By age eight, most children begin to see skin color through more adult eyes. In a sense, they are leaving the Garden of Eden, a place of racial tranquillity and limitless possibilities, and entering, with their new awareness (more accurately, acquired illusions), a world where their possibilities are restricted and people's perceptions and expectations of them can douse the flame of their dreams. As we shall see in the next chapter, nowhere is this new understanding of race more evident than in school.

CHAPTER NINE

How School Influences Older Children's Ideas About Race

Recently, a group of white parents in Riverside, California, vehemently protested naming their new school after Martin Luther King Jr. The parents expressed fears that King's name would evoke images of a "black" school and hinder their children's chances of getting into a good college.[1] Many would regard these white parents' objections to naming their children's school (expected to be two-thirds white) after King as reprehensible and racist. But sadly, it is also realistic. Too often, black schools are inferior; they lack the resources and support most white schools take for granted. Most of the good public schools in this country are located in wealthier districts; a disproportionate number of poor schools are located in low-income black neighborhoods.[2] One major way by which black children learn their social value, relative to children of other races, is through their school. By not providing equal educational opportunities to black children, this society sends a loud and clear message that they are not as valued as children of other races. This is a message many black children are able to pick up by the late primary school years.

CREATING ACADEMIC THROWAWAYS

Consider the case of fourth-grader Shannon, who was experiencing academic problems when I was brought in as a consultant on her case. I had known Shannon for a few years because I had been working with another child in her family. She had been a vivacious child interested in reading and writing little poems. The family had recently moved to a new neighborhood with a school that had a poor reputation.

From the first few weeks at the new school, Shannon's mother complained that her daughter didn't seem to be as interested in school as she had been at her former "better" school. Shannon's schoolwork was not as challenging as it had been at the old school. She didn't receive the impressive homework "packages" routinely distributed at her former school. School supplies seemed to be rationed; instead of bringing home books, Shannon brought home poor copies of textbook pages.

I encouraged Shannon's mother to talk with Shannon's teacher and, if that wasn't helpful, to talk with the principal. She was very reluctant to do so; in her experience, teachers and principals seldom listened to parents. As she had anticipated, her conversations with them were not helpful. They told her that they were doing the best they could given the limited resources they had. And they had a point: theirs was one of the poorer schools in the district. Shannon's mother believed that her daughter's only chance for a decent education was to transfer her to a better school—a formidable challenge in a district that allows few transfers. Shannon's situation is one that makes even the most optimistic person feel powerless.

I encountered a similar situation with ten-year-old Aaron, who had already begun a seemingly inexorable slide into school failure. The first time I listened to him read, my heart felt like it would break. Here was a fifth-grader with little knowledge of the basic rules of phonics. But I knew from his high level of motivation and quick grasp of the things I taught him that he was capable of doing well in school. Although he had known mostly school failure, Aaron was, remarkably, still eager to learn and touchingly grateful for the little time I spent tutoring him. Aaron's school had a poor academic and safety reputation; his mother said that her son had had only one "good" teacher since he started school, but she had no alternative but to keep sending him there. Since his mother didn't believe that Aaron learned much in school, she often kept him home.

Despite poor performance each year, he was automatically advanced to the next grade (this is called "social promotion"). He understood these promotions were a sham, and he had therefore become cynical about the need to do well in school. How in the world does society expect him, and other children like him, to compete academically with children who attend better schools?

The Widening Gap

Despite all the talk about black children's need for educational equality, there has been little noticeable improvement in the past few decades in many of the schools that serve them. It is widely recognized that many predominantly black schools are nowhere near equal to those of white children. In fact, "studies show that although there were school performance gains in the '70s and '80s, the performance gap between white and Asians on the one hand and blacks and Latinos on the other is again widening."[3] Robert Berdahl, chancellor of the University of California at Berkeley, who recently called for a recommitment to providing quality education to minority and poor children, acknowledges this sad truth: "We know, from an abundance of sources, that educational opportunities are not anywhere near equal—not in funding, not in facilities, not in teacher experience and not in access to college preparatory classes."[4]

I have consistently observed, and research confirms, that black children, like other children, in the early school years are naturally eager to learn. Research from the United Negro College Fund indicates that black children's achievement in the early grades is comparable to that of whites. However, a disturbing trend starts around the third grade for blacks compared to other races: black children begin to do poorly in grades and on national achievement tests.[5] For example, in Oakland and San Francisco, California, the average grade of middle school and high school black students is D+.[6] Blacks consistently score among the lowest groups on standardized tests of reading and math.

The roots of this problem are entwined in the history of racism, but the issue has grown into a tangled web of causes and effects. But if students lose interest in academics by the time they complete elementary school, as many black students do, it is difficult for them to regain that interest later, even if exposed to excellent teachers with adequate resources. They are likely to stay lost unless massive, and more costly, intervention efforts are made. Children who do not have an adequate foundation in the basic skills by the time they leave elementary school are simply unprepared to handle the more challenging work of high school; they'll always be playing catch-up.

Academic Achievement: "A White Thing"

As they begin to experience a sense of disconnection from school, children place less value on doing well in school. It is a well-documented fact that by the late elementary school years, some black children come to regard school success as a "white thing."[7] Black students who earn good grades are accused by their peers of "acting white." This expression, associating academic achievement with rejection of black heritage, does more harm to young blacks than any slogan coined by the Ku Klux Klan.

Some critics charge that black children do not do well in school because of the low value they and their parents place on education. This doesn't explain why most black children in their early years excel at school but later lose interest in pursuing school success. Some black children gradually learn that "the system" expects them to do poorly. As a result, they develop a defensive attitude, minimizing or dismissing the value of school success (this is similar to what psychoanalysts refer to as "reaction formation," a kind of defense mechanism).

In a newspaper story, Daniel Shaw, who a few years ago was a student at one of the worst elementary schools in a tough inner-city neighborhood, observed: "Most of the people I hung out with in the public school were very intelligent but they didn't have the support they needed." Daniel was one of the fortunate few in his neighborhood to receive academic and emotional support from an intensive tutoring program, Making Waves, that promised financial assistance for students who completed the program to attend college. Shaw said that kids like him "needed to know it's OK to be smart. Making Waves helps you realize that being smart is not a burden."[8]

Some people blame black parents' low valuation of education for their children's poor school performance and poor test scores.

In 1997, a University of Texas professor created a furor when he said that "African Americans and Mexicans can't compete academically with whites since they came from cultures in which failure is not looked upon with disgrace."[9] The assumption that black culture does not value academic achievement is outrageously false and inconsistent with the legacy of black struggle and survival in this county.

Education has long been equated with freedom. Since the slavery era, when it was illegal for blacks to learn to read and write (many slaves risked severe punishment to learn these skills), black families have passed on the value of education from one generation to the next. Studies consistently show that black parents continue to place a high value on education in spite of their children's low academic achievement.[10] Black students, too, have high educational expectations, although their actual achievement is lower. Social scientist Curtis Banks called this phenomenon the "attitude-achievement paradox."[11]

Parents whose children receive poor grades *do* bear some of the responsibility for their children's school performance. Research indicates that children's academic success is strongly associated with parents' involvement with their children's schooling.[12] Some parents, for a variety of reasons (including single parenthood and work responsibilities), are not as involved in their children's education as other parents. Parents of children with poor grades need to become more involved in their children's schooling. They can do so, for example, by making sure that their children attend school regularly. The best predictor of poor performance is the rate of absenteeism, one thing that black families themselves can control.

Before we condemn black parents who do not ensure that their children attend school regularly, however, we should try to "walk a mile in their shoes." Consider ten-year-old Aaron, whose mother often has an excuse ("The weather," "He woke up late," "I just didn't feel in the mood to get him ready") for not sending her son to school. Though a bright boy, Aaron has become accustomed to missing school.

Is this financially strapped single mother being irresponsible? A deeper look reveals that she doesn't send him to school regularly because her transportation is unreliable and she is afraid to allow him to walk to school because their neighborhood is unsafe.

Aaron's school has a poor academic reputation, children are promoted regardless of their grades, and few of them are expected to complete high school. Aaron's mother simply believed that it didn't make a difference whether Aaron attended school or not: "He didn't learn much anyway." She has a fantasy about sending Aaron to a school that has a good academic reputation in a neighboring district. However, even if Aaron were to qualify for that school, there isn't a school bus to take him there.

I expect that even though Aaron still expresses interest in school, sooner or later he will drop out. It's hard to say how much of the fault will lie with his mother. Often it's a feeling of powerlessness, not disinterest, that contributes to parents' lack of involvement in their children's education.

TEACHERS' EXPECTATIONS: THE POWER TO MOTIVATE OR TO DISCOURAGE

It wasn't until I was in the midst of writing this chapter that a memory buried deep in childhood resurfaced with painful clarity. Most of my educational experiences have been so positive that I rarely remember the time that I careened off course.

I started school in the second grade because I had advanced reading and math skills as a result of my mother's teaching. Second grade was a wonderful experience mainly because of an extraordinary teacher who made learning exciting and who made her students feel that they all were special. My third-grade experience, however, was an entirely different story. I went from being one of the best students in the second grade to being one of the worst in the third grade. Our teacher had a strict seating arrangement: "smart" students, mainly whites and Puerto Ricans, were seated in rows closest to the door, where the teacher directed most of her attention. Other students, marginal to poor students, mostly blacks, were seated on the far side of the room. I began the school year in the smart group, but thanks to playing around with my friends, I quickly landed in the group at the far side of the room. What I most remember about the teacher is her benign neglect. Unless we were noisy, she seldom engaged students in my section: we would rarely be called on to read aloud or to work out math problems on the blackboard. It didn't seem to matter to her that we frittered away time that should have been spent on our schoolwork by talking, telling jokes, and passing notes to each other. So much of my third grade was a fun-filled blur until the boom fell.

I had lost my class reader, and I knew that my mother could not afford a replacement. Fearing the consequences, I substituted a book with a cover that looked like my reader. Since the teacher rarely called on me to read, it took her a long time to notice the substitution. When she finally did ask me to read, I couldn't; the nicely covered book I held open during the reading period was one of my mother's nursing textbooks. Quite a fracas ensued when the teacher discovered the substitution; it was the first—and last—time my mother was called to school to deal with trouble I had gotten into. My mother had assumed that because I had skipped a couple of grades I would sail through school. She said the situation taught her never to take for granted that the school would look out for her children's education. But the lesson came too late for that year; I was held back in the third grade.

Over my years of consulting to families and schools, I have observed how chillingly easy it is for a student to become lost in the school system if he gets on a downward spiral as a result of a few simple missteps. Poor schools make it easier for children to lose their way. Minor school-related problems, if not appropriately addressed, quickly mushroom into bigger problems. If my mother hadn't aggressively intervened to set me back on the right course, I could have easily become part of the statistics on school failure that consign too many black students to a bleak future.

I have observed that the disconnection from school that I began to experience in the third grade happens to too many students who had begun school with an eagerness to learn. Like me, some of them learn early that there are teachers who do not expect them to do well in school, and so they conform to these expectations.

Teachers hold a unique role in our society. They are the gatekeepers to the American dream. If through words and actions they send the message that certain students are incapable of doing well in school, chances are good that these students will believe them. You may know of a famous study on the effect of teachers' expectations on school performance.[13] At the beginning of the school year, researchers informed the teachers that they had tested their students and determined their level of intelligence. They identified the students who were "smart." Guess what the researchers found when they returned at the end of the school year? The students they had identified as smart excelled at their schoolwork, and those who had not been so identified earned poorer grades. But it was all a ruse. The students had not been tested but had instead been randomly assigned intelligence levels! Yet by the end of the year, they had conformed to their teachers' expectations based solely on those arbitrary labels.

Black children are particularly vulnerable to their teachers' expectations because so many teachers believe that due to their race, parentage, or environment, black children are doomed academically. But there are also teachers who believe black children are capable of doing well in school, and such teachers can make a world of difference to their lives.

Bill Cosby, the famous black actor, said that his white sixth-grade teacher in an elementary school in Philadelphia "changed my life." Until he met her, he had gotten away with being the class clown instead of doing his schoolwork. But she refused to let him play in her class. Miss Mary B. Forohio, his teacher, remembers telling Cosby, "You've been acting up all your life since you came to this school." She told him that she expected him to change his ways in her classroom. Initially Cosby resented her: "Here was a kid who started out saying, 'If she messes with me I'm going to knock her out' and then [at] graduation feeling that I in fact could do things. I was very, very proud to have graduated from her class." His teacher, with the support of his mother, took a personal interest in him. She taught him how to channel his creative ability and energy into his schoolwork. Miss Forohio believed that "education can change the world one child at a time." She wanted Cosby "to have at least one teacher that he would never forget." Little did she know that she would have such a lasting positive effect on his life.[14]

It is important to point out that teachers' effectiveness in the classroom is largely a function of the school itself. Many fine teachers enter the profession intent on being dedicated teachers but are burned out by a system that makes too many unreasonable demands and provides too little support. So the problem of some teachers' low expectations is also a systemwide problem. Schools that are committed to improving the quality of education for black children must provide teachers with the support and training they need to do their job. Teachers perform one of the most important jobs in our society and should be properly recognized and compensated for it. Teachers who find that they are no longer doing the job that they want to do should seek help or join with other teachers and parents to advocate for educational reforms.

But teachers who find that they cannot effect change should choose another profession; to remain in the classroom and just go through the motions harms their students immensely. The widespread belief that many teachers, black as well as white, are mostly interested in collecting a paycheck is one of the most disturbing things I've learned in my conversations with black parents and students.

OBSTACLES TO SCHOOL SUCCESS

Besides possible negative experiences with teachers, there are other obstacles during the middle years that can rob children of academic success. These factors include the quality of schools, myths about blacks' intelligence, "black English" ("Ebonics"), and behavior management problems.

Quality of Schools

Whatever the academic handicaps some black children face at home, they are multiplied in the typical black school. It is hard not to conclude that the deck is stacked against black students' success in school. A black ten-year-old I know observed that compared to the school the white children attended, his school was not as big, the work was not as hard, and its playground didn't have trees. That they are being treated less well than other children is a painful fact for blacks to grasp when they are young. The realization that their education is not as good as that of whites (even when both races attend the same schools) is one of the major lessons many black children learn by the time they enter high school.

Over the years, I've heard many black parents complain about the disproportionate placement of their children in lower-ability and special education classes. Norman Chachklin, of the Legal Defense Fund of the National Association for the Advancement of Colored People (NAACP), summarizes this problem: "The overrepresentation of minority children in special education and their underrepresentation in gifted programs, and tracking or grouping practices in general, are major problems for African American children in many, many school districts."[15] Many people assume that black children are offered the same educational opportunities as white children when they attend the same school, but this is often not so.

Consider the scandalous situation that occurred in Morgan, Georgia. In 1994, the system's new white school superintendent, Corkin Cherubini, discovered something that he said "blew my mind." He unearthed the "persistence of school segregation under the guise of academic grouping." Beginning as early as kindergarten, black students, including those with higher grades and test scores than white children, were routinely "routed along separate tracks, with blacks often pushed into vocational and special education classes." When he tried to correct the situation, white parents vehemently protested. Cherubini received threatening messages; some whites accused him of being a traitor and pressured him to leave town. "With all of the debate raging over intelligence, race and genetics, he said it was clear that black students in his own school district were not given a chance. To him, this was not only immoral, but illegal."[16]

A 1993 nationwide study by the Rand Corporation revealed that such discriminatory academic practices as Cherubini uncovered in Georgia are more widespread than realized.[17] The study found that tracking, even at the primary school level, was highly linked to ethnicity rather than academic ability, as it is supposed to be. The study concluded that blacks' and Hispanics' lower achievement test scores, in subjects like math and science, can be at least partly attributed to the fact that they are more likely to be placed in classes for students with lower abilities. Compared to classes with bright students, classes with students with less ability had the least qualified teachers, lower-quality curricula, and poorer equipment. Being placed in these classes is often like being caught in quicksand: once in their grip, it is difficult to escape.

Once children are assigned to these classes, it is very difficult for them to move up to "regular" classes, much less to the classes for bright students.

In workshops that I've given on parenting and school, grown women have cried when recounting their children's experiences with school. Some blacks really believe that there is a conspiracy not to educate their children. And as you look around, you'd have trouble proving them wrong.

The Myth of Inferior Intelligence

Perhaps the most difficult stereotype black children have to deal with is that they are intellectually inferior to children of other races. Stereotyped as intellectually inferior in books like the controversial *The Bell Curve* that perpetuate the racist myth, black children gradually learn that because of their skin color, some people do not consider them as smart as other children.[18] This cruel myth has a major impact on children's developing self-concept and, more relevant to this discussion, on the quality of the education that they are offered. Educational opportunities made available to many blacks are not as extensive as those made available to children of other races.

The stereotyping of black children, regardless of the racial composition of their school, contributes greatly to their placement in less demanding classes. Even if they qualify for advanced college preparatory classes, such as those in math and science, black children are less likely than children of other races, with the exception of Latinos, to be placed in those classes. A study of a school district in California showed that only about half of the black students who scored in the top group on a standardized math test, compared to all of the Asians and 87 percent of the whites, were placed in algebra classes.[19] If blacks are excluded from advanced courses, they are at a disadvantage when competing for college. For example, a recent study showed that algebra is required for acceptance by most four-year colleges.[20]

There is *no* evidence that black children are inherently intellectually inferior to whites or children of other races. Intelligence itself is a much-debated and ill-defined concept. Renowned educator Howard Gardener has shown that intelligence is a multidimensional concept not easily captured in a single measure like an IQ test.[21] He has identified many different kinds of intelligence that are inherent in people of all races.

Studies on brain development during the early years show that environment exerts a tremendous influence on children's developing cognitive abilities.[22] Children who do not have the opportunity to grow up in environments that nurture their potential and attend schools that foster their abilities are at an enormous disadvantage compared to children who have these opportunities.

As a psychologist who over the years has done assessments of intelligence and academic achievement for hundreds of children of different races, I have observed what many studies have shown: the test differences some experts interpret as reflective of "race" are actually reflective of socioeconomic background. That is, children from higher-income families with educated parents tend to achieve higher scores on so-called intelligence and achievement tests. To compare the test scores of a child from a poor neighborhood attending a struggling inner-city school to the test scores of a privileged child in suburbia attending a well-endowed school is like comparing kiwis and cantaloupes; it just doesn't make sense. That this farcical debate about blacks' intelligence has been allowed to continue for so long is a testament to the enduring power of centuries-old racial prejudices used to justified blacks' enslavement in the first place. Schools that fail to educate their students properly and then claim that poor performance is the students' own fault should be held accountable for their students' failure. As the national group Education Trust concluded in a report on the educational gap among ethnic groups, "Students get the blame when they don't learn things that they were never taught."[23]

The Role of "Black English" ("Ebonics")

Schools' ineffectiveness in educating black children is also blamed on their intellectually impoverished background, which some teachers say is most evident in their limited speech and language skills. The long-simmering controversy about what contributes to some black children's poor language skills exploded onto the national scene in 1997 with the "Ebonics" controversy.

Some educators suggest that the nonstandard English some black children learn at home severely handicaps them in school. But that isn't necessarily true: many of us who come from homes where so-called black English was used excelled in English courses when we were taught standard English in school. Other educators suggest that black children would do much better in school if their teachers used black English to teach them. It is distressing to me to hear *black* educators advocating the use of nonstandard English by black students in their classwork. Although it is an appropriate teaching method to use nonstandard English as a bridge to teaching standard English, it is inappropriate to rely on nonstandard English *exclusively* because it undermines children's ability to learn communication skills that are essential for success at school and in the working world. The Ebonics controversy in Oakland, California, gained national attention when the Oakland School Board requested federal funds to integrate black English "as a separate language" into the standard school curriculum.

Many of us have different styles for communicating with family and friends and for communicating with our professional associates. It doesn't make one style superior to another; it's simply a recognition that different situations call for different communication styles. Children should not be told that they are renouncing their racial identity if they don't speak black English in all situations; rather, they should be encouraged to appreciate that using standard English is another step in joining the larger community of learned people. By the middle childhood years, children are very adept at adjusting their speech from one context to another. It is some adults who have trouble with it.

Behavior Management Problems

Another major obstacle to children's success in school is the unchecked behavior problems of a few unruly students. One of the most surprising things I've learned after several years of consulting to schools is that most young children who do poorly in school have behavior problems, not learning difficulties.

It is disheartening to see bright children do poorly on their schoolwork because their teachers are unskilled at managing students' behavior problems. Parents have told me that black children are less disciplined in the white teachers' classes. Some teachers, particularly whites, are intimidated by black children from low-income neighborhoods.

A mother of four children in elementary school told me that one day when she was visiting her children's school, she noticed that her daughter's third-grade teacher did not reprimand any of the children who were misbehaving. The mother tolerated the situation for as long as she could and then finally asked the teacher why he wasn't disciplining the unruly children. He told her that he couldn't "control" the class; the children "didn't listen" to him. With his permission, she took over the class for a brief time. It took her only a few minutes to get the children to focus on their schoolwork. She claimed that she, a high school dropout, knew much more about managing children's behavior than the teacher did.

Teachers are taught relatively little about behavior management. Research shows that in education schools, teaching discipline is not a top priority. Public Agenda, a public interest polling firm, found in a 1997 survey that "only 37 percent of education professors considered 'maintaining order and discipline' an important classroom priority. Only 30 percent say their college instructs future teachers in how to deal with rowdy, out-of-control students."[24] This is bad news for schools in low-income communities, which tend to have a larger proportion of less qualified teachers.

When teachers *are* trained how to discipline, the instructions some of them receive can be racist. In a newspaper story, a white teacher in a middle school in Berkeley, California, stated: "I learned that first of all, when a group of people are disenfranchised and you are a white person with power over them, you must be very careful. You can be overly lenient or you can become the oppressor."[25] This approach is a problem: too many teachers react more to students' color than to their status as students. So they bend over backward not to appear as the oppressor and in so doing allow students to escape the full consequences of their misbehaviors. Without proper discipline, students do not learn the skills necessary to function well in school.

Some teachers assume that it is best to respond leniently to black students' misbehavior because of the influence of "cultural sensitivity" pap that encourages them to tolerate language and behaviors that would not be allowed in these children's homes. For example, the white middle school teacher I quoted earlier reported that a black female student shouted at her, "I hate you, you ho," but she didn't know what to do. Cultural sensitivity instructors at teaching institutions are advising teachers that students' use of "ho" cannot be dealt with adequately unless the teacher understands the student's cultural values and is able to differentiate between "language designed to harm and language that is just throwaway, that is not meant to hurt anybody."[26] This is ridiculous! In any culture with which I am familiar, calling a woman a "ho" or a "whore" is an insult. Most blacks, regardless of social class, would not tolerate this language from an adult, much less from a child. A child who dares to call her mother or any female this word is likely to be severely disciplined. And when this gobbledygook is taught, what does it say about these educators' concept of black culture?

Those who teach that black culture tolerates its children's use of disrespectful language and behaviors to their elders simply do not know what they're talking about. Blacks in general place a high value on teaching children respect. As Star Jones, attorney and one of the hosts of the television talk show *The View,* said, "My grandmother taught me race is not an excuse for inappropriate behavior."[27] Schools that do not reinforce this value do a disservice to black children and their families.

Some teachers tell me that mental health services are desperately needed for children with school behavior problems. Many schools seem to regard counseling as a luxury, but it is actually a necessity for classrooms where a few difficult students make it hard for other students to receive an education. Some schools also have to deal with students and parents who dispute claims of students' misbehavior. Indeed, some teachers, especially white teachers, are afraid to discipline black children because they believe their parents will "go off" on them. This is a legitimate concern.

Sometimes during classroom observations, I've wondered what students and their parents would think if they could actually see how students are acting out in class. A video "report card" of students who habitually disrupt and otherwise misbehave in class would reveal to parents the magnitude of their children's problems. Some may say that this would be invasive, but I believe that desperate measures are needed for desperate situations. In many of these classrooms, the situation is truly desperate.

Parents, teachers, and students should sign an agreement prior to the beginning of the school year about the kind of behavior that is expected in the classroom. By early primary school, students are perfectly capable of understanding such an agreement. It is essential that parents believe that their children will be disciplined fairly and appropriately. If parents refuse to allow teachers to discipline their unruly children, they should be asked to transfer their children to schools that are more lenient. The support of other parents is also important. Most parents, regardless of race, do not want their children's education to be held hostage to a few troublemakers. Each child's major disciplinary decisions should be handled by a team that includes the teacher and classroom parents. Some parents may try to intimidate teachers, but they will think twice about using the same tactics on a parent who is "one of us."

Holding Schools Accountable

The debates on blacks' intelligence, black English, and behavior are smokescreens to divert attention from the more fundamental issue of schools that are failing our children. Today, fortunately, education is one of the top priorities on national, state, and local agendas. There is growing support among blacks for a school voucher system that will give them a greater choice of schools for their children. Critics, including politicians and some teachers' union representatives, argue that allowing parents to choose their children's school will close some schools and adversely affect public education.[28] But how can the situation be much worse than it presently is? Is it reasonable to assume that those districts where the average grade is D+ can get any worse if change is instituted?

Schools that do not adequately do their jobs of educating children deserve to be closed. No major business enterprise in our country that had as high a failure rate as the public schools that serve black children would be allowed to survive. Some school districts, with a large proportion of minority students with poor grades and test scores, have already begun to hold schools accountable for their students' performance. For example, Texas, which has a high proportion of minority and poor children, requires accountability from its schools. Minority students in Texas perform significantly better than similar students in California, where there is less accountability.[29] School districts across the country are waking up to the need for accountability: some are grading schools, and others are taking the extreme step of replacing the entire staff at schools whose students continue to perform poorly. In spite of these small, though promising, changes, there is still a long way to go before all children receive an equal education.

RACE IN THE CLASSROOM

By the late primary school years, most children are aware of race and know that it is a volatile issue. A few opportunistic students may use this knowledge to intimidate and bully other children. Some students begin to act out in school the racism they hear about, observe, or experience.

Racial bullies, much like other bullies, pick on children they deem vulnerable because of their appearance or demeanor to shore up their own fragile self-esteem. They tease or taunt other children using racial epithets. At this stage of development, however, children are not as likely to engage in major physical fights that involve other students, who choose sides along racial lines. Such fights are more likely to involve teenagers with strong racial or ethnic affiliations.

Unlike younger children, children in this age group fully understand the effect of racial epithets and disrespectful behavior on others. Often, however, what adults interpret as "racial" is actually something else. In most of the accounts I've heard, children in this age group express racism by teasing other children or by excluding them from their "group." Children should be taught how to handle being teased and how to respond to children who act out their racial prejudices.

Only occasionally in the primary school years do conflicts, passing as racial, erupt into anything other than name-calling or excluding children from play. For example, a group of white boys, in a mixed-race class, displayed a homemade Ku Klux Klan doll with a sign that read "Kill them all."[30] This is ridiculous juvenile behavior, behavior that would be laughable if it weren't so potentially dangerous. The students probably wanted to stir things up and attract some attention to themselves. They were not necessarily displaying the hatred such an act would imply were it perpetrated by an adult. The pranksters were suspended for a short period. In my view, they should have been given more severe punishments to teach them the seriousness of their actions.

One of the most egregious acts of "racism" committed by children in this age group was committed by a group of white and Latino boys, aged ten to twelve, who while shouting racial slurs viciously beat up a black boy in the school bathroom.[31] A white boy who came upon the scene following the attack said that when he saw the victim lying on the floor and the words "We hate Niggers" scrawled on the walls, he was too scared to get involved. "They're big kids," he said. "A lot of kids are afraid of being beat up by them." The students, arrested on hate crime charges, were the youngest persons to face such charges in California. However, the charges were eventually dropped, and the students were released to their parents' custody. These bullies had become accustomed to intimidating other children; in this instance, race was only an excuse for beating up this child.

Any child who has reached the age of reason and seriously injures another child should face criminal charges in a juvenile court and reap the consequences of his or her actions. When these crimes are dismissed as youthful indiscretions, children do not receive the help they desperately need to understand what they have done wrong, thus making them more likely to become lifelong criminals who think they have a right to pick on people they don't like.

Although none of the cases I've mentioned dealt with black perpetrators, black bullies too cause trouble for other students, including other blacks, whom they regard as easy prey. Bullies are bullies: race is just one of their many excuses for exerting power over others. I have heard of black students who hurl racial slurs at or threaten white students who they think "diss" (disrespect) them. Schools should act quickly and decisively when such abuses occur to make sure that students understand that their actions will be dealt with firmly. To do otherwise is to undermine the integrity of the school and to create an atmosphere hostile to learning.

If rules of behavior are in place to handle "racial" conflicts, school authorities can act quickly. Students should understand that violating school rules that require them to respect their fellow students will result in specific consequences. Policies should be fairly and consistently enforced.

Adults are more inclined to interpret any conflict between students of different races as racial, and they can become rattled when a conflict between students has racial overtones. If they retain their composure and objectivity, they'll realize that these conflicts are usually just another way for bullies to pick on the vulnerable. If race were not the spark, it would be something else: the victim's obesity, big ears, dress, unusual name, or whatever.

It can be helpful to have a student forum, like a student conflict resolution team or court, to handle conflicts between students. Children are sometimes more likely to see other children's racist words and behaviors for what they are: pettiness, envy, exploitation, or bullying. Working cooperatively on a student court or team to resolve conflicts, racial and otherwise, can also teach students important lessons about conflict resolution and citizenship.

Just as there are children who learn to sow the seeds of racial hatred, there are those who learn to cultivate racial harmony. A national poll found that most children at this age say that they have a friend from another race and would like to have other similar friendships.[32] Parents and teachers should do all they can to encourage children of different races to get to know each other at this stage of development when they are still open to forming such friendships. Anita Kurtz, when she was in primary school, founded Calling All Colors, an annual national racial-unity conference for students in grades three to eight.

When Teachers Are Accused of Racism

Although years ago, many white teachers blatantly discriminated against black students with impunity, it is harder today for any teacher to give a black student an undeserved grade, use racial slurs in reprimands, or indulge in any other behaviors suggestive of racism without risking serious consequences. If teachers use racist language or behave toward their students in ways even suggestive of racism, they jeopardize their jobs. (As mentioned earlier in this chapter, the most widespread—and harmful—form of discrimination remaining is the systematic exclusion of qualified blacks from advanced classes.)

Some white teachers are reluctant to discipline black students for fear that they will be accused of racism. News stories suggest that such fears may be justified. In one story I read, a black girl accused her teacher of using a racial slur while she was being disciplined; in another story, a black boy accused his teacher of kicking him. Such accusations elicit strong reactions from people who are prone to assume that all white teachers are racists. If parents are convinced that a teacher has indeed discriminated against a student, they should complain to the appropriate school officials. But parents have to be very careful to examine the veracity of similar allegations before taking them public and jeopardizing a teacher's job or inflaming racial tensions in the school and the wider community. Young children, who may or may not be telling the truth, do not realize the gravity of racial accusations. Schools should have in place a procedure to quickly evaluate and resolve students' complaints about teachers' use of inappropriate or abusive words and behaviors, racist or otherwise.

When I was in the seventh grade, I knew a student who blamed the bad grades he received on his teacher's racism. Other students I knew considered this teacher a fair person who went out of his way to help students. Chances are that the boy who cried racism received the grades he deserved. But his mother believed him and never bothered to ask the teacher his side of the story.

Some children learn early to use race as a crutch for their own lack of effort or other failings. Parents and other caregivers have to be very careful about not encouraging children to see themselves as victims. Help your children see themselves as capable of achieving the goals they set their minds to, but make sure they know that it will take lots of hard work, persistence, and dedication. Point to people, ordinary and famous, who experienced adversity, not only racial but other types as well, but triumphed over it and became better individuals in the process.

~

For black children, education offers a key to equality. If denied it, they cannot hope to keep pace in an increasingly competitive world. More than any other institution besides the family, the school has the power to influence children's attitude toward themselves for the good and to instill confidence in them about their potential. Unfortunately, too many schools shirk their responsibilities to black children. As we shall see in the next chapter, how children are prepared by their families, schools, and communities determines how confidently they are able to move into perhaps the most challenging period of their young lives: adolescence.

CHAPTER TEN

Preparing for Adolescence

The Lines Are Drawn

When I was a child, I spake as a child,
I understood as a child, I thought as a child:
but when I became a man, I put away childish things.
—1 CORINTHIANS 13:11

Tamara, a black girl, had been one of the most popular girls at the racially integrated school she had attended since kindergarten. She hung out with a group of girls of different races who considered each other best friends.

Little did Tamara know how radically things would change when she moved on to high school. From the first day she entered its gates, she sensed a racially charged atmosphere that came as a shock to her. Some of the black girls gave her withering glances whenever they saw her with whites and Latinas. Tamara discovered that she couldn't simultaneously be friends with blacks, Latinos, and whites. Blacks wanted her to choose sides. A few months into the school year, Tamara stopped going to regular school; she enrolled in the school's independent studies program. That way, she didn't have to choose sides.

The physical and psychological tumult that is adolescence is characterized by intense preoccupation with the ever-changing self. Adolescence is a time when issues relating to racial identity take center stage. Much of this is played out in high school, although for some individuals it can begin earlier. Whatever the racial composition of their high school—integrated, predominantly black, or predominantly white—black students are likely to confront racial issues to some degree as they come to terms with who they are and deal with the negative stereotypes concerning their race.

Students who attend predominantly black schools often escape the daily aggravation of racism that students at integrated and predominantly white schools may sense, if not confront. An eleventh-grader I know who attends a mostly black school in northern California could not recall one incident of racial conflict. However, she has observed that sometimes there are racial tensions between certain students and their white teachers. Some black students do have special difficulty dealing with authority figures, especially white ones.

Students at some mostly black schools are aware of the inferior quality of their schools, compared to schools attended mostly by whites. For example, the quality of the college preparatory courses at some black high schools is simply not on the same level as those available at many white schools, which have greater resources and a higher number of better-trained teachers. What message do black students receive from this disparity? They learn that white society believes that they are not as worthy of being educated as privileged whites are.

Schools with a strong white orientation pose a special challenge for black students. Without a secure sense of identity, black students at these schools can easily succumb to feelings of alienation. Black writer Kevin Powell recalls: "I went to an integrated school from kindergarten to the 12th grade and I can honestly say that I hated myself all the way from the time I had thoughts until I got to college. I learned nothing about myself as an African-American. . . . Self-hatred just festers and grows. . . . If you don't learn about your specific world you're not going to have any pride in yourself."[1] If the school is not sensitive to the needs of black students, they suffer.

Chris Rock, the comedian, was bused to a predominantly white school in New York because his parents believed he would receive a better education there than at their local predominantly black school. But Chris has described his experience at the white school as a living nightmare—practically every day, he was taunted and beaten up by white students. He never told his parents about his abuse, but he found the stress so overwhelming that he wet his bed until he was about thirteen. This school trauma still affects his relationship with whites: "It made me distrust white people as a whole people. Even to this day, if I'm in an environment and I'm the only black, I'll get nervous to the point that my nose will start bleeding sometimes 'cause I think something might happen."[2]

Some students can lose what some see as their black identity at a predominantly white school. A black mother complained on a television talk show that her son had lost his identity—he didn't talk, dress, or act like blacks, and even worse, he had become a *golf* fanatic! She blamed this change on the exclusive prep school her son attended. What did she expect when she sent him there, as she admitted, to get a better education? That he would absorb the academics and remain untouched by the social milieu?

Although I know some black students who thrived at predominantly white schools, it is difficult to do so unless the school is attuned to black students' identity issues. At private schools, social class can be a much greater distinction than race. A privileged black student may more resemble a privileged white student than a less privileged black. Unless these students maintain their roots in the black community, they risk becoming alienated from the so-called typical black.

Compared to the relative racial calm of predominantly black and predominantly white schools, some integrated schools are like a war zone. Students have to choose which side they're on. They are not allowed to fraternize with the "enemy" without being regarded as a traitor to "their side": their race. Students who did not experience the racial divide in the earlier grades can have a rude awakening.

Many black students who did not see themselves primarily in terms of their race in their younger years begin to do so in adolescence. Psychologist Beverly Tatum, in her book *"Why Are All the Black Kids Sitting Together in the Cafeteria?" and Other Conversations About Race,* says that racial identity does not become a major issue for most children until they reach adolescence.[3] This is consistent with children's psychosocial development. Psychologist Erik Erikson describes the principal task of adolescence as "forming an identity."[4] As black teenagers try to answer the question "Who am I?" they may for the first time seriously confront the reality of the status of their race in society. However, if parents and teachers have prepared them well, following advice like that provided in this book, their passage through this stage of development can be considerably smoother. Parents and teachers who are aware of the issues that teens will confront relating to their race are better equipped to help them deal adequately with problems and opportunities that may arise because of their race. These issues, ranging from dealing with the challenge of racial authenticity to handling racism in the classroom, are discussed in this chapter.

FORMING THEIR IDENTITIES

By adolescence, most blacks begin to identify themselves mainly by race, a major difference from younger children, who identify themselves primarily by gender. When psychologist Beverly Tatum, who is black, asked students to complete the sentence "I am ______," she found that black students are likely to fill in their race ("I am black/African American"), whereas white students tend to cite personality traits (for example, "I am shy").[5] Psychologist Cathleen Gray, who is white, obtained similar responses when she asked students, "Who are you?"[6] Black students exclusively defined themselves by their racial identity and white students by personality characteristics.

Seeing themselves primarily as blacks (or African Americans) is a crucial turning point in teens' development, for it signals the beginning of a lifelong awareness that many people regard their race as their defining feature. Many black adults say that they are forced to think of their race practically all the time as they go about in society. Research suggests that in a majority white culture, whites seldom think of their race.[7] Preoccupation with race, which is often forced on them, is a daily inconvenience for many blacks.

RACIAL AUTHENTICITY: HOW CAN YOU TELL WHO'S "REALLY" BLACK?

But what does it mean to be "black" or "African American"? (Black teens I've spoken with use both terms.) Teens have very definite ideas, yet rather vague criteria, about who is authentically black. Speech, dress, and attitude matter. Preferences in music have blurred now that teens of all races have acquired a taste for hip-hop, but music used to be an indicator of racial affiliation. Oprah Winfrey revealed on her talk show that when she was a young girl, she worried that her friends would find out that she liked the Beatles, particularly Paul McCartney.[8] Nonblacks also learn the many criteria make up the black stereotype. I had to chuckle when I heard that at a recent social gathering of high school girls (no blacks were among them), one white girl criticized her friend by declaring, "You dance like a white girl."

Nothing tells more about whether someone is authentically black than the people they hang out with. Although it's all right to have casual relationships (in class, on athletic teams, and elsewhere) with students of other races, when it comes to close friendships, "real" blacks stay with "the blood."

Studies show that high school students tend to associate mainly with students of their own race (at lunch and in classes, when they are not assigned seats).[9] A survey in *Teen People* magazine found that students "prefer hanging out with members of their own race—kids who speak like them, live near them and look like them—because that's where they feel they belong."[10] If in earlier grades students did not attend school or participate in activities with children of other races, it is unreasonable to expect them to feel immediately comfortable with students of other races when they are thrown together in high school.

The sense of identity of many nonblack high school students is linked to their group or clique. For whites, membership in groups is based primarily on shared interests, personality, or other similarities, as evident in groups like the popular crowd, the nerds, the jocks, and so on. But this is not the way things work for blacks and other racial or ethnic minorities. The glue that holds many minority students together is race or ethnicity. Blacks who go outside their group risk a cold shoulder, if not outright ostracism. As one black high school student put it, "People, especially teenagers, are afraid of what their friends will think if they hang out with people who are different from them."[11] So blacks who are interested in continuing friendships or forming new friendships with students of other races, especially whites, are likely to feel conflicted.

Sara, who is white, and her friend Chantal had been best friends since early primary school. When they entered high school, they were distressed not to be able to hang out together without causing problems in their relationships with other friends of their own races. Chantal's new black friends interpreted her friendship with a white girl as a rejection of them, and other blacks teased her about it. Sara's friends saw her as strange. Chantal and Sara's friendship foundered until they stumbled on a solution: they took their friendship underground. Away from school, they retained their intimacy, but once they hit the school steps, they became barely nodding acquaintances.

I have heard similar stories from several other former friends, who are now adults. They still mourn the loss of once cherished friendships and don't quite understand the reason why racial allegiance in high school proved stronger than the affectionate ties of childhood. Happily, I have also heard of many interracial friendships that did survive into adulthood despite racial pressures to end them. But for typical black students, having a close white friend raises questions about their racial authenticity. One of the major lessons of adolescence is "stick with your own kind!" Interracial friendships are for kids. When you enter high school, it is time to put your baby ways behind you.

I was reminded recently of the persuasiveness of this stereotype of authentic black behavior in American culture, not only among teens but also among adults—who should know better. The white president of the University of Florida reportedly called the incoming chancellor, his new boss, an "Oreo" in a conversation with colleagues at a party. He said that the black chancellor was effective in dealing with whites because he was "white on the inside." The president almost lost his job for this remark; it was saved by his supporters, including the new chancellor.[12]

The president is obviously not a black separatist or a racist. On the contrary, he has a reputation as a distinguished educator and is known to be sensitive to minority issues, including those affecting black students. Unfortunately, too many adults of all races share his attitude that blacks who are able to relate well to whites and who make it in the "white world" are somehow racially inauthentic. And these same adults do even more damage by passing this attitude on to their children and their students as they move through childhood and adolescence.

Losing opportunities to develop friendships with interesting people just because they are a different color can inhibit children's development and deprive them of many wonderful experiences. I noticed this problem particularly in college. Blacks who have had friendships with whites prior to college tend to be more open to interracial friendships. Conversely, black students who have had negative experiences with whites may view forming friendships with whites as "fraternizing with the enemy."

In the predominantly white women's college I attended in the Northeast, I had several wonderful friendships with black, Asian, and white students. I remember vividly how some of them reacted when I decided to run for student body president in my junior year. Some of my black friends tried to dissuade me from running, warning me that the predominantly white student body would never elect a black president (although there had been at least one before our time). I recall even more vividly the warning of a white friend, who on the eve of the election told me that because I wasn't a "blonde, blue-eyed cheerleader type," she didn't hold out much hope for my election. Luckily, I also had black and white supporters for whom the issue of race was not a consideration. Suffice it to say that I went on to enjoy one of the best years of my life as the student body president. When I think of what I would have missed if I had listened to the naysayers, I am grateful. But too many students miss out on dear friendships and great opportunities because they are, for various reasons, unable to see beyond race.

Oprah Winfrey, the talk show host, has described her college experience as less pleasant than it could have been because she did not share the views of some of the other black students, who had had different racial experiences prior to college.[13] It is important for students and parents to be aware of the problems different childhood experiences with people of other races can cause if teens plan to attend an integrated or predominantly white college.

INTERRACIAL DATING: TABOO?

For black teens to be regarded as authentic blacks, not only should their platonic friends be black, but their romantic interests should also be black. Surveys show that teens today are more likely to date outside their race than a generation ago. A 1997 *USA Today*/Gallup poll showed that 57 percent of teens said that they had dated someone of a different race, a big change from the 17 percent reported in 1980. But many teens still have a negative attitude toward interracial dating. The survey indicated that "black and white dating is most likely to cause trouble." Around a quarter of the black and white teens said they "would have a problem" with a white and black couple.

Some black girls find it particularly hurtful to see black guys dating white girls. At some subconscious level, they experience it as a rejection of themselves as attractive and worthy. This is understandable, since many black girls grow up seeing white females depicted as the ideal in feminine beauty. Blacks are relegated to an inferior status in terms of physical beauty and social status. A black girl who had a steady white boyfriend once told me that she still became annoyed when she saw black guys with white girls. She regarded this form of dating as rejection of black females.

Because of the myth of their sexual prowess, black guys are considered "a catch" by some white girls. As adults, black males are far more likely than black females to cross the color line to date and to marry (by a ratio of almost 2 to 1).[14] In high school, however, interracial dating is frowned on for both girls and guys. Rejecting interracial romantic alliances, and discouraging others from forming them, is one way teens can prove they are authentically black.

In spite of the racial tensions that rocked the interracial high school I attended in New York, some black and white students were friends. Interracial dating, however, was considered taboo; both blacks and whites were simply uncomfortable with the idea.

As a freshman in college, trying to find my bearings in the social mix, I succumbed briefly to the urge to prove myself to a fellow black student, who avoided close relationships with whites because of negative experiences she had had with them when growing up. Like some of the other blacks I knew, she had cordial relations with whites but tended to associate primarily with other blacks at this predominantly white college. Since she lacked the positive experiences that I had had with white friends in high school, her reluctance to cultivate white friends was understandable. Moreover, some of the white students were racially bigoted and did not encourage harmonious racial relationships.

One day, as this student and I were walking on campus, we encountered an interracial couple, a white girl and her black boyfriend. My companion said something to the couple to express her disapproval of their relationship and ended with an accusatory "Brotherrrr!" The couple looked stunned. I felt conflicted. This was my chance to show that I was as "black" as my friend, but these two people walking along, holding hands, minding their own business had not bothered us. But the unspoken pressure to show my blackness by also expressing disapproval was too much. I managed to squeeze out a convicting "Brotherrrr!" But I regretted saying it the instance I spoke.

For a long time after the incident, I felt miserable about my mean-spirited remark. It made me feel sad rather than validated. Like other teens who seeking acceptance from their peers, I had ignored childhood lessons about kindness and civility. I relearned a valuable lesson that day: racial validation should not come at the expense of hurting others.

Acceptance by other black schoolmates provides black teens a sense of belonging and security in high school and later in college that may be difficult to achieve otherwise in a school world that is often alienating for many blacks. But conforming to the expectations of the group can come at an exorbitant price if it requires teens to dress, act, speak, choose friends, and even think in a prescribed way. Who has the right to demand so much of anyone? Surely not real friends. In conforming to the stereotype, black students relinquish the freedom to be their true selves.

"SISTERS"

In her best-seller *Reviving Ophelia,* clinical psychologist Mary Pipher chronicled the dramatic and alarming changes that girls experience in early adolescence. Pipher convincingly argues that compared to a generation ago, girls today are having "more trouble" with adolescence as a result of disturbing cultural changes, including the trend to objectify and sexualize girls.[15] Pipher cites her own clinical experience and studies to show how girls, by succumbing to social pressures to deny their authentic selves, begin to lose their self-esteem, resiliency, optimism, and intellectual interests. Girls lose their "true selves" by conforming to societal expectations and becoming preoccupied with their appearance, especially their weight. Pipher suggests that the phenomenon she describes primarily affects white girls. Although she has little to say about black girls specifically, she does observe that having to deal with racism enables black girls from supportive families to do a better job of handling the challenges of adolescence and preserving their sense of self-worth: "Instead of weakening them, [dealing with race] gave them strength."[16]

Indeed, research indicates that the self-esteem of black female teens is generally higher than that of white female teens and girl teens of other races.[17] The reason, researchers believe, is that black teens are not as influenced as girls of other races by the traditional standards of beauty, particularly those relating to body weight. Psychologist Sumuru Erkut and her colleagues at Wellesley College found that compared to girls of other races, black girls scored highest on measures of self-worth, followed, in descending order, by Latinos, whites, and Chinese girls. Black teens view themselves as most socially successful and romantically appealing. I've talked to girls of other races who describe black girls as more "vivacious" and "independent." Erkut also found that, contrary to what is commonly believed, high academic achievement was the strongest predictor of self-worth for black girls.

Black girls may be losing their advantage in terms of self-esteem. Studies show that black females' healthier attitude toward their bodies may be becoming a thing of the past. A 1996 survey published in the professional journal *Pediatrics* is particularly alarming: it reported that black and white preadolescent girls were dieting at an almost identical rate (about 40 percent for both black and white girls).[18] A 1993 survey by *Essence* magazine revealed that more than half of the black women polled were at risk of developing an eating disorder.[19] Psychologist Audrey Chapman explained that body image has become a "class and generational issue. Middle-class blacks who are assimilated into the white culture—and teenagers too—want to be thin, thinner, thinnest."[20]

Compared with black males, black females growing up in inner cities are considerably less likely to get in trouble with the law, to abuse drugs, or to abandon their children. But there are troubling signs that this, too, is changing. Writer Joe Morgan points to the "exploding female prison population." He argues that we should not be surprised by this negative news: "Black girls are growing up in the same violent, materialistic, economically and spiritually impoverished environments as black boys."[21]

One of my black colleagues who conducts "empowerment and self-esteem" workshops for black girls aged twelve to eighteen reports that she sees a disturbing development in the preoccupations of the present generation of girls. Girls who came of age in the baby-boom generation supported the goals of the women's liberation movement: equal educational opportunities, equal employment opportunities, and equal pay.

Today's girls seem more interested in attaining a different sort of parity with guys. One of the most common questions girls ask her is, "Why can't we do what the boys do?" My colleague calls this "dysfunctional women's liberation." Females are interested in adopting the negative behaviors associated with males, like being "a player," dating three or four guys at the same time, and carrying on a "game," that is, convincing people to believe their lies. Mothers are increasingly dismayed to learn that their daughters are interested in adopting these disreputable attitudes and behaviors.

Girls are being pressured to become sexualized at increasingly younger ages. As the mother of a young teenager told me, her daughter and her daughter's friends' main interests seem to be dressing and "seeing how many guys they can get to like them or say they're cute." Much of this interest is normal for adolescent girls. However, the real problem is that the guys these girls are attracted to are more than ever interested in making quick scores than in becoming responsible adults. Such guys are not inclined to treat girls with the respect and kindness they deserve.

Like many parents, my friend would like her daughter to adopt "positive" role models like Maya Angelou, the author, and Susan Taylor, editor of *Essence* magazine and motivational speaker. Unfortunately, my friend complains, too often black girls choose as their role models women like the rappers Lil' Kim and Foxy Brown, who send messages that "it's OK to be tough, to wear stuff up half their butts, and to aggressively pursue boys."

Some teenage girls ignore consequences of adopting irresponsible male sexual behavior. Society still has a double standard: what is considered appropriate behavior for boys is not seen as appropriate behavior for girls. As my colleague says, "A guy can lay in the gutter, get up, brush himself off, and be a man, whereas if a girl does the same thing, people will say that she's a bitch or a slut." It is essential that girls become fully aware of the consequences of sexual behavior, one of the biggest of which is pregnancy.

Unwed pregnancy is a developmental hazard for teens. Statistics indicate that the teenage pregnancy rate for blacks, although declining in recent years, remains unacceptably high.[22] I must note that some black adult males bear equal, if not greater, responsibility for the problem. These men often prey on vulnerable, usually fatherless, girls, but they are rarely held accountable for the harm they cause to these teens' lives. I have never understood why experts label unwed teenage pregnancy a "teenage problem"; if it were addressed also as an "irresponsible adult male problem," perhaps more effective solutions would be found to deal with it.

The evidence suggests that teens who do not have educational and job opportunities are at higher risk for early pregnancy.[23] Having a child provides girls with a way to gain self-esteem when other avenues for doing so are blocked. In my own work with teenage girls, I continue to be amazed that giving birth accords many unwed teens instant social status *and* many adult privileges denied them prior to childbirth, including money of their own (thanks to welfare), freedom from curfews and other family rules, and permission to have overnight male company in their parents' homes. It is no wonder that girls who have little to begin with find motherhood so attractive.

Unless girls from economically disadvantaged backgrounds are offered substantially greater educational and employment opportunities, they will continue to be seduced by the immediate—even if temporary—boost to their self-worth that becoming a teenage mother provides. Simply reducing public assistance, as many of the welfare reform advocates prescribe, is not the answer. Economist Shelly Lundberg, author of a landmark study on premarital child rearing, observes: "The greater the person's prospects in life, the less likely she would get pregnant. But when you have no access to the labor market, no real chance of becoming productive, what you have left is bearing a child, which gives you personal satisfaction and social admiration. Cutting welfare benefits under these conditions has virtually no impact."[24]

Girls from more privileged backgrounds also face pressures to conform to cultural expectations, including becoming preoccupied with their appearance, having boyfriends, and being sexually active. Girls who are primarily interested in academic achievement and developing their other interests are made to feel out of sync with their peers. The fifteen-year-old daughter of a close friend told me, "There must be something wrong with me," since she does not have a boyfriend. She is a top student who is involved in many school and community activities, and she feels that she has a full and satisfying life. Although she has had crushes, she is not yet interested in having a steady boyfriend.

Not long after I had this conversation, a white colleague also told me that her teenage daughter felt that she and her friends were "not with it" since none of them had boyfriends. The impression many teenage girls absorb from the media is that girls their age should be "into boys," if not sexually active. But the media frequently distort reality, making attention-getting behaviors seem more prevalent than they actually are. Impressionable girls need people in their lives who can provide them with reality checks and guidance to counteract the power of the media as well as the negative influence of their peer group. Luckily, my friend's daughter has friends her age who share her values and goals. Girls who go against the cultural tide are less likely to feel alienated if they have supportive families and friends.

In general, black girls fare somewhat better than black guys in terms of the majority culture's perceptions and acceptance. Increasingly, however, they are facing many of the same stereotypes faced by black male teenagers. Nationwide efforts tend to focus on "saving" black males, "the endangered species," but it is important that people realize that black females also need to be shielded from similar perils.

"BROTHERS"

A father, speaking before President Clinton's advisory board on race in northern California, lamented, "As I watch my twelve-year-old son progress from being a cute, young black boy to an adolescent, in the eyes of many he's becoming what W.E.B. Du Bois called a 'black problem,' not for his action, but for just being black."[25]

As they leave their childhood years behind, black boys become saddled with negative stereotypes that can topple all but the psychologically strongest among them. Although they face some of the same challenges as black girls growing up in a race-conscious society, black males are pressured to conform to a more restricted image of the authentic black male.

The dominant male role model embraced by much of the youth culture is the "supermacho" male. Earning good grades, aiming for college, and having a regular job do not fit this image. Davey D. (aka Dave Cook), community action director and host of a radio program, *Street Knowledge,* in San Francisco, says that for black youth, "being black means not being intelligent, being black means wearing your pants in a baggy sort of way, having your hat on backward, acting like you're hard or ghetto."[26] He continues: "If you walk in with a suit and a tie and [have] good grades," other blacks might regard you as a "sell-out." Or as one black teen told me, "If you wear a suit, people will ask, 'Where's the funeral?'"

Teens who may personally reject the goal of becoming a supermacho male have to keep it to themselves. A fourteen-year-old from a low-income neighborhood told me that black guys at his school want to be known as the "baddest"; he would prefer to concentrate on his studies but believes that if he does, his friends won't think that he's cool and will make fun of him. Black males who express interest in earning good grades are seen as not "hard," even as "wimps," by their peers. Many teens have internalized the values perpetrated by the gangsta rap culture: you're not an authentic black if you go to school, have a job, and are faithful to your girlfriend.

For many male teens, self-esteem is related primarily to the number of their female conquests, the amount of cash they carry, and their athletic ability, particularly on the basketball court. It is no wonder that the goal of many young black males is to become either a rapper or a professional basketball player (even though there are only about 350 such players in the major leagues).

The image of black males that nonblack students have is also telling. Asked his impressions of the black males at his high school, a white student responded, "From the way they talk, most of the black guys come across as into proving they're the toughest." In the large integrated urban school he attends, there is only a handful of blacks in the college-prep classes. The white students notice that the few black guys in these classes do not conform to the image of the typical black male student in terms of manner (they tend to be more reserved), whom they associate with (their friends include students of other races), and how they dress ("They're not into designer clothes and sneakers like most of the other black guys. They're more into alternative clothes or their own thing"). However, academic advancement has a culturally imposed price: choosing not to conform to the stereotype of a black male can alienate these teens from their peers.

The journalist McCall, in his book *What's Going On,* expresses dismay that even young middle-class black males are adopting the dress, speech, and manner associated with poor blacks raised in the 'hood: he says it has become difficult to distinguish college students from thugs. "Many of them buy into the culture of obnoxiousness that is so pervasive among young blacks now." McCall blames the pervasive influence of the gangsta rap culture for imposing a "tremendous amount of peer pressure, even on young blacks who try to play it straight."[27]

Underlying black males' supermacho posture is a profound insecurity whose roots can be traced to the abuse (including lynching) black men have experienced in this society from the slave era to the present day at the hands of white males in authority, especially the police. (Consider the internationally publicized beating of Rodney King by several Los Angeles police officers.) Rather than become psychologically weakened by the negative stereotype of their race, many male teens retreat to the powerful part of their identity, their masculinity, and by so doing take on a supermacho persona in order to feel more secure.

But black male teens pay a high price for the supermacho image that some embrace and others have unfairly thrust upon them by a society that tends to simultaneously deify (consider sports legends like Michael Jordan and entertainers like Bill Cosby) and demonize black males. Black males are more likely than males of any other race to be viewed as troublemakers and to be harassed by the police. (A 1997 *Time*/CNN poll indicated that one-third of black teens feel they are treated unfairly by the police.)[28] Black males are more likely to be viewed suspiciously by people in public. For example, it is commonly known that people are more likely to cross to the other side of the street to avoid passing a group of black males (more than males of other races), and women are more likely to clutch their purses tightly in the presence of black males. As they enter their late teens and early twenties, black males are more likely than any other group to become involved in the criminal justice system (one in three young blacks is on probation, on parole, or in prison) and to die young. The suicide rate among black teens, previously low compared to that of white teens, has doubled in the past decade.[29]

Although considerable media attention is given to black teens who get in trouble, little is given to the many more black teens who lead productive lives in spite of the obstacles placed in their path. A student at a Catholic high school told me how difficult it is to live with the negative stereotype of the young black male. Like his other black schoolmates, he earns good grades and helps out in his community, but because of the color of his skin, some people mistake him for a thug. Some black teenagers see him as "selling out." But he is determined to pursue his dream of going to college. "What makes their choices better than mine?" he asks. His strength to deal with the challenges that he experiences comes from the support he receives from his parents, friends, and school.

Until society becomes a more hospitable place for black males, it is going to be difficult to induce those who find a sense of security in the image of the supermacho male to abandon their fantasy. And it is little more than an image, one reinforced by society's stereotypes and the limited choices that are available to many young blacks because of their poor educational and job opportunities. For example, a recent study showed that young black males who have jobs are no more likely to engage in violence than young white males, but the employment rate for young black males is considerably lower than that for their white peers.[30] Some of the teens I've spoken with, though they put on a good front of being supermacho, feel trapped by this persona and acknowledge that it is not really them. But peer pressure to "be cool" is so intense that it is difficult not to be swallowed up by the macho role unless the teen has a powerful counterforce, such as strong support from his family, school, or community, to enable him to resist the pull.

BEING BLACK: AN EXTRA BURDEN?

Black teens, females and males alike, should learn that there are many different ways to be black. They should not conform to the media-hyped negative image of black youth just because it seems like a "cool" thing to do. They should be allowed the freedom to be themselves. There is little doubt that the deck is stacked against black youth, especially as they enter adolescence. As one fifteen-year-old girl poignantly told me, "Until I got to high school, I didn't see any problem with who I am. But now, being black is like an extra burden. The other students expect you to choose sides. Teachers expect you to mess up and be dumb. If you're Asian or white, they think you're OK or they have to wait to figure you out. If you're black, they think they already know you. It's just not fair."

It all comes down to blacks' simply not being given the benefit of the doubt. Black youth learn that because of the color of their skin, they lug around a heavy burden of stereotypes about their intelligence, values, trustworthiness, behaviors, attitudes, and other characteristics held by people who have never even met them.

A 1997 *Time*/CNN poll indicated that 62 percent of black teens and 59 percent of white teens think racism is a "big problem."[31] Interestingly, however, when asked about its impact on their daily lives, nine out of ten black teenagers said racism had little impact (89 percent said racism was "a small problem" or "not a problem at all"). Twenty-three percent of black teenagers (compared to 16 percent of whites) said that they had been victimized because of their race. In marked contrast to their children, 53 percent of black adults say that they have experienced racial discrimination.

Perhaps the difference between teen and adult perceptions of racism can be attributed to adults' superior ability to recognize discrimination or to the fact that adults have had more years in which to experience it. Or perhaps the full brunt of racism isn't felt until adulthood, when one has to obtain a job, housing, bank loans, and so on. My impression is that the impact of racism in teens' lives is related to how they feel they are treated by their family, friends, school, and community. Teens who are fortunate enough to grow up in caring families, attend high-quality schools, and reside in supportive communities are more likely to be buffered against the impact of racism, even if they regard it as a "big problem," than those who do not have these advantages.

Black teens facing the challenges that being black presents in adolescence deal with them in various ways at different times in their personal development. William Cross, in his book *Shades of Black,* describes five stages of black identity development, the first two of which offer an understanding about how teens might negotiate what is for many of them a difficult time.[32] Teens at the first stage, which Cross describes as "pre-encounter," internalize society's messages about white superiority and black inferiority. As black teens mature and move to the second stage, "encounter," they may become militantly anti-white and pro-black. In early adulthood, blacks experience other stages as they work through issues relating to being black in a race-conscious society. By the final stage, "internalization-commitment," most blacks develop pride in their black identity and go on to build fulfilling lives in spite of the racism they continue to experience.

Parents as well as professionals who work with black teens need to understand that as teens adopt different strategies to deal with their identity issues, "acting white" at one time and becoming militantly black at another time, these behaviors are merely phases. For example, I've known teens who reject anything having to do with black stereotypes—speech, clothes, sports—and who were teased unmercifully for "acting white." I've also known young adults who went through a militantly black period when they embraced anything that was stereotypically black—fashion, speech, "attitude"—and rejected anything having to do with the "white oppressor." Years later, when I bumped into these individuals on the street in their business attire, they bore little resemblance to the person they were when they were struggling with black identity issues. So teenagers should not be demeaned or criticized for adopting different "racial" identities unless their behavior is harmful to themselves or others. With time and loving guidance, they will learn to accept themselves for who they are, racially and otherwise.

THE DILEMMA OF BIRACIAL TEENS

High school can be an especially challenging place for teens of mixed racial (black and other) ancestry. Not only are they expected to identify with black culture, but they often face intense pressure to repudiate the nonblack part of their identity. Tiger Woods, the golf champion, calls himself a "Cablinasian," a term that encompasses his complex racial heritage—Caucasian, black, Indian, and Asian. He is frustrated by people who insist that he identify himself as black: "My mother is from Thailand. My father is part black, Chinese and American Indian. So I'm all those. It's an injustice to all my heritages to single me out as black."[33] Some people interpret his refusal to identify as black as a rejection of black identity. Thais, unburdened by America's racial history, see it quite differently.

Most studies show that biracial teens have healthy self-concepts. For example, a study of biracial teens in San Francisco found that the majority of them had high self-esteem and were comfortable with their biracial identity.[34] Another study showed that contrary to popular perceptions, the vast majority of the biracial children did not see themselves as "marginal" but well anchored in their biracial identity.[35] However, many biracial teens have difficulties dealing with other people's need to define them racially.[36]

Popular singer Mariah Carey is the daughter of a black father of Venezuelan ancestry and an Irish-American mother. Her parents separated when she was very young. Like Tiger Woods, she faced problems from her peers because of her heritage. She has described her experience as "a very alienating thing for me. . . . It was hard growing up like that. But lucky for me, my mother never said anything negative about my father. She never discouraged me from having a good feeling about him. She always taught me to believe in myself, to love all the things I am."[37]

Carey said that she felt pressure growing up from people who insisted that she should identify as black: "I am very much aware of my black heritage, but I'm also aware of the other elements of who I am. And I think sometimes it bothers people that I don't say 'I'm Black.' . . . I have a mother who is 100 percent Irish who raised me from my birth and who is my best friend. So if I were to say that I'm Black only, that would be negating everything she is. So when people ask, I say I'm Black, Venezuelan and Irish, because that's what I am."[38]

I know a biracial (black and white) high school student who heard his black teacher criticize Carey for refusing to identify herself as black. He was concerned about the teacher's attitude toward Carey because he, like Carey, identified himself as biracial. He was bothered by people like his teacher who present only one side of biracial people: "They get mad at us for not calling ourselves black. But they forget to mention we don't call ourselves white either." He is uncomfortable with the demand of his peers, and society in general, that people like himself *must* choose sides.

However biracial teens choose to identify themselves, whether as biracial, black, or something else, it is crucial that they have the support of family and friends who accept them for who they are rather than who they would like them to be. Actress Halle Berry said of her mother, "The great thing about my mother is that even though she was white, she was really concerned about what would happen as I grew up as a black woman in this country, [and] she taught me a lot about where I came from and how to deal with racism. . . . Don't get mad about it, don't get militant about it, but make quiet change, you know. Live a good life and work hard at whatever you decide to do. And that's the best revenge, to succeed in a country where maybe people don't want to see us as a race succeed."[39]

People who claim to abhor racism play right into racists' propaganda when they insist that a drop of black blood makes a person black. This notion is inconsistent with the laws of genetics but consistent with old southern racist attitudes. In 1997, the federal government passed legislation allowing people for the first time in this country's history to indicate all their racial heritages on the census and other government forms. In a country that has for too long distorted and covered up issues relating to race, this legislation represents a refreshing move toward honesty. Some special interest groups, especially those that represent various racial minorities, fear that this change will dilute their political power, but in the long run such a change may prove healthier for the country. It may enable people to appreciate the fact that racial identity is more complicated than we have been led to believe. Most biologists say that race is biologically a "meaningless category." The

American Anthropological Association stated that "the concept of race is a social and cultural construction. . . . Race simply cannot be tested or proven scientifically."[40] Perhaps the change toward recognition of multiple ethnic backgrounds will hasten the healing of the animosity that often exists between blacks and whites. Perhaps we will all come to appreciate how intertwined our racial heritage—and our cultural destiny—really is.

~

A 1997 *Time*/CNN poll found that for black and white teens, "race is less important to them, both on a personal level and as a social divide, than it is for adults." The high school years offer a wonderful opportunity to harness the energies and imagination of teens to fight the racism that has for too long plagued our country. In the next chapter, we look at what parents, teachers, and school administrators can do to ensure that their students' generally more enlightened attitudes toward race prevail over the prejudices of their forebears.

CHAPTER ELEVEN

A Healthy High School Experience

You Can Make a Difference

There are many things parents and teachers can do to foster healthy development during high school. This chapter first discusses the academic challenges black teenagers face and then looks at ways parents can support their children's well-being, education, and development of positive racial attitudes. The chapter closes with suggestions for teachers and administrators to promote racial harmony in school.

HAVE PUBLIC HIGH SCHOOLS WRITTEN OFF BLACKS?

Many of the blacks I've talked with, students as well as parents and teachers, don't think that the average black student has much chance of receiving a decent education in most public high schools. Some students tell me that high school has become more a place to socialize than to get an education. One black student (who attends a parochial high school) opined that many blacks who attend the public high school in his area don't go to school to learn but "to kick it" (hang out) and "to be seen."

White students in the public high schools echo this view. They don't seem to regard blacks as serious students, perhaps because they are more likely to see them on sports teams than in their classes. Many whites—even some who are poor students themselves—believe that blacks are generally more interested in dressing well and socializing than in academic achievement.

The poor-quality schooling, low teachers' expectations, and school safety problems that black students face in the lower grades become magnified in high school. If a student has not acquired the academic skills and behavioral habits necessary for school success by the time he reaches high school, it is difficult, though not impossible, for him to chart a different academic course. The first day they enter high school, students are generally aware of their class assignments, supposedly based on their academic performance at their former schools. It is usually difficult for students to change classes, much less the ability level to which they are assigned (for example, honors, college preparatory, standard, basic, remedial). In too many schools, most black students are relegated to the lower academic tracks, even if they are more qualified than students of other races in higher tracks.

Brandon, a black high school student who unsuccessfully tried to enroll in classes at the highest ability level, puts it this way: "Once they [school officials] have you labeled, it's for keeps." Brandon lives in a very liberal northern California community and attends the same highly regarded, racially integrated school that his father attended. He notes that whites and Asians are usually in the honors or "regular" classes while blacks and Latinos are usually in the basic or remedial classes. Brandon's mother said that his school has changed little since his father's time: "It's basically two separate schools."

Brandon's mother acknowledges that students from more educated and economically privileged families are more likely to qualify for the honors classes. But she believes that race plays a major role in students' assignment to classes. Brandon's family is middle-class and well educated, with strong roots in the community. Brandon's father administers educational programs (including after-school tutorial classes) for minority students. Despite these advantages, Brandon feels that the academic deck is stacked against him because of his race. For example, he told me that in most of his classes (in the "regular" track), teachers usually "teach to" the whites and Asians. Teachers expect much less of blacks and Latinos than they do of students of other races. As Brandon puts it, "If African-American students ask a question, the teacher says they're disrupting the class, but if white students ask a question, it's because they're trying to learn."

Although Brandon is an articulate and intelligent teen, he has found it hard to overcome some teachers' preconceived notion that he's just another "dumb black student." The negative perceptions and expectations of teachers he observes are common obstacles that can derail the educational progress of students unless they have strong support from parents or other advocates.

Mrs. Richards, a college-educated black who works for the school system, told me that she was dismayed when she learned that her daughter, Vanessa, was not recommended to take algebra despite earning an A in her previous math class and a high score on the standardized math test. Mrs. Richards knew that if her daughter didn't take algebra and subsequent math courses, it would be very difficult for her to be accepted by the college of her choice.

Mrs. Richards asked Vanessa's teacher why her daughter wasn't recommended for algebra. The teacher explained that Vanessa's class participation was poor and said that she didn't think that Vanessa was "interested" in taking algebra. She told Mrs. Richards that if she had a problem with that decision, she should take her complaint to Vanessa's school counselor, which is exactly what Mrs. Richards did. After reviewing Vanessa's grades and standardized test scores, the counselor overruled the teacher and transferred Vanessa to algebra. Had Mrs. Richards not been a persistent and informed advocate for her daughter, her academic future would have been jeopardized.

If Brandon's and Vanessa's parents, with all their knowledge and resources, had difficulty getting their children into the appropriate classes in high school, what hope have less advantaged parents of securing a quality education for their children?

The superintendent of schools in Oakland, California, has observed that students who have advocates, usually parents who are skilled at dealing with the system, are more likely to be successful in school. Some black parents do not know how to recognize when their children are being shortchanged by the schools, much less what questions to ask or where to go for redress when their children are not receiving the education to which they are entitled. The superintendent has added child and family advocates to her staff to provide parents with expertise and support to enable them to counter the biases of the system so that their children can obtain the education they deserve.

Although there are some black students who enjoy the support of their school and experience academic success, too many others are allowed to drift. Parents and other caregivers must take an active role to ensure that their children are pointed in the right educational direction.

But it would be misleading to blame only the schools for the poor educational progress of some black teens. Students' own involvement in a youth culture that looks down on school success as well as some parents' lack of involvement in their children's schools also contribute to poor academic achievement. Children who feel emotionally nourished in their families are likely to have a better chance of doing well in school.

A recent groundbreaking study reported in the *Journal of the American Medical Association* indicated that contrary to the conventional wisdom, parents rather than peers have the most powerful influence on their children throughout the high school years.[1] Teens who feel loved, understood, and paid attention to by their parents are more likely to avoid risky behaviors like substance abuse, premarital sex, or violence. The study found that parents' positive expectations influenced their teens' behavior "powerfully" through the twelfth grade regardless of race, family income, or number of parents in the home. J. Richard Udry, the leader of the study, said, "Many people think of adolescence as a stage where there is so much peer influence that parents become both irrelevant and powerless. It's not so."[2] Black parents have more influence than they acknowledge in preventing their children from succumbing to the peer pressure of the youth culture.[3]

✷ WHAT PARENTS CAN DO TO RAISE HEALTHY TEENS

Be positive role models. If you want your teen to engage in positive behaviors, you have to set a good example. The values your children acquire are likely to be the ones they learn from observing you. They'll do as you do, not as you say to do. Walk the walk and save the talk.

Cultivate a caring relationship with your teens. They need you to be affectionate and to provide positive strokes just as much as when they were younger.

Have positive expectations concerning your teens' behavior. Unless they habitually give you cause, don't expect them to "mess up." Let your teens know specifically what kinds of behaviors you expect from them (like doing well in school, reaching for their goals, and avoiding premarital sex, drug use, and violence), and expect them to honor your wishes.

Be available for them. Your children should know that you are there for them when they need you. You may not be on the spot when they return from school, but it is important for them to know that there will be some time each day when you are available to listen to them and talk with them.

Provide supervision. Studies show that at least half of all juvenile crimes take place between the time school lets out and the time parents return home from work.[1] Teens should not be left to their own devices after school. If possible they should be involved in supervised activities with adults who are well trained to work with and discipline teens. To keep them busy when they do not have after-school activities, sit down with them and draw up a daily plan of activities (including homework and household chores) for them to do once they arrive home from school. Check daily to see that these activities are completed.

Keep them busy. They should be involved in as many extracurricular and community activities as they can manage without feeling stressed out. The busier they are, the less likely they are to succumb to the negative influences of peers who have too much idle time.

Encourage their spiritual growth. Whether you are members of an organized religion or simply believe in a divine being, having faith in a higher power gives meaning and purpose to teens' lives and provides an emotional shield few other alternatives offer. A major strength of black communities is local churches that encourage their members to keep this earthly life in perspective and to experience joys that are beyond anything that material comfort can provide.

~

Teens who grow up in nurturing families are more likely to be able to focus on doing well in school. The following is a list of things parents can do to support their teens' efforts to do well in school.

✱ HOW PARENTS CAN INCREASE THEIR CHILD'S CHANCES OF SUCCESS IN HIGH SCHOOL

Start preparing your child now to qualify for high school classes. Often school counselors are overwhelmed and are unable to give students the attention they need in choosing courses to qualify for the track they want to follow in high school. Network with parents of older students and the students themselves for information about your child's prospective high school's academic requirements and opportunities. By the sixth grade, you should know what math, language, and other courses your child needs. If her school doesn't offer them, make sure she gets them somewhere else—for example, at summer school.

Set high academic standards and help your teen meet them. Let your teen know that it is important to you that he earn good grades. Do all you can to support him in his efforts to achieve good grades.

Insist that your teen does her part. Students who regularly attend and participate in classes and who complete their homework assignments on time show teachers that they are sufficiently interested in their education to merit extra attention.

Do not burden teens with excessive family responsibilities. Some teens have told me that their parents expect them to do so many chores that they have little time to complete their homework and pursue their own interests. Parents who are burdened with financial and other obligations should be careful not to overwhelm their teens with too many demands that interfere with their homework. For example, they shouldn't expect older children to be full-time baby-sitters for their younger brothers and sisters. Remember: your teens are not their younger siblings' parents, and they should not be expected, except under the direst of circumstances, to take on the responsibilities of adulthood before their time.

Provide teens with a quiet and undisturbed place to study. Many homes are dens of distraction, with television or radio blaring and people wandering in and out. Teens who share bedrooms with brothers and sisters may be unable to retreat there to do their work uninterrupted. If you want your teens to do their homework well and study regularly, you'll need to support their efforts to do so. Make sure they have a set time and place to work, undisturbed by radio, television, or conversation. This sounds simple, but often it involves the cooperation of the whole family.

Encourage your teen to join a study group. A University of California study found that a major difference between college students who achieve high grades and those who did not was whether they participated in a study group.[5] The study also found that black students who did not do well academically were less likely than high-achieving students to be members of study groups. I've noticed that students who earn top grades in high school tend to work (on the phone or in person) with one or more of their classmates. So encourage your teen to do so, particularly in challenging courses.

Get your teen a tutor if your child is experiencing academic problems. Students who are trying hard but are still having difficulty with their schoolwork should obtain tutoring *as early as possible.* Make sure that the tutor understands and addresses your teen's specific academic problems. If you are unable to afford tutorial services, inquire whether your school district offers free or subsidized tutoring and mentoring services.

Be persistent. If your child qualifies for the courses in high school she needs to be eligible for a good college, make sure she gets into them. Don't take any excuses from teachers or school officials. Carry your case right up to the superintendent of schools, or even further, if you have to. Advocate for school reform.

Find a parents' advocate. If you don't know what questions to ask, whom to go to with specific complaints, or how to deal with the school bureaucracy, find someone (a relative, a friend, another parent, a paid advocate) who has the expertise to help you.

Make sure that your teen receives sound advice about college applications. The time for your child to start preparing for life after high school is when he starts high school. Overwhelmed counselors are too frequently unable, or unwilling, to provide the push some black students need before they will start to think about applying to college. So it is important that you encourage him yourself. Aliona Gibson, author of *Nappy: Growing Up Black and Female in America*, notes that none of her counselors encouraged her to go to college; they didn't think she was "college material." And yet Gibson graduated from the highly challenging, academically prestigious University of California at Berkeley. Gibson doesn't think the situation has changed since she was in high school: "It scares me because I think that there are kids just like me who won't get the encouragement [they need]."[6]

Help your child find a mentor. Some students do not have parents or other caretakers who have the time to support them actively in pursuing their educational goals. Such students can benefit enormously from having someone with whom they can regularly discuss school issues and who can encourage them when they are experiencing school problems. If there are no mentoring organizations in your area (or if there is a long waiting list, which is quite common), encourage your teen to ask someone he knows to be his mentor. Good candidates include an adult friend of the family, a librarian, a church member, a former teacher, or a retired professional. Many people welcome the opportunity to help a motivated young person reach for his dreams.

If all else fails, get tough. If you've tried everything and you still can't get your child the classes he needs, complain to the federal Office of Civil Rights. You could also consult organizations like the NAACP or the American Civil Liberties Union (ACLU) to assist you and other parents in filing a class action suit against your school district to compel it to improve the quality of the education at your child's school.

SUGGESTIONS FOR PARENTS ON HANDLING RACISM

I am pleased God has made my skin black; I just wish He made it thicker.[7]

—CURT FLOOD, EX-PROFESSIONAL BASEBALL PLAYER

How your teens view the role of race in their life depends a lot on you. They model their attitudes and behavior after yours. If you use race as a crutch for problems in your life, they will be inclined to do the same. Seeing themselves as victims of a racist society can become a lifelong habit.

Consider the case of Colin Ferguson, a black man who blamed all of his misfortunes on racism. In 1993, he randomly shot and killed several whites on a New York train. Ferguson had frequently complained to his black landlord that whites were the cause of his failures. But the landlord had a different perspective. "All black people are discriminated against. . . . Ask anyone and they'll tell you stories that would curl your hair. But you can't take everything in life and say it is the product of racism."[8]

Although Ferguson's case is extreme, some black people blame poor grades, low-paying jobs, difficult relationships, and other problems on racism. It's not always so. Encourage your teens to make sure they are doing all they can to uncover the true cause of their problems before blaming them on racism.

It is important to distinguish real from imagined racism. Wise parents teach their children to be careful not to interpret every slight as racist and to effectively handle actual racism in a manner that does not drag them down to the level of the bigots.

But other parents would be better off learning from their children. Consider the case of Venus Williams, the black tennis champion. She collided with another tennis player, a white, on a changeover during their game. Venus's father said that the incident was racially motivated. He called the other player a "big, tall white turkey." In contrast to her father, Venus "shrugged off the confrontation . . . [saying,] 'I thought we both weren't looking. . . .

It's not a big thing to me.'" Her father, his daughter's coach and manager, said that the tennis player who collided with Venus was lucky it was not his younger daughter, also a professional tennis player: "She would have been decked."[9] Now what would Venus have gained by "decking" the other player?

Parents who encourage their children to return what they perceive as racism with racism, and violence with violence, do them inestimable harm. The momentary satisfaction they may gain in besting their adversary may not be worth the risks to themselves or the cost to their dignity.

Handling racism is a challenge. The following list of suggestions will help your children respond to it constructively.

✷ CONSTRUCTIVE WAYS TO HANDLE RACISM

Ignore it. When someone is intent on causing a stir, few things are more infuriating than being ignored.

Use humor. Nothing takes the bite out an offensive remark better than humor. Told that her hair looked "puffy" by a white classmate, a black girl responded, "Yeah, I overdid it with the helium this morning."

Prepare a clever comeback. One girl told me that when a guy called her a name, she responded, "Thank you for sharing." A boy teased by a classmate for being dark responded, "The blacker the berry, the sweeter the juice." Such comebacks rob annoying little yappers of their bite.

Defuse the situation with a conciliatory response. The biblical advice "A soft answer turneth away wrath" is worth remembering. Countering an annoying or mean remark with a gentle response can be disarming.

Channel anger constructively. The best way to combat bigots is to invest the energy you could use to get back at them to do something that makes you feel good. Dancing to a bigot's tune is a waste of time.

Complain effectively when an annoyance becomes a major problem. Teens should learn how to complain effectively—in person, on the phone, or by letter—about anyone who discriminates against or harasses them. I've seen people who respond to rude behavior by angrily "telling off" the culprits in public. All this does is draw more attention to their own disrespectful behavior rather than direct attention toward the racists. It is human to become angry with offensive people, but don't whine, scream, or yell. It is important to stay in control of your temper if you want to achieve a just resolution to problems caused by bigots. *Keep the focus on the perpetrator's offense,* not on your behavior. (There are books available on how to complain effectively.)

Avoid verbal and physical confrontations whenever possible. A wise saying points out that "you can't throw mud without some ending up on you." If someone hurls racial epithets at you and you do the same to them, the other guy has won. He's brought you down to his loathsome level. Physical action should be considered only as a last resort. If you feel physically threatened, call the police.

Think before reacting to bigots' words and behaviors. After a provocation, teens should ask themselves the following questions:

Am I certain this is an instance of racism? Give others the benefit of the doubt. People who act positively are more likely to be treated positively by others, even those who may have ill intent.

Is the offense worthy of a response? How important is the grievance? If it's not a big deal, let it go. It doesn't mean you're not tough enough to handle the situation. Rather, you're not stupid enough to let bigots decide when you get mad or lose control. Remember, choose your own battles; don't let others choose them for you.

What is my role in the racial confrontation? Some people are quick to interpret other people's insensitive or rude behavior as racism, but these same people often don't see how they themselves contributed to the confrontation. If you want respect yourself, it is important to give it to others. Even when confronted with racism, it is best to act to deescalate the situation.

What is my goal? Safety should be a foremost consideration. Do not get sucked into a confrontation to satisfy a racist's perverse need to prove who is better, stronger, or whatever.

What is the most effective strategy to handle the situation? Often it is far more effective if someone in authority—a schoolteacher, a principal, a store manager, or if necessary the police—handles a racist's behavior.

Are the consequences worth the hassle? Some people feel it is their right to retaliate forcefully against racists who pick on them. But retaliation can come at a high price. Taking on more problems just for the momentary satisfaction of getting back at a racist is not worth the effort. Remember, living well is the best revenge.

PLAYING THE RACE GAME IN HIGH SCHOOL

Besides parents, high schools play an important role in helping teens cope in a race-conscious society. Since teens are more likely to experience racial antagonism in high school than at any previous time in their schooling, it is important that their schools be prepared to handle conflicts between students of different races and ethnicities.

Often teachers and school officials are not prepared to deal with bullies or opportunistic students who initiate conflicts with students of another race. Many students tell me that bullies often get away with their behavior because their victims are afraid to report them. Often intimidated students believe they will have more problems if they report them. Bullies are unlikely to be given more than a slap on the wrist anyway. These problems abound whether or not the victims are of a different race.

Conflicts between students of different races may be minor skirmishes involving teasing and taunting or silly but harmful pranks like displaying hooded dolls, nasty graffiti on hallway and restrooms walls, and inserting racist words or codes in yearbooks. When students assault each other, it can escalate to major violence. Many of the conflicts that have attracted national attention started out as a conflict between two individuals or a small group of students, usually males, of different races. The conflicts are often engendered by minor personal irritations rather than anything racial. However, when such conflicts occur, they can quickly erupt into major crises if school officials are unprepared and unskilled in handling them. Students of different races take sides in the wake of negative rumors and growing publicity.

For example, consider the conflict that arose in the fall of 1997 at northern California's Carlmont High School, the model for the racially tense school in the movie *Dangerous Minds.* The student population is almost equally divided between whites and minorities (30 percent of whom are bused in from a nearby low-income community).

Although there had been several racial conflicts during the initial phase of busing when whites protested the admittance of minorities to their schools, such conflicts had diminished in recent years. Racial tensions erupted when a white student discovered his car broken into and his stereo stolen. His friends retaliated by breaking the headlights of a Latino student's car though there was no evidence that a Latino was responsible for the theft. The conflict spread when racist graffiti (containing racial slurs against minorities) was sprawled on school buildings, minority students were harassed on campus, and a group of white students taunted and teased minority students when they were returning to their neighborhood on the school bus. Black students were drawn into the conflict when they were also teased and harassed by whites.

Carlmont's principal said, "We can't pretend racism doesn't exist or isn't a concern in kids' minds. Maybe this will give us an opportunity to deal with an issue that not only the schools, but all of society is constantly dealing with."[10]

Unfortunately, Carlmont's reaction is typical of that of many other schools. School officials wait until an incident erupts before dealing with the racial tensions that are simmering just below the surface of their students' school days. Then they deal with the conflicts only in a superficial manner. As discussed earlier in this book, most teachers and administrators are not trained to manage students' ordinary behavioral problems, much less ones that have the added inflammatory power of race. Like many student perpetrators at other schools, the Carlmont students who triggered the conflict seemed to have received relatively mild discipline, given the gravity of their offenses: at least a dozen students were given one-day at-home suspensions. Most of the estimated sixty students who were involved in the name-calling received even milder discipline. Some of the black students believed that the school's response should have been firmer. As one black student said, "I feel we need an apology. We didn't write anything on the walls about them."[11]

It is distressing how unprepared many school officials are to deal with conflicts between students of different races. From the stories I hear and read about, it seems that most students who instigate conflicts with students of a different race receive little more than a slap on the wrist.

During the much publicized struggle to desegregate the schools in the civil rights era, black students were subjected to teasing, taunts, and even physical assaults by white students and their families who did not welcome them at their schools.

REVERSE RACISM IS NOT THE ANSWER

Sadly, some black youths have learned these racist lessons well. Some of them pick on other students simply because they are of a different race. I have heard of several stories of white students who were intentionally bumped into in school hallways, teased, and subjected to other intimidating behaviors. White teachers, too, are not exempt from such insults. I recently heard of a white teacher who was sitting in a classroom talking to a student when an object was thrown at her, hitting her feet. She flinched but did not report the black male student whom she saw fleeing the scene.

Some black students who protest the loudest about white racism are blind to their own racism. Black racists are just as loathsome as white racists. Despite what some people say—that blacks can't be racist because they don't have power—black youth who believe that it is their right to be offensive or abusive to a person because of their race or ethnicity are indeed racists. The ability to intimidate and cause another person pain is power.

Some people wonder whether black youths, in their anger at the historical abuse of their race, have become unsympathetic to the suffering of other historically persecuted groups. For example, a few years ago, there was a public outcry when it was reported that black high school students, on a field trip to view the film *Schindler's List,* disturbed the theater audience when they erupted in laughter at the depiction of Jews, including young children, being tortured and killed by their Nazi tormentors.[12] In the aftermath of the publicity the situation generated, the film's director, Steven Spielberg, visited the Oakland, California, high school and discussed the situation with the students, who said that their reactions to the film had been distorted.

Recently I heard of a similar reaction to the viewing of *Schindler's List* in an integrated high school class, also in northern California. Students viewed the film in several installments over a week. At the initial showing, some of the black students in the class laughed during the scenes of the torture of the Jews. Protest from a few white students who made comments like "It wasn't funny" were drowned out by the laughter of these students. Fortunately, the film was shown over several days, and with each passing day, students' criticism of these students' laughter became bolder. On the final day, it disappeared altogether after two black students, who had not participated in the laughter, loudly criticized the laughing students.

The student who told me about this incident said it was one of the most dramatic transformations he had ever seen. The laughing students who were silenced by the black students ceased being disruptive and gave their full attention to the film. By its conclusion, they seemed genuinely distressed by the suffering depicted in the film. My sense is that these students got permission from other blacks to drop the facade of indifference at the suffering of people of another race. They showed their heartfelt empathy for others when they believed they no longer had to conceal their true feelings with laughter in a misguided effort to appear "cool."

White racism cannot be effectively fought with black racism. That simply pulls blacks down to the same level as racist whites. Writer Carlos Fuentes said, "We only hurt others when we're incapable of imagining them. I believe cruelty is the inability to assign the same feelings and values to another person that you harbor in yourself. All of those figures in Hitler's regime were kind to their wives and children, but then they were able to turn around and kill children because they were Jewish."[13]

At some schools, racial separatism is less a product of students' choice than one of tradition. In extreme cases, the school administration arranges things so that students not only attend different classes but also have different social functions, including proms. Some students even attend separate graduation ceremonies.

At Randolph County High School in Wedowee, Alabama, the principal canceled the prom after he learned that many students planned to attend it with a date of a different race. (Many of the students admitted that they told the principal this just to see his reaction.) The same principal called a biracial student, who later sued him, a "mistake."[14] How are students of different races expected to get along when their principal sets such a poor example?

In 1990, at Pear County High School in Fort Vasely, Georgia, after years of being denied requests that the school change its policy of holding separate proms for blacks and whites, students (with the help of some parents) finally obtained permission to attend the same prom. A white parent admitted that there was "fear of the unknown, and even a deeper fear of that unexpressed sexual thing." But the students did not see things the way the adults did. As one student said, "The way we saw it, it was not a black and white thing with us. We just wanted to have our prom together. Now we really are proud, we've changed tradition."[15]

High school offers a golden opportunity to deal head on with the issue of racism in this society. But too many schools squander this opportunity. Developmental psychologist Jean Piaget characterized this stage of a person's life, ages twelve to eighteen, as "formal operations," a time when students are capable of abstract thinking and envisioning possibilities not limited by the present state of the world.[16] Teens can begin to see the world not as it is but the way they would like it to be. It is not surprising that it was young people, both black and white, who were at the forefront of the struggle for civil rights in the 1960s and 1970s. Many older blacks had been psychologically beaten into submission by years of oppression. Older whites were accustomed to a tradition of racial complacency. It was the youth who could most plainly envision a future that was free of racial strife.

Perhaps the promise of youth is best embodied by black teenager Keisha Thomas, who a few years ago shielded a white man who was being viciously beaten by blacks.[17] They had mistaken him for a member of the Ku Klux Klan, who were marching in the vicinity, because of the color of his skin. By throwing herself between him and the blows of his attackers, this heroine was proclaiming that he was a human being deserving of kindness regardless of the color of his skin. The energies and imagination of this stage can be marshaled to promote racial evil, as in the case of organizations like the skinheads and Aryan Youth, or to promote racial harmony, as is the case of dozens of student organizations across this country that are dedicated to racial understanding.

The following are some suggestions for promoting racial harmony in high school.

WHAT HIGH SCHOOLS CAN DO TO PROMOTE RACIAL HARMONY

Two of the most typical ways schools have promoted racial harmony are by offering lessons in black history during Black History Month and by offering workshops in cultural sensitivity, or what is called "diversity training." But as Cynthia Tucker, editorial writer for the *Atlanta Constitution,* points out, teaching black history separately marginalizes it. Tucker argues that black history "should be woven intricately into American history. Anything else reduces American history to myth."[18]

Diversity training tends to deal superficially with the major issues that divide students along racial and ethnic lines. Too often, diversity training emphasizes racial and ethnic groups' differences rather than the commonalities that unite them. Frequently, such training focuses on the *anger* blacks (and other minorities) feel about being victimized and the *guilt* whites feel about the privilege they have because of their race. But students need to be taught how to manage rather than inflame these emotions so that they can improve race relations in their high school and in society at large.

Black students need to learn strategies to channel their anger into obtaining a good education in high school and pursuing their options beyond high school. Holding white students accountable for the racism of previous generations of slaveholders and other oppressors when many (if not most) of these white students are descended from immigrants who came to the United States after the Civil War is counterproductive. White students who believe they have done nothing to feel guilty about can understandably become resentful of blacks and less inclined to see the role they may play in perpetuating a race-conscious society.

It is infinitely more productive for high schools to foster an atmosphere in which all students are expected to get along and to teach them ways they can contribute to making society a more hospitable place for all its citizens. Schools should substitute "human sensitivity workshops" for "cultural sensitivity workshops" and "humanity training" for "diversity training."

✱ SUGGESTIONS FOR FOSTERING INTERRACIAL HARMONY

Promote human sensitivity. Encourage students to treat each other with respect and kindness. Students should be taught that their feelings about other students and faculty are their own affair, but they are required to talk and behave respectfully toward others whether they like them or not.

Students should be required to sign a contract indicating their agreement to abide by their school's rules of behavior (as detailed in their student handbook). Consequences for violating these rules should be enforced swiftly and fairly.

Let students get to know each other in natural settings. Schools that genuinely seek to foster racial harmony should invest more in extracurricular activities like bands, newspapers, glee clubs, talent shows, dances, and sport teams (ones that allow students with varying abilities to participate rather than just the best athletes). By participating together in such activities, students learn to know one another as people, not as members of a racial group.

Expose the common myths about the races. It is important that students be provided with information that debunks the stereotypes about blacks and other minorities, including those related to intelligence, social behavior, and class status. I have known whites who were astonished to learn that most black Americans are not poor, that two-thirds of blacks are working class or middle class, that most drug addicts are not black, and that blacks are not the major cause of violence in this society (a sociologist suggests that the United States would still be the most violent county among developed countries even if all blacks were to move elsewhere).[19] Myths fuel racist ideology. To be informed citizens, students need to know the facts before they complete high school.

Conduct class discussions on the exploitation of racial and ethnic differences in various countries. Examine how the racist strategy has been used to polarize and exploit people by power seekers around the world. The underlying point is that no racial or ethnic group has a monopoly on virtue or vice—all groups have oppressed other groups to achieve their selfish ends, some more successfully than others.

Teach students to think critically about information they receive about different races. Encourage students to question the negative information they have learned about different races. Assign readings from James Loewen's excellent book *Lies My Teacher Told Me.*[20] It shows how traditional history has provided a distorted picture of blacks and other minorities.

Appoint students to a conflict resolution team or student court. Every school should have a conflict resolution team or student court where students are encouraged to resolve their own conflicts. All students should be required to serve on this team or court.

Encourage students to generate strategies to respond to racism. Many people are uncomfortable listening to negative racial stereotypes or ethnic jokes but, as one white person wrote to a newspaper, they "go along to get along." Studies show that if only one person in a group dissents, even mildly, to the negative words or behavior of other members of the group, it emboldens others in the group to express their disagreement.[21] Let students know that they have a responsibility to combat racism in their everyday lives. As British statesman Edmund Burke said: "The only thing necessary for evil to triumph is for good men to do nothing."

✱ HOW TO RESOLVE "RACIAL" CONFLICTS AMONG STUDENTS

Implement procedures for defusing racial conflicts. Schools that are skilled at managing students' conflicts in general are better able to manage racial conflicts. Often a conflict is tagged "racial" only because it involves students of different races. It is important to prevent racial incidents before they occur and to intervene quickly in those that do erupt to prevent them from becoming full-blown racial conflicts. Too many schools wait until a crisis occurs before developing a procedure to deal with students who stir up racial trouble. Have one in place *before* problems arise:

Establish rules for dealing with student conflicts, regardless of the race or ethnicity of the students involved.

Implement all rules fairly and consistently without regard for a student's race, ethnicity, or social class.

Closely monitor students who are intent on fomenting trouble between racial groups.

Make the "punishment" fit the "crime." Often school officials are too lenient with offending students. Students who deface school property (for example, yearbooks damaged by racial epithets) should be required to give restitution or to clean up racist graffiti. In-school suspensions that require students to work with a counselor on addressing their racist behavior are preferable to out-of-school suspensions that some students view merely as vacation time.

Learn from experience—your own and that of other schools. Racist students are often troubled individuals who act out their racism in predictable ways, for example, by being verbally abusive, using the printed word (for example, newspapers, yearbooks, flyers, posters, graffiti on buildings) for racist ends, or initiating cowardly, childish pranks (for example, displaying black dolls with their heads in nooses). Some students are bolder and will physically attack their victims. Develop strategies to deal with the common ways students choose to express racism. Refine your strategies with experience.

Be careful about talking to the media. The media can blow an initially minor conflict way out of proportion, leading to an escalation of racial tensions in the school and the greater community. Some school officials and students say things in front of the camera that they wouldn't ordinarily say. In March 1998, a minor conflict between black and Latino students in California's Hayward

High School's parking lot blew up into three days of racial unrest at the school. Some school officials and students became angry at the media; they claimed that the racial tensions were fanned by the sensational stories created by the media when it descended on the school. A student reacted cynically to the sudden media attention: "I think it's a waste of time. I think it's stupid. They're just trying to make our school look bad. There's a mural in the library [about racial harmony] we've been working on for two years. We've been asking the news [media] to come, but they won't come out, and then there's a stupid little fight and they're out here an hour later. . . . We get all the recognition for the bad stuff that goes on here and nothing for the good stuff."[22]

Growing up happy and healthy in our society is a challenge for any child, but it can be especially tough for the black and biracial child. As they leave what for many of them is the more sheltered world of childhood and encounter the demands of adolescence, they become increasingly aware of a world that values them less than their fairer-skinned peers.

Learning to deal with this knowledge can make or break them. Families and schools can do much to strengthen children to face the challenges they are likely to encounter because of their race. Children need to know that they do not have to conform to stereotypes to prove their racial authenticity. They can strive to do well in school and still be black; they can be friends with students of other races and still hold on to their racial identity; they can dream different dreams and still be authentically themselves. Encouraging children to expand their horizons, and by so doing transcend the limitations of racism . . . that's what will make for a better world.

Epilogue

. . . and a little child shall lead them.
—Isaiah 11:6

As children grow up, we expect them to increase in wisdom. For most of us in most things this is true, but not in matters of race. Working on this book has taught me that in dealing with race, children are generally wiser than adults. Young children are developmentally inclined to treat people based on their character, as revealed by their actions, rather than on the color of their skin. As they grow older, this wonderful quality is lost to many of them as they learn some of the racial bigotry of previous generations.

My six-year-old son right now is quite sensible about skin color. He seldom refers to people by their color and treats people as he finds them. It's a joy to see how his interactions with different people are untainted by racial stereotypes. How I wish he could hold on to his racial innocence—but it will be difficult to do so growing up in our race-conscious society.

My teenage daughter remembers how once she was as oblivious to race as her younger brother, but by high school, she had become aware of the tyranny of racial typecasting. The other day, she mused, "I wonder what would happen if children were brought up without being told about all that old racial stuff." She sees the absurdity of our country's obsession with race, but she would admit that she has to be vigilant not to let race influence her own perceptions of different people.

Her attitude gives me hope. We are not able to prevent her from being affected by racism, given its prevalence in this society, but her father and I try not to pass on color prejudices and racism to our children. She was raised to see racial diversity as an asset—as she says, "It makes people more interesting"—rather than something to bemoan. As she grows older, she will need to remain anchored in her beliefs to withstand the negative messages that society sends about blacks and other minorities. With the appropriate guidance, all children can learn to question and reject toxic messages that for too long have helped perpetuate deep color and racial divisions in our country.

This book's main goal has been to guide parents, educators, and others in raising emotionally healthy black and biracial children. A major point of *I'm Chocolate, You're Vanilla* is that young children who feel negative about their color are most likely to have been adversely influenced by people close to them. Young children are *not* naturally inclined to feel negative about their race. Indeed, in their early childhood, they are developmentally incapable of grasping the idea of race at all. Given proper nurturance, young children—the irrepressible egocentric characters that they are—are naturally predisposed to like themselves.

The burden of white racism is with us still. But some blacks do not realize that they help perpetuate this burden by repeating, often unconsciously, the color prejudices passed down from the slavery era. As Aliona Gibson writes in *Nappy: Growing Up Black and Female in America,* "A lot of horrible things go down in the black community about light-skin vs. dark-skin."[1]

This is a wake-up call from the front line. As a psychologist, I am frustrated when I see black children, born every bit as gifted as children of other races, thwarted from realizing their full potential by the time they reach early adolescence. Despite the tremendous progress blacks have made in this country, their children continue to be beset by limits telling them who they are and what they are capable of becoming. It is ironic that these limits are imposed not only by the racism that endures in institutions like schools but inside some of their own communities as well. Blacks must be vigilant not to pass on any negative stereotypes about their race. Many children learn from their own families and communities negative stereotypes about blacks' physical attractiveness, abilities, and potential. There is only so much we as individuals can immediately do about institutional racism, but there is a whole lot we can do *now* about the color prejudices and standards that exist in our own communities.

We need to work for comprehensive cultural changes so that a person's worth is not determined by skin color or race. We need to redefine what it means to be black or African American in a way that allows our children to grow up free to be their true selves, rather than be pressured to conform to some stereotype. We must reject the racist notion that being black means having certain inherent abilities, preferences, lifestyles—and limitations. Nobel Laureate Toni Morrison observes: "When you know somebody's race, what do you know? Virtually nothing."[2]

We need to reexamine our parenting practices—in some of which linger a vestige of slavery, an expectation that black children must grow up tougher than white children in order to deal with the obstacles they will face. As a psychologist, I am finding that some of our parenting practices, far from strengthening our children, weaken them. One of the things most of the children I've counseled have in common is a deep yearning for gentle parenting. A black middle-class friend told me that she was unsettled recently by her eleven-year-old daughter's remark: "I wonder what it's like to be white." This is a child who is growing up in a loving home but is bothered by how other black children are disciplined in public. She has observed that they are more likely than white children to be yelled at, hit, and generally belittled by their caregivers. She believes that white children have it easier. This is a perception that is shared by many black children whom I have met over the years. Our children should grow up believing that they are as precious as any other children.

We need to make our communities, as many of them once were, the port in the storm, rather than the center of turbulence. Writer Gwendolyn Parker said that growing up in a nurturing black community with strong role models strengthened her as a child to deal with racial bigotry: "I didn't even know white people until I was about nine. That was really when I first began to experience prejudice. And as a result I had to locate the problem and I knew the problem wasn't me because I had grown up with examples of black doctors, lawyers, bankers, real estate developers. These are people in the community that I could see."[3]

Finally, those of us who do so need to stop teaching our children that all whites are our enemy. The anger some of us harbor toward whites is understandable given centuries of oppression and injustice. But if we become like white racists, they win—for they will have robbed us of our humanity just as they have lost theirs to their irrational and poisonous hatred. Author Patricia Rayburn recalled, "All my life, I'd point at white people saying , 'You need to fix you.' . . . But to change the world you need to change yourself." Rayburn realized that her anger at whites "wasn't hurting them—it was killing me."[4]

Any fixing that needs to be done has had to start with us. For too long, blacks have been neglected by the national agenda. All over the country, there are promising efforts to rebuild our families, schools, and communities. Nothing less is at stake than the future of our children and the survival of blacks as a people.

It is high time for all of us, Americans of all races, to work for a climate of racial healing so that our children will have the chance to grow up in a society that is committed to living up to its ideal of racial equality. Let us begin this promising new millennium afresh by letting go of anachronistic racial animosities and creating a legacy of racial harmony.

Ultimately transcending racism means recapturing the perspective of young children, who are able to see beyond people's color to their shared humanity. Martin Luther King Jr.'s stirring words have the ring of prophecy: "The problem of race remains America's greatest moral dilemma. When one considers the impact it has upon the nation, its resolution might well determine our destiny."[5]

Appendix

Stages of Race Awareness

Stage	*Racial Self-Identification*	*Racial Constancy*	*Origin of Racial Identity*	*Racial Classification*	*Racial Attitudes*
I. Racial Innocence Age 3 and under	Most children are unable to accurately identify their skin color, much less their race/ethnicity.	Children reside in a fantasy world where anything is possible, including changes in skin color and gender.	Children are unaware of the biological origin of their skin color.	Children are unable to correctly categorize people by race/ethnicity.	Preschoolers are developmentally inclined to see people as individuals rather than as members of racial/ethnic groups.
II. Color Awareness Ages 3–5	When asked, "What color are you?" children are just as likely to describe the color of their clothes as their skin. Children may accurately identify their skin color using words like *brown*, *white*, *pink*, *tan*, and *black*. Some children also use familiar words related to food like *chocolate*, *peach*, and *vanilla*.	Children believe that if they desire, they can change their skin color by magical means like wishing and painting.	Preschoolers believe that God, their parents, or they themselves have used magical means to produce their color.	Children may accurately group people by skin color but not by race. Children describe others in their own terms like *chocolate*, *vanilla*, *pink*, and *peach*. Some children use other words like *lemon girl* (for an Asian girl) and *cherry girl* (for a red-haired white girl). All light-complexioned people, including Asians, whites, and blacks, are seen as "white." Children describe people as "brown" who have medium-brown complexion; "black" is used only to describe dark-skinned people.	Children are predisposed to be friendly to anyone who acts positively toward them. Children at this stage continue to see people of their own and other races without skin color and racial prejudices. However, children who are routinely taught racial bigotry begin to form negative association with certain skin colors.

Stage	*Racial Self-Identification*	*Racial Constancy*	*Origin of Racial Identity*	*Racial Classification*	*Racial Attitudes*
III. Awakening to Social Color Ages 5–7	Children can accurately identify their skin color and begin to make relative skin-color distinctions, like *light-skinned* and *dark-skinned.* Most children are unable to reliably identify their race/ethnicity.	Children *begin* to perceive that their skin color is a permanent feature of their bodies and understand that the effect of the sun on the skin is only temporary.	They begin to grasp the connection between their color and their mother's and expect skin colors of family members to be similar. However, they do not yet fully comprehend the genetic basis of skin color.	Children *begin* to understand that skin color means something more than mere color, but they are inclined to categorize people by color, rather than race or ethnicity. They use conventional terms—*brown, black, white*—to describe people. *Black* is used to describe only brown- and dark-skinned blacks and *white* to describe Asians and whites. When asked, children can identify Chinese people. Children begin to use ethnic labels, like Puerto Rican and Italian, sometimes inaccurately.	Although they do not yet fully understand them, children begin to adopt skin-color prejudices of their family and friends as well as those presented by the media. For example, children may begin to express a preference for light or dark skin and to see "white" or "black" people as negative stereotypes.
IV. Racial Awareness Ages 8–10	Children can accurately identify their race/ethnicity using terms like *black* and *African American.* Some biracial children say they are "part" black or African American and "part" another race, like white.	Children comprehend that racial/ethnic identity is permanent.	Children understand the genetic basis of racial/ethnic identity. Unlike younger children, they understand the reason members of the same family can have different skin tones.	Children rely not only on skin color but also other physical cues, such as hair color and textures, as well as facial features to determine a person's group—white, black or African American, Chinese, and so forth. As they mature, children realize that physical cues can be unreliable in determining some people's race. Children begin to also rely on more subtle cues—including social and behavioral ones—when making racial/ethnic identifications.	Unless they are sensitively taught not to prejudge people based on their race, children may adopt full-fledged racial stereotypes, common in the culture and their own racial/ethnic group.

Notes

INTRODUCTION

1. D. P. Hopson and D. S. Hopson, *Different and Wonderful: Raising Black Children in a Race-Conscious Society*. New York: Simon & Schuster, 1992. For a comparative review of many of these studies on black children's low self-esteem, see W. Cross, "Black Identity: Rediscovering the Distinction Between Personal Identity and Reference Group Orientation." In M. Spencer, G. Brookins, and W. Allen (eds.), *Beginnings: The Social and Affective Development of Black Children*. Hillsdale, N.J.: Erlbaum, 1985.
2. K. Clark and M. Clark, "The Development of Consciousness of Self and the Emergence of Racial Identity in Negro Preschool Children," *Journal of Social Psychology*, 1939, *10*, 591–599; K. Clark, *Prejudice and Your Child*. Boston: Beacon Press, 1963.
3. Hopson and Hopson, *Different and Wonderful*.
4. See Cross, "Black Identity," for a comprehensive review of many of these studies: F. Aboud, "The Development of Ethnic Self-Identification and Attitudes" In J. Phinney and M. Rotheram (eds.), *Children's Ethnic Socialization: Pluralism and Development*. Thousand Oaks, Calif.: Sage, 1987; M. Alejandro-Wright, "The Black Child's Development of the Concept of Race," unpublished paper, Harvard University Graduate School of Education, 1975; M. Alejandro-Wright, "The Child's Development of the Concept of Race: A Socio-Cognitive Development Study," paper presented to the Society for Research in Child Development, March 1979; M. Alejandro-Wright, "The Child's Development of the Concept of Race," doctoral dissertation, Harvard University Graduate School of Education, 1980; M. Alejandro-Wright, "The Child's Conception of Racial Classification: A Socio-Cognitive Developmental Model" In Spencer, Brookins, and Allen, *Beginnings;* L. Semaj, "Reconceptualizing the Development of Racial Preference in Children: The Role of Cognition" In W. Cross and A. Harrison

(eds.), *The Fourth Conference on Empirical Research on Black Psychology.* Published by Africana Studies Center and NIE, U.S. Department of Health, Education and Welfare, 1979.

5. G. Kamiya, "Complex Rage of John Edgar Wideman," *San Francisco Examiner,* Jan. 9, 1994, p. D3.
6. "The Two Nations of Black America," Frontline, PBS Television, Henry L. Gates Jr. (correspondent), Feb. 10, 1998.
7. As told to actor James Wood, *Today,* NBC, Dec. 24, 1996.

CHAPTER ONE

1. L. Kohlberg, "A Cognitive-Developmental Analysis of Children's Sex-Role Concepts and Attitudes" In E. Maccoby (ed.), *The Development of Sex Differences.* Stanford, Calif.: Stanford University Press, 1966.
2. H. Ginsburg and S. Opper. *Piaget's Theory of Intellectual Development.* (2nd ed.) Englewood, N.J.: Prentice Hall, 1979, p. 223.
3. L. Kohlberg and D. Ullian, "Stages in the Development of Psychosocial Concepts and Attitudes. In R. Friedman, R. Richart and R. Vanole (eds.), Sex Differences in Behavior. New York: Wiley, 1974, *75,* 89–164; R. Slaby and K. Trey, "Development of Gender Constancy and Selective Attention to Same-Sex Models," *Child Development,* 1975, *46,* 849–856.
4. Kohlberg, "Cognitive-Developmental Analysis"; m. Spencer,"Personal and Group Identity of Black Children: An Alternative Synthesis. *Genetic Psychology Monographs,* 1982,*106,* 59-84.
5. T. McMillan, "Hers," *New York Times,* Nov. 8, 1987, p. 20.
6. A. Bernstein and P. Cowan, "Children's Concepts of How People Get Babies," *Child Development,* 1975, *46,* 77–91.
7. T. Moore, "Family Colors," *San Francisco Examiner,* May 7, 1995, p. 2.
8. P. Ramsey and L. Myers, "Salience of Race in Young Children's Cognitive, Affective and Behavioral Responses to Social Environments," *Journal of Applied Developmental Psychology,* 1990, *11,* 49–67; M. Van Parys, "Preschoolers in Society: Use of Social Roles of Sex, Age and Race for Self and Others by Black and White Children," paper presented at the biennial meeting of the International Society of Behavioral Development, Toronto, 1981; P. Ramsey, "The Salience of Race in Young Children Growing Up in an All-White Community," *Journal of Educational Psychology,* 1991, *83,* 28–34.
9. D. Britt, "Love Overcomes Fear and the Color of Skin," *San Francisco Chronicle,* Oct. 12, 1994, p. E8.

CHAPTER TWO

1. Hopson and Hopson, *Different and Wonderful,* p. xix.
2. J. Piaget, *The Child's Conception of the World.* Totowa, N. J.: Little Field, Adams & Co., 1969.
3. B. Payton, "Black like Me" In D. Wickham (ed.), *Thinking Black: Some of the Nation's Best Black Columnists Speak Their Minds.* New York: Crown, 1996, p. 176.
4. M. Riggs (director), *Black Is, Black Ain't: A Personal Journey Through Black Identity.* 1995. Videotape.
5. A. Gibson, *Nappy: Growing Up Black and Female in America.* New York: Harlem River Press, 1995, p. 3.
6. J. Kaufman, "Here She Is, Ms. Tiny Miss," *People,* Sept. 26, 1988, p. 49.
7. T. B. Brazelton, "Families Today," *San Francisco Chronicle,* Apr. 18, 1994.
8. H. Kohl, *Should We Burn Babar? Essays on Children's Literature and the Power of Stories.* New York: Free Press, 1995.
9. M. Cimons, "One Woman's Uphill Quest to Make and Sell Toys for Black Kids" *Oakland Tribune,* July 17, 1988, p. C1.
10. T. McMillan, *Waiting to Exhale.* New York, Viking, 1992, pp. 274–275.
11. A. Ashe and A. Rampersad, *Days of Grace.* New York: Ballantine Books, 1993, p. 142.
12. Ibid.
13. C. Marshall, White Christmas a Dream That's Changing for Minorities," *Oakland Tribune,* Dec. 23, 1991, p. A13.
14. Dr. Bruce Bridges, NAACP member, *Day and Date,,* Dec. 15, 1995.
15. M. Sanchez, "Ethnic Santas Deck the Halls," *San Francisco Chronicle,* Dec. 25, 1993, p. A10.
16. M. Locke, "Kids Bring Wishes to Rainbow of Santas," *San Francisco Chronicle,* Dec. 18, 1994, p. C15.
17. Ibid., p. C15.
18. R. Ellison, *Invisible Man.* New York: Modern Library, [1952] 1992.
19. R. Lyons, "Ralph Ellison, Author of Invisible Man, Is Dead at Eighty," *New York Times,* Apr. 17, 1994, p. 38.

CHAPTER THREE

1. K. Russell, "Growing Up with Privilege and Prejudice," *New York Times Magazine,* June 14, 1987, p. 24.
2. P. Pierce, "Still Trying to Fight It," *Parade Magazine,* Jan. 3, 1993, p. 6.

3. S. Nazario, "When White Parents Adopt Black Babies, Race Often Divides," *Wall Street Journal,* Sept. 12, 1990, p. A8.
4. R. J. Simon, H. Altstein, and M. S. Melli, *The Case for Transracial Adoption.* Lanham, Md.: American University Press, 1994.
5. Nazario.
6. B. Mandel, "When Love Conquers City Bureaucracy," *San Francisco Examiner and Chronicle,* April 24, 1994, p. B14.
7. Simon.
8. National Adoption and Information Clearinghouse fact sheet circa 1997.

CHAPTER FOUR

1. Frederick E. Patterson Research Institute, *The Status of Education in Black America,* Vol. 2: *Preschool to High School.* Washington, D.C.: Frederick E. Patterson Research Institute, 1997.
2. L. Gregory, "Kwanza: 7 Days—7 Principles," *San Francisco Examiner,* Dec. 26, 1993.

CHAPTER FIVE

1. R. Coles, *The Story of Ruby Bridges.* New York: Scholastic, 1995; H. Marshall (adapt.) and T. Johnson (teleplay), *The Ruby Bridges Story.* New York: Disney Press, 1997.
2. Payton, "Black Like Me," p. 175.
3. Gibson, *Nappy,* p. 148.
4. E. Kitt, *Alone with Me,* Chicago: Henry Regnery Co., 1976.
5. R. Carroll, *Sugar in the Raw: Voices of Black Girls Growing Up in America.* New York: Crown Books, 1995, p. 128.
6. *The World Almanac and Book of Facts, 1998.* Mahwah, N.J.: World Almanac Books, 1997, p. 962.
7. G. Knight, *Between Each Line of Pain and Glory: My Life Story.* New York: Hyperion Books, 1997.
8. A. Moody, *Coming of Age in Mississippi.* (5th ed.) New York: Dell, 1968, pp. 38–39.
9. Contact Patty Green at: Ginger Kids, Inc., 610 Main Street, Suite 210, Buffalo, New York, 14202.
10. L. Derman-Sparks and the ABC Task Force, *Anti-Bias Curriculum Tools for Empowering Young People.* Washington, D.C.: National Association for the Education of Young Children, 1989.
11. *Starting Small,* free booklet by Teaching Tolerance, 400 Washington Aveue, Montgomery, AL 36104.
12. J. Lee, *Sally Jessey Raphael,* ABC, Feb. 8, 1994.

13. P. Ramsey and L. Myers, "Salience of Race in Young Children's Cognitive, Affective and Behavioral Responses to Social Environments," *Journal of Applied Developmental Psychology*, 1990, *11*, 49–67; M. Van Parys, "Preschoolers in Society: Use of Social Roles of Sex, Age and Race for Self and Others by Black and White Children," paper presented at the biennial meeting of the International Society of Behavioral Development, Toronto, 1981; P. Ramsey, "The Salience of Race in Young Children Growing Up in an All-White Community," *Journal of Educational Psychology*, 1991, *83*, 28–34.
14. Dr. Laura Schlessinger, radio talk show, rebroadcast May 26, 1996.

CHAPTER SIX

1. E. Erikson, "Eight Stages of Man" In *Childhood and Society*. New York: Norton, 1950; E. Erikson, *Identity, Youth and Crisis*. New York: Norton, 1968.
2. M. Straus, D. Sugarman, and J. Giles-Sims, "Spanking by Parents and Subsequent Antisocial Behavior of Children," *Arch. Pediatrics Adolescent Medicine*, vol. 151, Aug. 1997.
3. "National Report," *San Francisco Chronicle*, Apr. 8, 1998, p. A3.
4. J. H. Franklin, *The Militant South*, Cambridge, Mass.: Harvard University Press, 1956; E. Ball, *Slaves in the Family*, New York: Farrar, Straus & Giroux, 1998.
5. J. Comer and A. Poussaint, *Raising Black Children*. New York: Plume, 1992, p. 53.
6. A. Richman, "Oprah," *People*, Jan. 12, 1987, pp. 49–55.
7. See various articles by B. Perry in *The Advisor: Bulletin of the American Professional Society on the Abuse of Children*, 1993, *6*(1–2).
8. K. Bryson, "Current Population Reports, Household and Family Characteristics," U.S. Census Bureau, March 1995.
9. J. Wallerstein and J. Lewis, *The Long-Term Impact of Divorce on Children: A First Report from a Twenty-Five-Year Study, Family and Conciliation Court Review, 36* (3), July 1998, pp. 368–383.
10. N. Marone, *How to Father a Successful Daughter*. New York: McGraw-Hill, 1988.
11. J. Scanzoni, *The Black Family in Modern Sociey*, Boston: Allyn and Bacon, 1971.
12. A. Kardiner and L. Ovesey, *The Mark of Oppression*, New York: Norton, 1951.
13. C. Tucker, As I See It, "A Letter to Martin Luther King III," *San Francisco Chronicle*, Nov. 8, 1997, p. A20. (Reprinted from the *Atlanta Constitution*.)
14. W. Goldberg, *Book*, New York: William, Murrow and Co., 1997.
15. L. Hughes, "Mother to Son" In A. Bontemps (ed.), *American Negro Poetry*. (Rev. ed.) New York: Hill & Wang, 1974.

16. J. Coleman, *Long Way to Go: Black and White in America.* New York: Atlantic Monthly Press, 1997.

CHAPTER SEVEN

1. J. Johnson, *The Autobiography of an Ex-Colored Man.* New York: Penguin Books, 1980, pp. 10-11.
2. American Association of University Women, *How Schools Shortchange Girls: A Study of the Major Findings of Girls' Education.* Washington, D.C.: American Association of University Women, 1972.
3. R. Jerome, "Cast Away," *People,* Aug. 4, 1997, pp. 40-45.
4. C. Page made this remark on a San Francisco radio show while promoting his book, *Showing My Colors,* New York: HarperCollins, 1996.
5. "School Choice: No Easy Answers," *San Francisco Chronicle,* Aug. 29, 1997.
6. Frederick E. Patterson Research Institute, *Status of Education in Black America,* Vol. 2.
7. V. Wagner, "Schooled in Black Culture,"*San Francisco Examiner,* Apr. 28, 1996, p. A1.
8. D. Goleman, *Emotional Intelligence.* New York: Bantam Books, 1995.
9. S. Fulwood, "Policy on Integration May Face Test," *Los Angeles Times,* July 13, 1997, p. A1.
10. M. McCabe, "A Decade of Opportunity," *San Francisco Chronicle,* Mar. 8, 1996, p. 1.
11. N. Asimov, "A New Breed of School Is Born," *San Francisco Chronicle,* Sept. 16, 1997, p. A15.
12. J. Marshall, "Test Scores Analysis Shows State Schools Doing Well," *San Francisco Chronicle,* Sept. 9, 1997, p. 1.
13. R. Elmore and D. Burney, "Investing in Teacher Learning," National Commission on Teaching in America's Future, 1998.

CHAPTER EIGHT

1. See Appendix for description of Stages of Race Awareness
2. *Oprah,* ABC, Mar. 11, 1994.
3. S. Spielberg, interview with B. Walters, ABC, Mar. 21, 1994.
4. *Oprah,* ABC, date not available.
5. M. Rosenberg and R. Simmons, *Black and White Self-Esteem: The Urban School Child.* Washington, D.C.: American Sociological Association, 1972; R. Taylor, "Psychosocial Development Among Black Children

and Youth: A Reexamination," *American Journal of Orthopsychiatry,* 1976, *46,* 4–19.

6. Piaget, *Child's Conception of the World.*
7. K. Cunningham, "Say It Loud," *People,* May 23, 1994, p. 128.
8. "A Different World: Children's Perceptions of Race and Class in the Media," Children Now, Oakland, Calif., 1998.
9. T. Moore, "Racism on Television Gets Static from Kids," *San Francisco Chronicle,* May 7, 1998, p. A2.
10. D. Hampton, "Will Power," *Essence,* July 1997.
11. N. McCall, *What's Going On.* New York: Random House, 1997, p. 58.
12. H. Gates Jr., *Colored People: A Memoir.* New York: Vintage Books, 1995; J. Cochran, *Journey to Justice.* New York, Ballantine Books, 1996; Knight, *Between Each Line.*
13. H. Lee, "Formula for Change and Hope," *San Francisco Chronicle,* Dec. 30, 1997, p. A16; R. Mills, *The Health Realization Model: A Community Empowerment Primer,* Alhambra: California School of Professional Psychology, 1993.

CHAPTER NINE

1. "White Parents Resist Naming School for King," *San Francisco Chronicle,* Jan. 5, 1998, p. A20.
2. E. Bonner, "Report Shows Urban Pupils Fall Short on Basic Skills," *New York Times,* Jan. 8, 1998, p. A12.
3. Editorial, "The Great Divide in American Education," *San Francisco Chronicle,* Feb. 1, 1998, p. 6.
4. T. Walker, "UC Chancellor Puts Focus on Poor Kids," *San Francisco Chronicle,* Jan. 24, 1998, p A14.
5. Frederick E. Patterson Research Institute, *Status of Education in Black America,* Vol. 2.
6. "Oakland Schools in Flux," *San Francisco Chronicle,* Aug. 8, 1997, p. A22.
7. S. Farden and J. Ogbu, "Black Students' School Success: Coping with the Burden of Acting White," *Urban Review,* 1986, *18,* 176–206.
8. T. Moore, "College Bound Since 5th Grade," *San Francisco Chronicle,* May 30, 1997, p. 1.
9. "Law Professor Attacked for Remarks on Race," *San Francisco Chronicle,* Sept. 16, 1997, p. 3.
10. Frederick E. Patterson Research Institute, *Status of Education in Black America,* Vol. 2.
11. W. Banks, G. McQuater, and J. Hubbard, "Toward a Reconceptualization of the Social-Cognitive Basis of Achievement Orientation in

Blacks" In A. Boykin, A. Franklin, and J. Yates (eds.), *Research Directions of Black Psychologists.* New York: Russell Sage Foundation, 1979, pp. 294–311.
12. J. Comer, "Home-School Relationships as They Affect Academic Success in Children," *Education and Urban Society,* 1984, *16,* 323–337.
13. R. Rosenthal, *Pygmalion in the Classroom: Teacher Expectations and Pupils' Intellectual Development.* New York: Irvington, 1992.
14. *Dateline,* NBC, Jan. 16, 1998.
15. E. Harrison and E. Stanley, "Georgia Educator Fights to Desegregate Schools," *San Francisco Chronicle,* Dec. 28, 1996, p. A5.
16. Ibid.
17. "Racial Harm Is Found in School Tracking," *New York Times,* Sept. 20, 1990; J. Oakes, M. Selvin, L. Karoly, and G. Guiton, "Educational Matchmaking, Academic and Vocational Tracking in Comprehensive High Schools," RAND, 1992.
18. R. Herrstein and C. Murray, *The Bell Curve: Intelligence and Class Structure in American Life.* New York: Free Press, 1994.
19. "How the Disadvantaged Are Further Disadvantaged in School," *San Francisco Chronicle,* Feb. 1, 1998, p. 6.
20. "Math Adds Up to College, Report Says," *San Francisco Chronicle,* Oct. 21, 1997, p.1.
21. H. Gardner, *Frames of Minds: The Theory of Multiple Intelligence.* New York: Basic Books, 1983.
22. S. Greenspan (with B. Benderly), *The Growth of the Mind and the Endangered Origins of Intelligence.* Reading, Mass.: Addison-Wesley, 1997; S. Blakeslee, "Studies Show Talking with Infants Shapes Basis of Ability to Think," *New York Times,* Apr. 17, 1997, p. 14.
23. "Great Divide," p. 6.
24. M. Robinson, "What Causes School Violence," *Investors Business Daily,* Nov. 12, 1997, p. A36.
25. S. Winakur, C. Marinucci, and G. Lewis, "The War on Youth Violence: Teachers Fleeing the Classroom," *San Francisco Examiner,* Nov. 28, 1994.
26. Ibid., p. 14.
27. *The View,* ABC Television, Dec. 10, 1997.
28. J. Brooke, "Minorities Flock to Cause of Vouchers for Schools," *New York Times,* Dec. 26, 1997, p. 1.
29. "Great Divide," p. 6.
30. B. Evengelista and J. Frost, "Doll Stirs Race Tension at Junior High School," *OaklandTribune,* Apr. 18, 1989.
31. J. Woolfolk, "8 Boys Arrested During School in San Jose Hate-Beating," *San Francisco Chronicle,* May 29, 1993.

32. "Today's Kids Want Racial Harmony," *Good Housekeeping,* Feb. 1993, p. 119.

CHAPTER TEN

1. K. Powell, *This Is America,* PBS, Jan. 2, 1998.
2. C. Rock, *60 Minutes,* CBS, Apr. 19, 1998.
3. B. Tatum, *"Why Are All the Black Kids Sitting Together in the Cafeteria? and Other Conversations About Race.* New York: Basic Books, 1997.
4. Erikson, "Eight Stages of Man"
5. Tatum, *"Why Are All the Black Kids . . . ?"*
6. C. Gray, *This Is America,* PBS, Jan. 2, 1998.
7. M. Goldberg, *Skin Deep: Black Women and White Women Write About Race.* New York: Doubleday, 1995.
8. *Oprah,* ABC, date not available.
9. Tatum, *"Why Are All the Black Kids . . . ?"*
10. K. Baker, "The Race Divide," *Teen People,* Mar. 1998, pp. 41–43.
11. Ibid., p. 4X.
12. "Chief Quits over 'Oreo' Remark," *San Francisco Chronicle,* Jan. 17, 1998.
13. *Oprah,* ABC, date not available.
14. U.S. Census Report, 1992.
15. M. Pipher, *Reviving Ophelia.* New York: Ballantine Books, 1994.
16. Ibid., p. 280.
17. S. Erkut, M. Fern, J. Fields, and R. Sing, "Raising Confident and Competent Girls: Dimensions of Self-Esteem," working paper, Wellesley's Centers for Women, Wellesley, Mass., 1998.
18. G. Schreiber, M. Robins, R. Striegel-Moore, E. Obarzanek, J. Morrison, and D. Wright, "Weight Modification Efforts Reported by Black and White Preadolescent Girls," National Heart, Lung, and Blood Institute Growth and Health Study, *Pediatrics, 96* (1), July 1996.
19. M. Browne, "Dying to Be Thin," *Essence,* June 1993, pp. 86-129.
20. J. Schneider, "Mission Impossible," *People,* June 3, 1996, p. 3.
21. J. Morgan, "The Bad Girls of Hip-Hop," *Essence,* Mar. 1997, p. 79.
22. A. Holmes, "Quality of Life Is Up for Many Blacks, Data Say," *New York Times,* Nov. 18, 1996, p. 1.
23. R. MacLeod, "Can Welfare Reform Reduce Pregnancy Rates?" *San Francisco Examiner and Chronicle,* Mar. 5, 1998.
24. Ibid.
25. L. Freedberg, "Race Panel Gets an Earful in San Jose," *San Francisco Chronicle,* Feb. 11, 1998, p. A3.
26. A. Vaziri, "Rebel with a Hip-Hop Cause," *San Francisco Chronicle and Examiner,* Feb. 8, 1998.

27. N. McCall, *What's Going On,* pp. 66–67.
28. C. Farley, "Kids and Race," *Time,* Nov. 24, 1997, pp. 88–91.
29. Ibid.; "Two Societies," *Newsweek,* Feb. 23, 1998; *San Francisco Chronicle,* Apr. 1998; P. Belluck, "Black Youths' Rates of Suicide Rising Sharply, Studies Find," *New York Times,* Mar. 20, 1998, p. A1.
30. D. Eliot, "Serious Violent Offenders: Onset, Developmental course and Termination," *Criminology, 32* (1), pp. 1-21, 1994.
31. Farley, "Kids and Race"
32. W. Cross, *Shades of Black: Diversity in African-American Identity.* Philadelphia: Temple University Press, 1991.
33. H. Nasser, "Varied Heritage Claimed and Extolled by Millions," *USA Today,* May 8, 1997, p. 1.
34. J. Gibbs and A. Hines, "Negotiating Ethnic Identity Issues for Black-White Biracial Adolescents" In M. Root (ed.), *Racially Mixed People in America.* Thousand Oaks, Calif.: Sage, 1992.
35. C. Kerwin, J. Ponterotts, B. Jackson, and A. Harris, "Racial Identity in Biracial Children: A Qualitative Investigation," *Journal of Counseling Psychology,* 1993, *40,* 221–231.
36. C. Cauce and others, "Between a Rock and a Hard Place: Social Adjustment of Biracial Youth" In Root, *Racially Mixed People in America.*
37. Norman, "Mariah Carey," *Ebony,* Apr. 1994.
38. Ibid.
39. S. Murray, "She's as Solid as a Rock," *San Francisco Chronicle,* June 2, 1994, p. E1.
40. C. Petit, "No Biological Basis for Race, Scientists Say," *San Francisco Chronicle,* p. 4.

CHAPTER ELEVEN

1. M. Resnick and others, "Protecting Adolescents from Harm: Findings from the National Longitudinal Study on Adolescence Health." *Journal of the American Medical Association,* 1997, *278,* 823–832.
2. B. Vobejda, "Love Conquers What Ails Teens, Study Finds," *Washington Post,* Sept. 10, 1997, p. A1.
3. "Parents Remain Major Influence on Teen Behavior Well into Their Teen Years: Study," *Jet,* Sept. 29, 1997.
4. Ibid.
5. U. Treisman, "Mathematics Achievement Among African American Undergraduates at the University of California, Berkeley," *Journal of Negro Education,* 1990, *59,* 463–478; U. Treisman, "Studying Students Studying Calculus: A Look at the Lives of Minority Mathematics Stu-

dents in College," *The College Mathematics Journal, 23* (5), pp. 362-372, 1992.

6. Gibson, *Nappy.*
7. C. Flood, *SPORTS FINAL,* NBC Television, San Francisco, rebroadcast Jan. 20, 1997.
8. R. McFadden, "A LongSlide from Privilege Ends in Slaughter on a Train," *New York Times,* Dec. 12, 1993, p.2.
9. "Father of Tennis Star Venus Williams Charges Racism During Recent U.S. Open," *Jet,* Sept. 29, 1997, pp. 49-50.
10. J. Wildermuth, "Racial Incidents Rock School in Belmont," *San Francisco Chronicle,* Oct. 28, 1997, p. A13.
11. Ibid.
12. "Laughter At Film Brings Spielberg Visit," *New York Times,* April 13, 1994, p. B9.
13. J. Smith, "Carlos Fuentes' Literature Is History in the Making," *San Francisco Examiner,* Apr. 24, 1994, p. B13.
14. E. Harrison, "Principal's Race Comments Spur Small Uproar," *Los Angeles Times,* Mar. 16, 1994, p. A1.
15. M. Milloy, "Not Just Another Prom Night," *San Francisco Chronicle,* May 10, 1990, p. A13.
16. Piaget, *Child's Conception of the World.*
17. "Guardian Angel," *People,* July 8, 1996, p. 86.
18. C. Tucker, "Black History Set-Asides Serves Neither History nor Blacks," *San Francisco Chronicle,* Feb. 14, 1998.
19. M. Sanchez-Jankowski, *Islands in the Street: Gangs in American Urban Society,* Berkeley: University of California Press, 1991.
20. J. Loewen, *Lies My Teacher Told Me.* New York: New Press, 1995.
21. T. Mitchell, *People in Organizations.* New York: McGraw-Hill, 1978.
22. *12 O'Clock News,* FOX Television, San Francisco, Mar. 13, 1998.

EPILOGUE

1. Gibson, *Nappy,* p. 147.
2. T. Morrison, *Sixty Minutes,* CBS Television, March 1998.
3. G. Parker, *This Is America,* PBS, date not available.
4. D. Britt, "Forgiveness Begins with Disarming Rage," *San Francisco Chronicle,* Oct. 6, 1996, p. C20.
5. M. L. King Jr., *Ethical Demands of Integration,* 1963, p. 117.

About the Author

Marguerite N. A. Wright is a licensed psychologist who specializes in the developmental and psychosocial issues of low income and minority children. She is a staff psychologist at Children's Hospital Oakland in California. She also teaches in the Children and the Changing Family program of the University of California Berkeley Extension.

Wright received her B.A. degree in psychology from Wheaton College, Norton, Massachusetts; her doctorate in human development from Harvard University; and completed a post-doctorate in developmental psychology at Yale University. She resides in northern California with her husband and their four children.

Index

R

S

T

CPSIA information can be obtained at www.ICGtesting.com
Printed in the USA
BVOW000423160713

325992BV00004B/4/P